Global Development Horizons 2011

Multipolarity: The New Global Economy

Global Development Horizons 2011

Multipolarity: The New Global Economy

THE WORLD BANK
Washington, D.C.

© 2011 The International Bank for Reconstruction and Development / The World Bank

1818 H Street NW
Washington DC 20433
Telephone: 202-473-1000
Internet: www.worldbank.org

1 2 3 4 14 13 12 11

This volume is a product of the staff of the International Bank for Reconstruction and Development / The World Bank. The findings, interpretations, and conclusions expressed in this volume do not necessarily reflect the views of the Executive Directors of The World Bank or the governments they represent.

The World Bank does not guarantee the accuracy of the data included in this work. The boundaries, colors, denominations, and other information shown on any map in this work do not imply any judgement on the part of The World Bank concerning the legal status of any territory or the endorsement or acceptance of such boundaries.

ISBN: 978-0-8213-8692-7
eISBN: 978-0-8213-8693-4
DOI: 10.1596/978-0-8213-8692-7
ISSN: 2221-8416

Cover image: Untitled, by Marc Pekala, 2010
Cover design: Financial Communications, Inc., Bethesda, Maryland, United States

Contents

Boxes

Figures

Tables

Foreword

THE WORLD ECONOMY IS IN THE midst of a transformative change. One of the most visible outcomes of this transformation is the rise of a number of dynamic emerging-market countries to the helm of the global economy. It is likely that, by 2025, emerging economies—such as Brazil, China, India, Indonesia, and the Russian Federation—will be major contributors to global growth, alongside the advanced economies. As they pursue growth opportunities abroad and encouraged by improved policies at home, corporations based in emerging markets are playing an increasingly prominent role in global business and cross-border investment. The international monetary system is likely to cease being dominated by a single currency. Emerging-market countries, where three-fourths of official foreign exchange reserves are currently held and whose sovereign wealth funds and other pools of capital are increasingly important sources of international investment, will become key players in financial markets. In short, a new world order with a more diffuse distribution of economic power is emerging—thus the shift toward multipolarity.

Throughout the course of history, major economic transitions have always presented challenges, as they involve large uncertainties surrounding identification of emerging global issues of systemic importance and development of appropriate policy and institutional responses. It is in this context that the World Bank is launching a new report, *Global Development Horizons (GDH)*.[1] The new report serves as a vehicle for stimulating new thinking and research on anticipated structural changes in the global economic landscape. To retain this forward-looking orientation and to serve the World Bank Group's mandate of development and poverty alleviation, it is envisaged that future editions of GDH will be dedicated to themes of importance to the emerging development agenda and global economic governance, including changing global income inequality, increasing economic insecurity, global population aging, and the future shape of development finance.

The inaugural edition of GDH addresses the broad trend toward multipolarity in the global economy, particularly as it relates to structural changes in growth dynamics, corporate investment, and international monetary and financial arrangements. Multipolarity, of course, has different interpretations within different spheres of contemporary international relations. In international politics, where much of the discussion has been focused, the debate centers on the potential for a nonpolar world, in which numerous national concentrations of power exist but no single center dominates (as opposed to the bipolar global political environment that defined the Cold War era). In the realm of international economics, multipolarity—meaning more than two dominant growth poles—has at times been a key feature of the global system. But at no time in modern history have so many developing countries been at the forefront of a multipolar economic system. This pattern is now set to change. Within the next two decades, the rise of emerging economies will inevitably have major implications for the global economic and geopolitical landscape.

---

1. GDH now contains the thematic analysis that previously appeared in *Global Development Finance* and *Global Economic Prospects*. *Global Economic Prospects* will continue to be produced, but without the thematic chapters, and *Global Development Finance* will be focused on data.

In a world of progressively more multipolar economic growth and financial centers, policy makers will need to equip themselves with the tools and capabilities to effectively capitalize on opportunities while simultaneously safeguarding their economies against the risks that remain stubbornly high as the global economy struggles to find a stable footing. Within the realm of immediate concerns, the tragic earthquake and tsunami that hit Japan in March 2011, the political turmoil gripping much of the Middle East and North Africa, and the financial tremors emanating from the European sovereign debt crisis are all likely to exact a heavy toll on global financial markets and growth. Seen against the backdrop of a sub-par global growth trajectory, high levels of unemployment in many advanced and developing economies, and rising inflationary pressures in many emerging and low-income economies, these events call for further bold, concrete actions to shore up confidence and establish the underpinning for bankers to lend, and for businesses to invest in equipment and technology that will boost productivity, create jobs, and generate long-term growth. Indeed, it is through rising investment and economic growth that productive jobs will be created to absorb the large youth cohort in the Middle East and North Africa region and elsewhere, that earthquake-shattered parts of Japan will be rebuilt, and that fiscal consolidation in the United States and Europe will become more achievable.

The transformation of global patterns of economic growth is also driving a change in the international monetary system. At the current juncture, the U.S. dollar remains the most important international currency, despite a slow decline in its role since the late 1990s and abandonment nearly forty years ago of the Bretton Woods system of fixed exchange rates (in which the dollar officially anchored the world's currencies). But the dollar now faces growing competition in the international currency space. Chief within this space is the euro, which has gained ground in recent years as a currency in which goods are invoiced and official reserves are held, while the yen and pound represent only single-digit shares of official reserves In the longer term,

the size and dynamism of China's economy and the rapid globalization of its corporations and banks will position the renminbi to take on a more important international role. By 2025, the most probable global currency scenario will be a multipolar one centered around the dollar, euro, and renminbi. This scenario is supported by the likelihood that the United States, the euro area, and China will constitute the three major growth poles by that time, providing stimulus to other countries through trade, finance, and technology channels and thereby creating international demand for their currencies.

The potential for rising competition among power centers that is inherent in the shift to a more multipolar world makes strengthening policy coordination across economies—developing and developed—critical to reducing the risks of political and economic instability. In the years leading up to the financial crisis, the role of international economic policy making was confined to managing the symptoms of incompatible macroeconomic policies, such as exchange rate misalignments and payments imbalances. As capital markets have been liberalized and exchange rates made more flexible, balance of payments constraints on national economies have been considerably eased, shifting policy coordination toward the more politically sensitive spheres of domestic monetary and fiscal policy.

For its part, the international financial community must recognize that it has a complex burden to shoulder in ensuring that the least developed countries (LDCs) are guarded against the volatility that could accompany the transition to a multipolar order. Many LDCs are heavily reliant on external demand for growth and, hence, their ability to manage their external relations becomes critical. For those with floating exchange rate regimes, a critical element would be the development of the necessary institutional policy frameworks, market microstructure, and financial institutions that can ensure the smooth functioning of foreign exchange markets. Aid and technical assistance from international financial institutions have the potential to cushion volatility in these economies as they adapt to the global forces involved in the transition to a multipolar world.

Finally, the World Bank believes that a publication geared toward stimulating new thinking and research on the implications of a changing global landscape should embed change in its own format and design. Thus, GDH will consist of both a hard copy publication and a companion website (http://www.worldbank.org/GDH2011) that will serve as an extension of the paper publication. This website will be a platform for the report's underlying data, methodology, blog postings, and relevant background papers. The site will also include an interactive feature that will allow visitors to explore the scenarios described in GDH. This is in line with the Bank's agenda to "democratize" development via our Open Data Initiative and greater emphasis on open knowledge exchange (http://data.worldbank.org). In the future, the site will also serve as a repository of related research papers from the broader development community, as well as a vehicle for interactive debate and networking with various think tanks, business associations, and policy establishments concerned with long-term global economic change and its implications for development policy and discourse.

Justin Yifu Lin
Senior Vice President and Chief Economist
The World Bank

Acknowledgments

THIS REPORT WAS PREPARED BY the Emerging Global Trends team of the World Bank's Development Prospects Group (DECPG). Mansoor Dailami was the lead author and manager of the team. The report was prepared with direction from Hans Timmer and under the general guidance of Justin Yifu Lin, World Bank Senior Vice President and Chief Economist.

The Overview was written by Mansoor Dailami with contributions from other team members. Chapter 1 was written by Jamus Jerome Lim and Jonathon Adams-Kane. Dominique van der Mensbrugghe was the architect behind the computable general equilibrium modeling using the World Bank's Linkage model. Mohsin S. Khan (Peterson Institute for International Economics and formerly with the International Monetary Fund) provided input and direction for the current account modeling, John Baffes offered technical advice on commodities, and Thorsten Janus (University of Wyoming) provided technical comments on measures of multipolarity. Chapter 2 was written by Mansoor Dailami, Jacqueline Irving, and Robert Hauswald (American University) with written contributions from Sergio Kurlat, Yueqing Jia, and William Shaw. Chapter 3 was written by Mansoor Dailami and Paul Masson (University of Toronto) with contributions from Hyung Sik Kim, Sergio Kurlat, Gabriela Mundaca, and Yueqing Jia.

The report also benefited from the comments of the Bank's Executive Directors, made at an informal board meeting on April 21, 2011.

Many others provided advice, inputs, and comments at various stages of the report's conceptualization and preparation. Ann Harrison coordinated the review process within the Development Economics Vice Presidency and provided substantial comments and advice. Shahrokh Fardoust commented on the report at its various writing stages. Marcelo Giugale, Manuela V. Ferro, Jeffrey D. Lewis, and Jon Faust (John Hopkins University) were peer reviewers at the report's concept paper stage. Manuela V. Ferro, Jeffrey D. Lewis, Marcelo Giugale, Kalpana Kochhar, and Joshua Aizenman (University of California at Santa Cruz) were discussants at the Bank-wide review. In addition, within the Bank, comments were provided by Augusto de la Torre, Ritva Reinikka, Indermit Gill, Ahmad Ahsan, Asli Demirguc-Kunt, Ivailo Izvorski, Linda Van Gelder, Willem van Eeghen, Shantayanan Devarajan, Akihiko Nishio, Merrell Tuck-Primdahl, Ana Fernandes, Aaditya Mattoo, Hiau Looi Kee, Maggie Chen, Hinh Dinh, Vivian Hon, Jean-Jacques Dethier, Volker Treichel, Luis Serven, and David Rosenblatt.

Outside the Bank, invaluable help was received from many experts through meetings, discussions, and presentation of the report's early findings. They include Dale Jorgenson (Harvard University), Philip Turner (Bank for International Settlements), and Ajay Shah and Ila Patnaik (National Institute of Public Finance and Policy, India).

The online Global Development Horizons website was produced by David Horowitz, Jamus Jerome Lim, Rebecca Ong, Sarah Crow, and Katherine Rollins. Technical help in the production of the website was provided by Roula Yazigi and Vamsee Krishna Kanchi, and Augusto Clavijo provided support for formatting figures and tables for the final version of the report. Background papers and related research are available on the website (http://www.worldbank.org/GDH2011).

Dana Vorisek edited the report. Rosalie Marie Lourdes Singson provided production assistance to the Emerging Global Trends team and to Merrell Tuck-Primdahl, Rebecca Ong, Cynthia Case, and Swati Priyadarshini Mishra, who managed dissemination activities. Book design, editing, and production were coordinated by Cindy Fisher, Denise Bergeron, Santiago Pombo-Bejarano, and Patricia M. Katayama, of the World Bank Office of the Publisher.

Glossary

THIS REPORT INTRODUCES terminology that is not commonly found in World Bank publications. This glossary defines some of the key terms and definitions used.

Growth pole: An economy that significantly drives global growth.

Growth polarity: A measure of the extent to which an economy's growth spills over to global growth, along trade, finance, technology, and migration channels.

Potential growth pole: An economy that has the potential to be a growth pole in the future, including those that have been identified as current growth poles.

Potential emerging economy pole: Potential growth poles that are also emerging economies.

Multipolarity: The existence of more than two growth poles in the world economy, measured as the degree of concentration of growth polarity (the lower the concentration, the greater the degree of multipolarity).

Advanced economies: Economies that have traditionally been identified as industrialized nations: Australia, Canada, the economies of the euro area and EU-15, Iceland, Japan, New Zealand, Norway, Switzerland, and the United States of America. Used interchangeably with the term developed economies, when in contrast to developing economies, and with the term global North, when in contrast to the global South.

Developing economies: Economies listed as low-income, lower-middle-income, and upper-middle-income according to the World Bank official classification.

Emerging economy/market: Economies with relatively high levels of economic potential and international engagement, broader than traditional Dow Jones, FTSE, JPMorgan Chase and MSCI classifications: Algeria, Argentina, Azerbaijan, The Bahamas, Bahrain, Barbados, Belarus, Brazil, Bulgaria, Chile, China, Colombia, Costa Rica, Croatia, Czech Republic, Dominican Republic, Ecuador, Arab Republic of Egypt, El Salvador, Estonia, Georgia, Ghana, Guatemala, Hungary, India, Indonesia, Jamaica, Jordan, Kazakhstan, Kenya, Republic of Korea, Kuwait, Latvia, Lebanon, Lithuania, Malaysia, Mexico, Mongolia, Morocco, Nigeria, Oman, Pakistan, Panama, Peru, Philippines, Poland, Qatar, Romania, Russian Federation, Saudi Arabia, Singapore, South Africa, Sri Lanka, Thailand, Trinidad and Tobago, Turkey, Ukraine, United Arab Emirates, Uruguay, República Bolivariana de Venezuela, and Vietnam.

AFR/SSA, EAP, ECA, LAC, MNA, SAR: The official World Bank classifications of these regions (Africa, East Asia and Pacific, Europe and Central Asia, Latin America and the Caribbean, Middle East and North Africa, and South Asia), including high-income countries located within these regions.

Abbreviations

ADRs	American Depository Receipts
AIM	Alternative Investment Market
ASX	Australian Securities Exchange
BIS	Bank for International Settlements
BITs	bilateral investment treaties
BRIC	Brazil, the Russian Federation, India, and China
BRIICKS	Brazil, the Russian Federation, India, Indonesia, China, and the Republic of Korea
CBO	U.S. Congressional Budget Office
EC	error components
ECB	European Central Bank
EFSF	European Financial Stability Facility
EFSM	European Financial Stability Mechanism
EM	emerging market
EOI	export-oriented industrialization
EU	European Union
FDI	foreign direct investment
GATS	General Agreement on Trade in Services
GATT	General Agreement on Tariffs and Trade
GDP	gross domestic product
GGB	German government bond
GMM	generalized method of moments
GNI	gross national income
HBS	Harrod-Balassa-Samuelson
ICOR	incremental capital-output ratio
ICRG	International Country Risk Guide (PRS Group)
IDRs	Indian depositary receipts
IE	International Enterprise (Singapore)
IEA	International Energy Agency
IFS	International Financial Statistics (IMF)
IIPs	international investment positions
IMF	International Monetary Fund
ISI	import substituting industrialization
IV	instrumental variables
LDCs	least developed countries
LSE	London Stock Exchange
M1	notes and coins in circulation
M2	money holdings
M&A	merger and acquisition
NASDAQ	a U.S. stock exchange (formerly National Association of Securities Dealers Automated Quotations)

NYSE	New York Stock Exchange
OECD	Organisation for Economic Co-operation and Development
PMG	pooled mean group
PPP	purchasing power parity
R&D	research and development
SDR(s)	Special Drawing Right(s)
SGX	Singapore Stock Exchange
SWFs	sovereign wealth funds
TFP	total factor productivity
USEIA	U.S. Energy Information Administration
WDI	World Development Indicators (World Bank)
WIPO	World Intellectual Property Organization

All dollar amounts are U.S. dollars unless otherwise indicated.

Overview

SWEEPING CHANGES ARE AFOOT in the global economy. As the second decade of the 21st century unfolds and the world exits from the 2008–09 financial crisis, the growing clout of emerging markets is paving the way for a world economy with an increasingly multipolar character. The distribution of global growth will become more diffuse, with no single country dominating the global economic scene.

The seeds of this change were planted some time ago. Over the past two decades, the world has witnessed emerging economies rise to become a powerful force in international production, trade, and finance. Emerging and developing countries' share of international trade flows has risen steadily, from 26 percent in 1995 to an estimated 42 percent in 2010. Much of this rise has been due to an expansion of trade not between developed countries and developing countries, but among developing countries. Similarly, more than one-third of foreign direct investment in developing countries currently originates in other developing countries. Emerging economies have also increased their financial holdings and wealth. Emerging and developing countries now hold three-quarters of all official foreign exchange reserves (a reversal in the pattern of the previous decade, when advanced economies held two-thirds of all reserves), and sovereign wealth funds and other pools of capital in developing countries have become key sources of international investment. At the same time, the risk of investing in emerging economies has declined dramatically. Borrowers such as Brazil, Chile, and Turkey now pay lower interest rates on their sovereign debts than do several European countries.

As investors and multinational companies increase their exposure to fast-growing emerging economies, international demand for emerging-economy currencies will grow, making way for a global monetary system with more than one dominant currency. The growing strength of emerging economies also affects the policy environment, necessitating more inclusive global economic policy making in the future.

This broad evolution under way in the global economy is not without precedent. Throughout the course of history, paradigms of economic power have been drawn and redrawn according to the rise and fall of states with the greatest capability to drive global growth and provide stimulus to other countries through cross-border commercial and financial engagements. In the first half of the second millennium, China and India were the world's predominant growth poles. The Industrial Revolution brought Western European economies to the forefront. In the post–World War II era, the United States was the predominant force in the global economy, with Germany and Japan also playing leading roles.

In more recent years, the global economy has begun yet another major transition, one in which economic influence has clearly become more dispersed than at any time since the late 1960s. Just as important, developing countries have never been at the forefront of multipolarity in economic affairs. During the forecast period of *Global Development Horizons (GDH) 2011*—from 2011 to 2025—the rise of emerging economies will inevitably have major implications for the global economic and geopolitical hierarchy, just as similar transformations have had in the past.

Increased diffusion of global growth and economic power raises the imperative of collective management as the most viable mechanism for addressing the challenges of a multipolar world economy. The key differences that the management of a multipolar global economy will present relative to the postwar era of the U.S.-centered global economic order relate to the distribution of the costs and responsibilities of system maintenance and the mechanisms for sharing the special privileges and benefits associated with being a global growth pole. In the postwar era, the global economic order was built on a complementary set of tacit economic and security arrangements between the United States and its core partners, with developing countries playing a peripheral role in formulating their macroeconomic policies and establishing economic links with an eye toward benefiting from the growth dynamism in developed countries. In exchange for the United States assuming the responsibilities of system maintenance, serving as the open market of last resort, and issuing the most widely used international reserve currency, its key partners, Western European countries and Japan, acquiesced to the special privileges enjoyed by the United States—seigniorage gains, domestic macroeconomic policy autonomy, and balance of payments flexibility.

Broadly, this arrangement still holds, though hints of its erosion became evident some time ago. For example, the end of the postwar gold exchange standard in 1971 heralded a new era of floating currencies (formalized by the Jamaica Agreement in 1976), a trend that has not been limited to developed countries. Particularly since the East Asian financial crisis of 1997–98, developing countries have increasingly floated their currencies. Changes in currency use have also occurred. As Europe has followed a trajectory of ever-increasing economic integration, the euro has come to represent a growing proportion of international transactions and foreign exchange reserve holdings. At the same time, developing economies' increased trade flows and the gradual opening of their economies to foreign capital have benefited developing economies handsomely, boosting their growth potential and tying their economic and financial stakes to the continuation of a liberal global order. In the unfolding global economic environment, in which a number of dynamic emerging economies are evolving to take their place at the helm of the global economy, the management of multipolarity demands a reappraisal of three pillars of the conventional approach to global economic governance—the link between economic power concentration and stability, the North-South axis of capital flows, and the centrality of the U.S. dollar in the global monetary system. Such a reappraisal offers much in advancing the debate on the future course of international development policy and discourse.

In anticipation of the shape of the future global economy, this first edition of *Global Development Horizons* aims to map out the emerging policy agenda and challenges that an increasingly multipolar world economy poses for developing countries.

Emerging Growth Poles Will Alter the Balance of Global Growth

The coming decades will see global economic growth increasingly being generated in emerging economies. By 2025, global economic growth will predominantly be generated in emerging economies. Although many high-income countries are only gradually recovering from the financial crisis, most developing countries have swiftly returned to their fast precrisis growth trend. China was one of the first economies to emerge from the crisis, and it returned quickly to around 10 percent growth. India experienced a stronger contraction, but also attained more than 10 percent growth in 2010, and the government is putting in place an ambitious new Five Year Plan (with improved policies and necessary investment programs) to keep growth at that level. Latin America sharply rebounded in 2010, after contracting sharply in 2009. Even Sub-Saharan Africa is expected to return quickly to almost 6 percent annual growth, similar to its performance in the years before the crisis. Even in the absence of such exceptionally high growth rates in the developing world, the balance of global growth is expected to shift dramatically.

The changing role of developing countries will come with major transformations to their economies, corporate sectors, and financial systems. These changes are likely to occur in a wide variety of scenarios. The baseline scenario considered in *GDH 2011*—which is derived from longer-term historical trends and from forward-looking components such as anticipated changes in demography, labor force growth, saving patterns, and educational levels—offers a lens into the possible transformations to come. This scenario envisions average growth over the next 15 years that will be substantially lower than the highs of 2010. However, emerging economies will still, collectively, expand by an average of 4.7 percent per year (more than twice the developed world's 2.3 percent rate) between 2011 and 2025. (Given the considerable uncertainty underlying long-term growth projections, the baseline scenario includes error bands to emphasize the wide range of possible outcomes). By 2025, six major emerging economies—Brazil, China, India, Indonesia, the Republic of Korea, and the Russian Federation—will collectively account for more than half of all global growth. Several of these economies will collectively account for more than half of the global growth rate. This new global economy, in which the centers of growth are distributed across both developed and emerging economies, is what *GDH 2011* envisions as a multipolar world.

Altering this balance calls for productivity growth in emerging economies and realignment of demand away from external sources

Even with a moderation of growth in developing countries, successful realization of the baseline scenario presented in *GDH 2011* is dependent on several important changes to the character of growth in emerging economies. In particular, strong future growth performance of emerging markets depends critically on these economies' ability to sustain improvements in technological dynamism—often referred to as total factor productivity (TFP)—and to successfully transition toward internal sources of demand.

Historically, economic progress in emerging economies has followed one of two paths. The first, which characterizes economies such as China, India, and Russia, is one in which TFP growth is a major contributor to economic growth. The second path, which has recently been common among the economies of Latin America and Southeast Asia, is one in which growth is led by the rapid mobilization of factors of production. Yet even in the former case, TFP

growth has been largely due to the rapid adoption of existing technologies, economywide factor reallocation, and improvements in institutional governance, rather than progress in pure innovative capacity. The long-run viability of fast-paced growth in emerging economies will thus depend, in part, on the ability of emerging economies to enhance their indigenous innovation through investments in human capital and through the creation of appropriate institutional mechanisms to stimulate expenditure on research and development (R&D).

Innovation and innovative capacity are already rising in emerging economies. Since 2000, China and India have invested heavily in R&D; expenditures on R&D accounted for 1.4 percent of gross domestic product (GDP) in China and 0.8 percent in India, about an order of magnitude greater than that shown by peer economies in their respective income groups. The siting of major research facilities in China by Microsoft, the invention of the Nano microcar by Indian firm Tata, and the continued string of aeronautical breakthroughs in Russia suggest the emerging-economy giants' strong potential for fostering growth through technological advancement.

Rapid growth in the major emerging economies will also need to be accompanied by a realignment of growth away from external sources and toward internal demand—a process that is under way in many cases. In China, for example, consumption is projected to rise from the current 41 percent of national income to 55 percent by 2025, much closer to the level of developed countries. Similar increases are also likely to occur in the emerging economies of Eastern Europe. Latin American economies, where the consumption share of income is already 65 percent and is expected to remain at that level, will be the exception to this trend. The sharpest declines in savings rates are likely in East Asian and Eastern European economies, where population aging will be at a more advanced stage. In Eastern Europe, rising levels of consumption are likely to occur concomitantly with relative declines in investment shares, consistent with the declining labor force in several countries. As a result, current account deficits could narrow in those countries. Conversely, account surpluses in several Asian countries could be reduced with the declining savings rates. Together with rising domestic savings in the United States after the financial crisis, the more prominent role of emerging economies coincides with a narrowing of global imbalances, which indeed is part of the baseline scenario.

Sustaining higher consumption shares of output in emerging economies will be key in consolidating the transition from externally driven to internally driven growth and will require an expansion of the middle class, which, in turn, will call for emerging-market policy makers to usher in broad financial sector development and to improve domestic social safety nets. To meet demand for more diverse consumption goods, increasing numbers of small and medium enterprises are required, together with open trade relations.

As the international trade shares of the emerging and developed world converge, global wealth and asset holdings will shift toward emerging economies

As a group, emerging economies are likely to experience significant increases in their international trade flows by 2025, in terms of both imports and exports. The value of Indonesia's exports, for example, is likely to double between 2010 and 2025, while the value of its imports is expected to be more than one-and-a-half times higher by 2025. Global trade is forecast to expand as a share of global output over the same time period, from 49.9 percent of output to 53.6 percent.

These current account paths mean that major emerging economies are likely to collectively take on a large and rising net asset international position (albeit at a diminishing rate) in their holdings of investments in developed economies (which, in turn, are expected to build equally large net liability positions). Global wealth and asset holdings will thus shift further toward emerging economies with surpluses, such as China and major oil exporters in the Middle East. This adjustment is already reflected in the current financial landscape: International reserves held by emerging economies topped $7.4 trillion

in 2010 (approximately three times the $2.1 trillion in reserves held by advanced economies), and the share of cross-border mergers and acquisitions (M&A) by firms based in emerging economies in 2010 was 29 percent ($470 billion) of the global total.

The road ahead for emerging economies—while cautiously positive—will nevertheless entail downside risks of both a short- and a long-term nature. If economies with historically low TFP contributions are unable to raise their productivity levels through institutional reform and technological innovation, the existing two-track global economy may fracture even further into a slowly divergent growth path between advanced economies, low-productivity developing economies, and high-productivity developing economies. Similarly, if outward-oriented emerging economies with weak internal demands are not successful in increasing their consumption share, capital in these economies may eventually be channeled toward increasingly unproductive, low-yielding investments. The run-up in commodity prices since 2003 may also become persistent, which could potentially derail growth in developing countries that are especially commodity intensive. On the upside, if emerging economies successfully navigate their rising per capita incomes, provide necessary infrastructural improvements, and facilitate corporate sector reform, the baseline scenario may underestimate emerging economies' future growth potential. Finally, unexpected economic and geopolitical developments may introduce fundamental uncertainty of a nature that is impossible to develop scenarios for.

Emerging-Market Multinationals Becoming a Potent Force in Reshaping the Process of Industrial Globalization

Long relegated to second-tier status, emerging-market companies are becoming powerful forces and agents of change in the global industrial and financial landscape. Trends in foreign direct investment (FDI) flows are one indication of this shifting status. Between 1997 and 2003, companies based in emerging economies engaged in cross-border investment through M&A deals of $189 billion, or 4 percent of the value of all global M&A investments over the period. Between 2004 and 2010, that amount increased to $1.1 trillion—17 percent of the global total. Since 2003, approximately 5,000 firms based in emerging markets have established a global presence through 12,516 greenfield investments of $1.72 trillion. More than one-third of FDI inflows to developing countries now originate in other developing countries: Of the 11,113 cross-border M&A deals announced worldwide in 2010, 5,623—more than half—involved emerging-market companies, either as buyers or as takeover targets by advanced-country firms. As they venture overseas, companies based in emerging markets tend to seek assets that will help them accomplish one or more of several goals: diversification of their growth, a larger global market share, exploitation of growth opportunities not available in their domestic economies, or freedom from an unfavorable domestic economic climate.

As they pursue growth opportunities abroad, corporations based in emerging markets play an increasingly prominent role in global business, competing with firms based in advanced countries for natural resources, technology, and access to international markets. Many emerging-market firms often have an advantage over advanced-country firms in navigating difficult policy environments in other developing countries, because they have experienced similar conditions in their home countries. These two trends, together with the overall strengthening of South-South trade links, will ensure that South-South investment continues to expand. Further, M&A activity by emerging-market firms in developing countries is on the rise and is becoming an important source of FDI. Because such transactions typically occur within close geographical proximity, they will not only deepen regional economic ties, but also accelerate the integration of low-income countries into the global economy. Emerging-market firms have also been active in South-North acquisitions, especially in advanced economies with sophisticated equity markets and favorable growth prospects. The annual value of cross-border M&A transactions undertaken by emerging-market firms is forecast to more than double by 2025, while the annual number of cross-border M&A deals is expected to more than triple (from fewer than 2,500 in 2011 to almost 8,000 in 2025). This trend outpaces the underlying GDP growth rates in emerging-market firms' home countries.

The development of emerging-market firms into a potent force for globalization in their own right will have important implications for cross-border capital formation, technology generation and diffusion, and financing of commercial activities. A number of innovative and dynamic emerging-market firms are on a path toward dominating their industrial sectors globally—much in the same way that companies based in advanced economies have done over the past half century. Many emerging-market firms have already begun overtaking their advanced-country competitors in terms of the priority accorded to developing innovative technologies and industrial processes, with 114 firms from emerging economies ranking among the top 1,000 firms worldwide by R&D spending as of 2009, twice as many as five years earlier. This is a particularly noteworthy accomplishment given that the private sector traditionally has not been the main financier of R&D in developing countries. In 2025, a luxury sedan is as likely to be a Hyundai or Tata as a Mercedes or Lexus, is as likely to be powered with fuel from Lukoil or Pertamina as from ExxonMobil or BP, and is as likely to be financed by China's ICBC (Industrial and Commercial Bank of China Ltd.) or Brazil's Itaú as by Citi or BNP Paribas.

There are strong signs of mutually reinforcing links between commercial and financial globalization

The shift in economic and financial power toward the developing world is also reshaping cross-border corporate finance, transforming emerging-market firms into significant participants in international capital markets. The progress of a growing number of developing countries in improving the soundness and transparency of domestic institutions and policies has enabled their firms to gain increased access to international bond and equity markets, and at better terms, in their efforts to expand globally. Nearly two-thirds of emerging-market firms that have been active acquirers since the late 1990s—those firms that have undertaken 10 or more acquisitions—have tapped international markets to access one or more forms of financing through syndicated loans, bond issues, and equity listings. As evidence of the mutually reinforcing links between commercial and financial globalization, a growing number of emerging-market firms undertake at least one cross-border acquisition within two years of accessing international capital markets. International bond issuance, in particular, by borrowers based in emerging markets has grown dramatically since the mid-1990s and is now one of the main sources of capital inflows for those countries. Since 1995, a large number of emerging private companies have engaged in high-profile global bond market transactions, with 80 of them issuing bonds over $1 billion each, of which 10 were issuances of over $2 billion. Some prominent issuers include Petrobras International Finance Company of Brazil, América Móvil of Mexico, Novelis Inc of India, and VTB bank of Russia. Over the next decade and beyond, there is likely to be significant scope for emerging-market companies to further expand their access to international capital markets and at more favorable terms.

In emerging-market economies such as Brazil, Chile, and Mexico, where local capital markets have seen considerable growth and maturity in recent years, companies have the capacity to fund their growth through a more balanced mix of local and international capital market issuance. Furthermore, in some emerging growth poles, particularly those in Asia, signs already exist that their local capital markets are evolving into regional financing hubs. During the next decade and beyond, as local consumer demand continues to rise in the fastest-growing emerging markets and as local capital markets in those countries become deeper and better regulated, manufacturing and consumer goods firms based in developed countries can be expected to also seek access to capital markets in emerging markets. Cross-listings of securities by developed-country firms, although initially motivated by the desire to raise their firms' brand recognition, will be followed by issues that tap large pools of available savings in emerging markets.

From a policy perspective, the growing role and influence of emerging-market firms in global investment and finance may make it more possible—and indeed, critical—to move forward with the sort of multilateral framework for regulating cross-border investment that has been derailed several times since the 1920s. In contrast to international trade and monetary relations, no multilateral regime exists to promote and govern cross-border investment. Instead, the surge of bilateral investment treaties (BITs)—more than 2,275 BITs were in place in 2007, up from just 250 in the mid-1980s—has provided the most widely used mechanism for interstate negotiation over cross-border investment terms, including access to international arbitration of disputes. Though BITs have proven to be suboptimal from an economic point of view, there are reasons to believe that their proliferation and the associated experience of formulating, negotiating, and implementing them across a large number of developed and developing countries have set the stage for transition into a multilateral framework. The elimination of investment restrictions through BITs, for example, may be supportive of more general multilateral liberalization efforts. Moreover, BITs have also set the stage for complementary institutional advancements at the global level. Indeed, the International Centre for the Settlement of Investment Disputes (ICSID) has experienced growing demand for cross-border investment dispute settlement services—cases registered with the ICSID averaged 25 per year between 2001 and 2010, up from an average of about two cases per year between 1981 and 1990. This increase in demand has allowed the maturation of an institutional infrastructure that is well positioned to serve as an important foundation, especially on legal aspects, for a multilateral framework in the future.

Multipolar International Economy to Lead to a Larger Role for the Euro and, in the Long Term, for the Renminbi

Rapid growth in emerging-market economies has led to enormous wealth creation and substantial accumulation of their net claims on the rest of the world, raising the profile of emerging markets in the international financial system as a result. Developing and emerging countries held two-thirds of the world's $9 trillion of official foreign exchange reserves as of late 2010, compared to only 37 percent of reserves held at the end of 2000. Sovereign wealth funds and other pools of capital in developing countries have become a major source of international investment. Between 2010 and 2025, the collective net international investment position of major emerging markets is projected to rise to a surplus of more than $15.2 trillion (in 2009 dollars) under the baseline scenario presented in *GDH 2011*, offset by a corresponding deficit in today's advanced economies.

Even though the role of emerging markets in international finance is growing, there is a great disparity between their economic size and their role in the international monetary system. At present, no emerging economy has a currency that is used internationally—that is, one in which official reserves are held, goods and services are invoiced, international claims are denominated, and exchange rates are anchored—to any great extent. Virtually all developing countries are exposed to currency mismatch risk in their international trade and investment and financing transactions. Addressing these disparities in the international monetary system needs urgent attention, in terms of both the management of the system (here, the International Monetary Fund [IMF] continues to play a leading role) and the understanding of long-term forces shaping the future workings of the system.

International currency use exhibits considerable inertia and is subject to network externalities, rendering currencies already in widespread use the most attractive. For now, the U.S. dollar remains the chief international currency, despite a slow decline in the proportion of global reserves held in dollars since the late 1990s. But the dollar now faces several potential rivals for the role of international currency. At present, the euro is the most credible of those alternatives. Its status is poised to expand, provided the euro area can successfully overcome the sovereign debt crises currently faced by several of its member countries

and can avoid the moral hazard problems associated with bailouts of countries within the European Union.

Looking further ahead, as emerging economies account for an ever-growing share of the global economy and participate more actively in cross-border trade and finance, one sees that their currencies—particularly the renminbi—will inevitably play a more important role in the international financial system. A larger role for the renminbi would help resolve the disparity between China's great economic strength on the global stage and its heavy reliance on foreign currencies. On one hand, China is the world's largest exporting country and holds the largest stock of foreign exchange reserves by far ($2.9 trillion held as of end 2010). On the other hand, China faces a massive currency mismatch because transactions by its government, corporations, and other entities with the rest of the world are almost entirely denominated in foreign currencies, primarily U.S. dollars. With private entities in China not able to directly address the currency mismatch, the task falls to the government. In moving to address such issues, Chinese authorities have undertaken the internationalizing of the renminbi on two fronts: (1) developing an offshore renminbi market and (2) encouraging the use of the renminbi in trade invoicing and settlement. Such initiatives are beginning to have an effect in laying the foundation for the renminbi taking on a more important global role.

Building on this unfolding reality, *GDH 2011* presents three potential scenarios for the future of the international monetary system: a status quo centered on the U.S. dollar, a multicurrency system, and a system with the Special Drawing Right (SDR) as the main international currency. The most likely of the three scenarios is the multicurrency system. Under this scenario, the current predominance of the U.S. dollar would end sometime before 2025 and would be replaced by a monetary system in which the dollar, the euro, and the renminbi would each serve as full-fledged international currencies. This expected transition raises several important questions. First, how will developing countries, the majority of which will continue to use foreign currencies in trade of goods and assets, be affected by a move to a multicurrency system? Second, can a multipolar economic system—with its dangers of instability—be managed within the existing institutional arrangements, or is a more fundamental reform of the system necessary? Third, what can be done to smooth the transition to multipolarity, short of fundamental reform of the international monetary system?

A more multipolar international monetary system will still involve currency risks for most developing countries

The dollar-based international monetary system of the present and the likely multicurrency system of the future share a number of defects inherent to a system based on national currencies. The fundamental problem is an asymmetric distribution of the costs and benefits of balance of payments adjustment and financing. Countries whose currencies are key in the international monetary system benefit from domestic macroeconomic policy autonomy, seigniorage revenues, relatively low borrowing costs, a competitive edge in financial markets, and little pressure to adjust their external accounts. Meanwhile, countries without key currencies operate within constrained balance of payment positions and bear much of the external adjustment costs of changing global financial and economic conditions. This asymmetric distribution of the cost of adjustment has been a major contributor to the widening of global current account imbalances in recent years. It has also produced a potentially destabilizing situation in which (a) the world's leading economy, the United States, is also the largest debtor, and (b) the world's largest creditor, China, assumes massive currency mismatch risk in the process of financing U.S. debt. Another shortcoming of the current system is that global liquidity is created primarily as the result of the monetary policy decisions that best suit the country issuing the predominant international currency, the United States, rather than with the intention of fully accommodating global demand for liquidity. This characteristic means that the acute dollar shortage that developed in the wake of the Lehman Brothers collapse in 2008, which particularly affected non-U.S. banks, was in many respects worse than the dollar shortage of the 1950s.

In a multipolar global economy, it is likely that dissatisfaction with a national currency–based system will deepen. But from a monetary policy perspective, the creation of a system in which global currency decisions are made on a truly multilateral level—that is, with the explicit agreement of a large number of countries—is not likely; as such, a new system would require countries to cede national sovereignty over their monetary policy. The great deal of inertia in the current international monetary system based on national currencies is also a factor, as is the expectation that a more diffuse distribution of global economic power is likely to render cooperation on any sort of economic policy across borders more difficult.

In the years leading up to the financial crisis, the role of international economic policy making was confined to managing the symptoms of incompatible macroeconomic policies, such as exchange rate misalignments and payments imbalances. As capital markets have been liberalized and exchange rates made more flexible, balance of payments constraints on national economies have been considerably eased, shifting policy coordination toward the more politically sensitive spheres of domestic monetary and fiscal policy. Unless a country's borrowing and trade are concentrated in one of the three key currencies, instability in exchange rates between the key currencies will lead to fluctuations in competitiveness and the value of assets and liabilities, impeding that country's economic policy making and potentially jeopardizing the welfare of its residents. Thus, countries without leading currencies will need to step up their efforts to hedge against exchange rate volatility. This will be the case for developing countries, in particular.

Some of the challenges facing the international monetary system could possibly be managed through increased use of the SDR. Established by the IMF in the 1960s as an international reserve asset and unit of account, the SDR is currently valued in terms of a basket of four major international currencies—the euro, Japanese yen, pound sterling, and U.S. dollar. Enhancing the role of the SDR in the international monetary system could help address both the immediate risks to global financial stability and the ongoing costs of currency volatility. From an operational perspective, there are two main ways to increase use of the SDR. The first would be to encourage official borrowing denominated in SDRs. A second avenue would be to formalize central bank currency swap facilities using the SDR, which would be useful during a financial crisis, or perhaps to adjust the composition of the SDR basket to include the renminbi or other major emerging-market currencies. Over time, the SDR could serve as a natural hedge, especially for low-income countries that lack developed financial markets.

Nevertheless, a multilateral approach will remain the best way to manage global economic policy making

In a world of progressively more multipolar economic growth and financial centers, interdependency will be the operating norm even more than at the present, bringing new challenges for economic diplomacy, national economic policy making, and management of transnational capital channeled across national borders. The potential for rising competition among power centers that is inherent in the shift to a more multipolar world makes it especially important to improve the design of policy coordination across economies—both developing and developed. More generally, as global economic integration increases, so, too, do spillovers of monetary and fiscal policies across countries. Thus, policy coordination is needed not only to improve the average performance of the global economy, but also to avert the attendant risks. Countries should move quickly to better coordinate their responses to global imbalances, to improve financial regulation, and to expand mutual surveillance of macroeconomic policies. To the extent that the vulnerability that comes with interdependence can be managed through appropriate responses by international institutions and multilateral agreements—such as the provision of emergency financial assistance and commitments to open-door policies to ensure access to international markets—interdependence can lead to a shared increase in global prosperity.

Even in the absence of fundamental reform in international policy coordination, a number of concrete steps could be taken to further the

coordination framework put into place by the Group of 20 (G-20) and to preserve the gains made in central bank collaboration and harmonization of financial regulations during the 2008–09 financial crisis. Importantly, coordination should focus on outcomes that would be mutually beneficial to a large number of countries—that is, on international public goods, such as environmentally friendly technologies—rather than on zero-sum variables, in which a gain for one country implies a loss for another. Only by recognizing that multilateral coordination has welfare-enhancing benefits for all will countries voluntarily take into account the concerns of other countries.

Multipolarity to Bring Benefits and New Challenges to the Developing World

A more multipolar global economy will, on balance, be positive for developing countries as a whole—though not necessarily for each of them individually. Growth spillovers—flowing from trade, finance, migration, and technology channels—will induce technological transfer, spur demand for exports, and improve the terms of trade in developing countries as well as enable them to develop their domestic agricultural and manufacturing industries. For example, since 1990, bilateral trade flows between the least developed countries (LDCs) and the major emerging economies have increased threefold; trade with emerging economies now accounts for a greater share of LDCs' bilateral trade flows than their trade with major advanced economies. Moreover, a more diffuse distribution of global growth will also create new external growth drivers, meaning that idiosyncratic shocks in individual growth pole economies will have less impact on the volatility of external demand in those countries than at present. This characteristic was evident in the aftermath of the 2008–09 financial crisis, when cross-border M&A originating in emerging economies accounted for more than a quarter of the value of all deals in 2009 and 2010. Greater multipolarity could also have a tangible effect on patterns of foreign aid, as increased aid disbursements by emerging economies push official development assistance to even greater shares of gross national income in LDCs.

The effect of an increasingly multipolar global economy is likely to differ across countries, however, and LDCs—many of which are heavily reliant on external demand for growth—are at the greatest risk of not being able to adapt to risks created by the transformation. LDCs that are net importers of commodities and mineral resources may face higher global prices because of increased global demand for raw materials. Even in cases where LDCs are net commodity or resource exporters, export-biased growth in LDC economies runs the risk of immiserizing growth. For LDCs with floating exchange rate regimes, critical elements of their response to a more multipolar global economy will be development of institutional policy frameworks, market microstructure, and financial institutions that can ensure the smooth functioning of foreign exchange markets.

Multilateral institutions can play a role in ushering in this new multipolar world by providing technical assistance and promoting policy-learning forums that enhance understanding of the process of transition to a multipolar world economic order. Efforts to raise awareness and equip policy makers in developing countries with the necessary policy tools and financial capacity would help the policy makers to better position their countries in response to expected future challenges and risks, while capitalizing on their countries' strengths and opportunities. Aid and technical assistance from international financial institutions to LDCs also have the potential to cushion the economic shocks and lessen volatility in the LDCs' economies as they seek to adapt to the global forces involved in this transition.

Furthermore, cross-border investment could also benefit from a multilateral framework similar to the World Trade Organization. Meanwhile, the IMF is well positioned to take the lead in guiding reforms in the international monetary system, including providing support for the design of coordination mechanisms for a multicurrency regime that would limit currency volatility and, hence, help LDCs mitigate external exchange rate risks.

Major transitions such as the one currently underway in the global economy always present challenges, because they involve large uncertainties and necessitate complex policy responses. The transition at hand is not just a matter of leaving behind old economic paradigms. Rather, it is about establishing the appropriate mindset and the proper policy and institutional responses—in developing countries, developed countries, and multilateral institutions—to facilitate the transition to, among other matters, better development outcomes. Developing countries have made considerable progress in integrating themselves into, and expanding their profile within, the traditional channels and institutions of international trade and finance. But much work remains to ensure that developing economies adapt to the transition now under way in the global economy in a manner that allows them to share the burden of system maintenance commensurate with their increased stakes in an open international system. It is also critical that major developed economies simultaneously craft policies that are mindful of the growing interdependency associated with the increasing presence of developing economies on the global stage and leverage such interdependency to derive closer international cooperation and prosperity worldwide.

1

Changing Growth Poles and Financial Positions

THE GLOBAL ECONOMY OF 2025 IS likely to look significantly different from that of 2011. Today's emerging economies will, in real terms, account for 45 percent of global output, compared with about 37 percent in 2011 and 30 percent in 2004. These countries will account for about as great a volume of international trade and investment flows as the developed world, and the drivers of global growth will be not only developed giants, but also major developing countries such as China and India, which are likely to experience rapid growth between 2011 and 2025. Emerging economies also will hold a greater proportion of global wealth, as measured by net international investment positions (IIPs).

Shifts in global economic power are not new. Throughout the trajectory of economic history, each phase of global growth has been driven by a small set of countries. From the start of China's Tang dynasty to the Ming dynasty (600–1600), China was a dominant force in the global economy, accounting for a quarter of its output and as much as a third of its growth. The Renaissance saw the beginning of the rise of economies in Western Europe—beginning with Italy, Portugal, and Spain and then, with the advent of the Industrial Revolution, Belgium, France, and Great Britain—accompanied by a transformation of incomes, production, and trade. In the decades following World War II, the mutually reinforcing engines of American innovation and strong consumer demand propelled the United States to the position of the world's foremost economic power, with Germany, Japan, and the former Soviet Union also playing leading roles.

As the world exits the 2008–09 financial crisis, the global economy appears poised to transition to a new set of growth poles—defined in this book as an economy that significantly drives global growth—with some hitherto "emerging" economies prominent among them. Although growth in the advanced economies remains sluggish—a phenomenon that has been described as a "new normal" (El-Erian 2009)—developing economies have recovered from the crisis and are exhibiting robust growth. Global growth in the first quarter of the 21st century thus is likely to be driven by the sustained rise of China, India, and other emerging economic powerhouses. This chapter explores the economic and financial implications of this shift in greater detail. The main messages of chapter 1 are as follows:

- *Under the most likely baseline global economic scenario presented here, emerging economies will become increasingly important engines of global growth between 2011 and 2025.* The combined real output of six major emerging economies—Brazil, the Russian Federation, India, Indonesia, China, and the Republic of Korea (the BRIICKs)—will match that of the euro area by 2025. Growth in emerging markets will, in this scenario, average 4.7 percent over 2011–25, compared with the developed world's growth of 2.3 percent, and will be accompanied by a significant realignment of consumption, investment, and trade shares. The shares of global trade flows accounted for by emerging and advanced economies will converge rapidly, with each group accounting for roughly half of all global trade by 2025, contrary to the current situation in which the advanced economies represent the majority of both exports and imports. In some major emerging economies, these structural changes are already under way.

- *The changing landscape of growth drivers in the world economy points toward a distribution of economic size and growth that is more diffuse: a multipolar world.* In the 2004–08 period, the United States, the euro area, and China served as the world's main growth poles. By 2025, emerging economies, including Brazil, India, Indonesia, and Korea—along with advanced economies such as Japan and the United Kingdom—are likely to join these three poles in accounting for much of the world's growth activity. But to sustain their growth momentum and serve as true growth poles, emerging economies will need to undertake structural changes that will generate self-sustaining, internally driven growth through a combination of sustained productivity advances and robust domestic demand. This undertaking calls for saving rates consistent with investment opportunities, capital that is efficiently allocated and utilized, and the ability not only to adopt new technologies but also to drive innovation.

- *The potential emerging economy growth poles are far from a monolithic group, with their rapid rise to power characterized by the diversity of their development pathways.* East Asian growth poles, such as China and Korea, historically have been heavily reliant on exports to drive growth, whereas in Latin American growth poles, such as Brazil and Mexico, domestic consumption has been more important. With the emergence of a substantial middle class in developing countries and demographic transitions underway in several major East Asian economies, stronger consumption trends are likely to prevail, which in turn can serve as a source of sustained global growth. Strong investment trends also have the potential to drive global growth going forward, and to increase productivity in emerging economies. In many large emerging economies, the structural changes that will drive changes in their consumption and investment trends are already under

way. Just as important, variations in aggregate demand brought about by changes in the configuration of the world's growth poles may have significant impacts on the prospects of least developed countries (LDCs), which are often reliant on external demand for their growth.

- *As a group, potential emerging economy growth poles are having an ever-greater impact on global investment, trade flows, and external imbalances.* There have already been tangible shifts in global trade and investment patterns, most notably in the greater volume of South-South flows. Yet the unfolding dynamics of global imbalances will depend as much on the policies adopted by governments as they do on private trade and capital flows responding to such policies. Efforts to promote financial market development, for example, can help reduce oversaving behavior and facilitate adjustment in countries running very large current account surpluses; similarly, enhancing the business environment for exporting can help deficit countries rein in their current accounts.

Growth Poles and the Global Macroeconomy in the Postcrisis Era
The emergence of new poles

In the years leading up to the global financial crisis of 2008–09, many developing economies were beginning to display their economic vitality and dynamism. Emerging developing-world powerhouses such as Brazil, Russia, India, and China—the so-called BRIC economies (O'Neill 2001)—began to challenge the economic power of the G-7, accounting for an ever-increasing share of global trade, finance, and labor flows.

The financial crisis has accelerated this trend. With postcrisis economic performance in developing countries undeniably stronger than in developed countries (developing economies as a whole grew by 1.5 percent in 2009, compared to a decline of 3.4 percent in developed countries) and near-term growth forecasts suggesting that developing and emerging economies will continue to expand considerably faster than their high-income counterparts, the global growth poles are beginning to expand beyond developed economies.

China and India are likely to be the main flag bearers among emerging-market growth poles in the years ahead. This is especially so for China, which overtook Japan as the world's second-largest economy in 2010 and Germany as the world's largest exporter in 2009. In the medium term, the proportion of global economic growth represented by other emerging countries such as Brazil, Indonesia, Korea, and Russia likely will increase dramatically. Together with China and India, these countries—epitomized by the BRIC economies but not limited to them—will increasingly become the world's major consumers, investors, and exporters, affecting both the developed world and the LDCs with which they interact.

From poles to the periphery: Channels by which poles drive global growth

Although widely used in the policy community, the term "growth pole" remains somewhat ambiguously defined (box 1.1). This book conceives of a growth pole as an economy whose growth spills over to—and thus helps drive—the growth process in other economies. To that end, this book applies a quantitatively based definition that depends on the contribution of the economy to global growth, adjusted by the strength of linkages from domestic to global growth.[1] In this fashion, a growth pole not only is a hive of economic activity, but also is able to stimulate economic activity in the countries with which it has strong links.

Because the focus of this chapter is on the transmission of real economic growth (and associated implications of this growth for economic policy), the definition of a growth pole employed here departs from definitions of polarity and distribution of power that are more commonly found in fields of study such as political science and international relations (Felsenthal and Machover 1998; Mansfield 1993).[2] The distribution of economic influence, nonetheless, has

practical implications for issues of international policy coordination, policy choices, and international monetary relations, all of which are addressed in chapter 3.

A number of economic transmission channels are supported by both theory and empirical evidence. Since technological progress is a key driver of sustainable, long-run growth (Romer 1990; Solow 1956), channels of technological diffusion are central to growth spillovers. These channels include flows of knowledge through trade, finance, and migration, as well as more direct transfers of technology embedded in physical capital and technological knowledge embodied in human capital (figure 1.1). For example, foreign direct investment (FDI) from the United States to China may lead to indirect technology transfer via the building of U.S.-designed manufacturing plants and equipment, although a more direct transfer of know-how may occur in the use of capital-intensive technology; through training of operational line workers, back-office staff, and management; and through learning by local suppliers.

In addition to technological diffusion, growth spillovers can be promoted through the transfer of institutional advances that shape incentives to develop or adopt new technologies, or through the release of constraints that prohibit the adoption of technologies (Acemoglu, Johnson, and Robinson 2005; Rodrik, Subramanian, and Trebbi 2004). Although such transfer of institutional practices is undoubtedly important, the transfer tends to come about slowly and often is difficult to measure accurately.

To some extent, the transfer of institutional practices can be captured indirectly in data on a potential growth pole's growth rate and economic size. It is plausible that when reform of economic institutions promotes growth, people in other countries take notice and demand similar reforms of their governments. Moreover, the larger the economy in which the reforms and growth take place, and the more rapid the growth, the more conscious people in other countries likely will be of these events, assuming all else is held constant. Trade, capital flows (particularly FDI), and international migration also may facilitate some transfer of institutional advances, reinforcing the more

BOX 1.1   What is a growth pole? Defining poles in theory and practice

In this book, a growth pole is defined as an economy whose domestic growth helps drive the growth process in other economies. This definition is motivated in part by a desire to focus on the importance of economic dynamism and progress—the "growth" part of the expression—while capturing the important role of spillover externalities, knowledge transfer, and gains from exchange (the "pole" part of the term). However, given the lack of consensus on the definition of a "growth pole," it is useful to examine alternative conceptualizations of the term.

The term "growth pole" was first introduced in the context of economic growth by François Perroux in 1949. Initially, the expression was used in reference to agglomerations of firms or industries in which growth is concentrated and that had linkages to each other and to peripheral firms. Since then, the term has been applied to an increasingly varied set of related concepts, with "growth pole" quickly taking on a spatial or geographic dimension. These concepts differ mainly in terms of the space in which poles are identified. In discussions of regional development policy, for example, cities where economic growth is concentrated came to be known as growth poles, with the aspects of vertical linkages and external economies of scale remaining central to the concept. In fact, the study of tensions between forces supporting greater agglomeration versus specialization spawned the field of economic geography (Fujita, Krugman, and Venables 1999; World Bank 2009b).

The idea of growth polarity then became extended to the global scale, while simultaneously becoming somewhat enmeshed with the concept of polarity—sites of concentration of geopolitical power and influence—being developed in the international relations literature. This connection is due in part to the intuitive idea that geopolitical influence stems ultimately from

economic size; still, to clearly define a "growth pole," the concept must be unlinked from that of geopolitical influence per se. The concept of *global growth poles* also differs somewhat from the idea of growth poles conceptualized in regional, national, or geographic space, to the extent that the nature of international economic linkages differs from linkages within national or regional economies, and not merely in terms of scale.

Even when a global scale is specified, the expression "growth pole" is not always used consistently. Some generalizations, however, can be made as to the term's qualitative meaning. In this book, a global growth pole is broadly defined as an economy in which global growth is significantly concentrated and that drives growth in other economies sufficiently to have an impact on the growth of the world economy as a whole. Thus, a quantitatively based definition of a global growth pole depends on the growth rate of the economy relative to the growth rate of the world economy, and on the strength of linkages between domestic and global growth (see annex 1.1).

In establishing this definition for identifying global growth poles, countries are the natural units to consider, mainly due to aggregation of relevant data at the country level. However, in some special cases in which a group of countries is highly integrated—as is the case for an economic and monetary union, for example—it is probably justifiable to consider the entire group as a potential pole. If this approach is taken, clearly defined criteria are required to group countries consistently. This book aggregates the economies of the euro area, the two CFA franc zones (independently), the Eastern Caribbean dollar zone, and the South African Multilateral Monetary Area as single economic units. In addition, China and its special administrative regions of Hong Kong and Macao are classified as a single economic unit.

traditional knowledge and technological transfer roles of these channels.

Trade is a major channel by which growth is propagated from growth poles to periphery economies. The more commercial exchange domestic firms have with foreign firms, the more industrial and technological knowledge the domestic firms

acquire; hence, the evolution of technological progress and comparative advantage are interlinked and jointly determined (Grossman and Helpman 1991a). Trade in intermediate goods may function as a channel of technology diffusion and spillover in a second, weaker way: intermediate goods embody technologies, so importation

FIGURE 1.1   Channels of growth spillovers from a growth pole

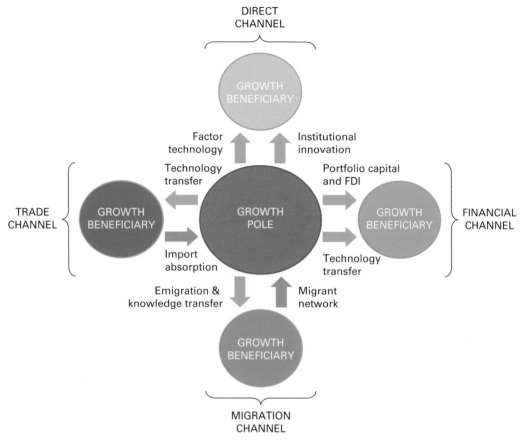

Source: World Bank staff calculations.
Note: Arrows point to direction of flow, whereby growth from a pole can influence growth elsewhere, while annotations indicate the specific growth stimuli transferred to the beneficiary of the pole.

of intermediate goods can reduce costs of product development and production of new products (Eaton and Kortum 2002; Grossman and Helpman 1991b; Rivera-Batiz and Romer 1991).

The broad implication that trade is an important channel of technology diffusion is supported by a small body of empirical research. For example, in East Asian economies, firm openness is associated with subsequent advantages in firm-level productivity (Hallward-Driemeier, Iarossi, and Sokoloff 2002). Although empirical support is greater for importation than for exportation as a significant channel of technology diffusion to the country in question, a growth pole nevertheless may drive growth in a periphery economy simply by absorbing its exports and driving expansion of exporting industries. Exportation

also is associated with intraindustry reallocation of production from low-productivity firms to high-productivity firms and, in some industries, with market size effects stemming from increasing returns to scale (Krugman 1979; Melitz 2003). Thus, it is possible that growth is driven by bidirectional trade—that is, by importing from a growth pole and by exporting to a pole.

Capital flows, particularly FDI, have the potential to be an important channel of technological diffusion. FDI flows from multinational parent companies to subsidiaries (or greenfield investments) have the potential to directly transfer technological knowledge, or at least result in indirect knowledge transfers from subsidiaries to other firms in the host country through labor turnover or technology embedded in intermediate goods and services (Du, Harrison, and Jefferson 2011; Ethier 1986; Fosfuri, Motta, and Rønde 2001; Markusen 2004; Rodríguez-Clare 1996). FDI also may promote growth through channels other than technology diffusion, such as real-location of production to the most productive sectors within an economy or to the most productive firms within sectors. More broadly, financial openness can promote growth, especially when such liberalization is combined with complementary institutional reform, which spurs domestic financial market development and fosters growth (Beck and Levine 2005; Quinn and Toyoda 2008). Thus, capital flows, indeed, can be another important channel through which growth poles drive global growth.

The empirical evidence that FDI is an important channel of technological diffusion is somewhat mixed. Large intraindustry spillovers are found primarily in case studies of high-technology FDI projects, as in the case of microchip-maker Intel in Costa Rica (Larraín, López-Calva, and Rodríguez-Clare 2001) and other technology sectors (Keller and Yeaple 2009). Firm-level studies using broader industry samples typically find evidence of only small intraindustry spillovers

(Griffith, Redding, and Simpson 2004; Haskel, Pereira, and Slaughter 2007). In some cases, there is also evidence of vertical spillovers. In Lithuania, for example, technological spillovers from FDI occur through backward linkages from partly foreign-owned firms to their domestic suppliers, but not from fully foreign-owned firms (Javorcik 2004).

Given that technological knowledge is difficult or impossible to codify fully, meaning that some technological knowledge is transferred only from person to person, the mobility of labor also plays a role in promoting knowledge spillovers. Empirical evidence supports the hypothesis that both migration and short-term business travel facilitate diffusion of tacit technological knowledge. International labor mobility promotes not only knowledge flows to the firms that hire immigrants, but also knowledge spillovers to other firms in the economy (Hovhannisyan and Keller 2010; Kim, Lee, and Marschke 2009; Oettl and Agrawal 2008). The stock of migrants may induce network effects from increased trade and knowledge transfer (Kerr 2008; Kerr and Lincoln 2010; Rauch 2001) and serve as a source of growth for the recipient nation, as migrants tend to be self-selected as industrious and seeking opportunity (McCraw 2010). Historically, emigration has been associated with the onset of modern economic growth in Europe—a phenomenon sometimes termed the "mobility transition" (Hatton 2010).

Evolving growth poles in the global economy

Over the course of two millennia, large swings in global growth leadership have occurred. Until the first half of the second millennium, China and India were the world's predominant growth poles.[3] Starting in the 1500s, Western Europe began its unrelenting rise, accounting for a rising share of total global output (Maddison 2007) and playing a growing role in shaping global growth dynamics. This is evident from examining these countries' *simple polarity index*, which measures a country's contribution to global growth (figure 1.2).[4]

Although Western Europe retained its position as the predominant growth pole through much of the first half of the 20th century—in large part

FIGURE 1.2 Historical evolution of simple growth polarity, selected economies, 1–2008

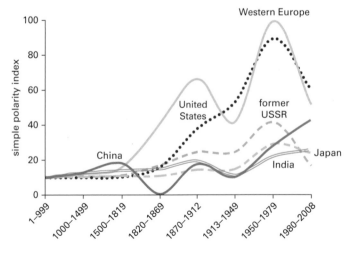

Source: World Bank staff calculations, from Maddison 2003.
Note: The simple polarity index was calculated from size-weighted (compound) GDP growth rates measured in 1990 international Geary-Khamis dollars normalized to the maximum and minimum of the full 1–2008 period.

due to robust growth in France and Germany—countries such as Japan, the United States, and the former Soviet Union also became growth poles during that time. Also evident in figure 1.2 is the general upward trend in the simple growth polarity index, a reflection of the long-run acceleration in global growth that began in the mid-millennium and persisted until the 1970s.

Though the large industrial economies of today were undeniably the drivers of global growth during the 20th century, this trend appears to be changing. Using a measure of polarity that captures growth spillovers via trade, finance, and technology channels—defined as a country's *multidimensional polarity index*—the downward trend in the indexes of large advanced economies is evident (figure 1.3, panel a). Japan's multidimensional polarity index fell sharply after the bursting of its asset bubble in the early 1990s and never again approached its previous level. In a similar fashion, the polarity indexes of the United States and the euro area moderated during the late 1990s and 2000s.

In contrast, the multidimensional polarity indexes of key emerging countries appear to be synchronously rising (figure 1.3, panel b). With the exception of China, however, these polarity indexes are still one to two orders of magnitude smaller than those of advanced countries. Nevertheless, China's polarity exceeded, in absolute terms, that of the euro area and the United States in the 2004–08 period, and the combined value of the real multidimensional polarity indexes for the five highest-ranked emerging countries (China, Korea, Russia, India, and Singapore) was about the same as that of the five highest-ranked advanced economies (table 1.1, column 1).

What is most striking about potential growth poles among the emerging economies is the distinction of China: the only emerging economy that undeniably can be classified as a current growth pole. This is the case regardless of whether growth is measured according to alternative metrics; China, for instance, has a slightly lower relative polarity if one corrects for changes to a country's real exchange rate over time (table 1.1, column 2),[5] but has much greater relative polarity when growth is adjusted to capture actual purchasing power (table 1.1, column 3).

FIGURE 1.3   Modern evolution of multidimensional growth polarity, selected advanced and emerging economies, 1969–2008

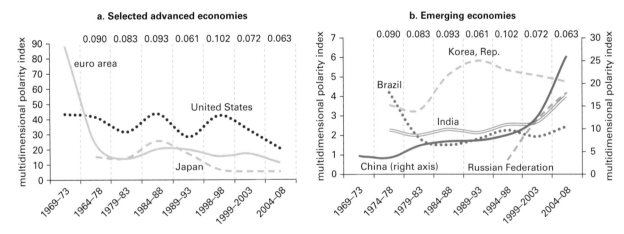

Sources: World Bank staff calculations, from IE Singapore, IMF Direction of Trade Statistics (DOT), IMF International Financial Statistics (IFS), World Bank World Development Indicators (WDI), and World Intellectual Property Organization (WIPO) Patentscope databases.

Note: The multidimensional polarity index was generated from the first principal component of trade, finance, and technology-weighted growth shares, measured in constant U.S. dollars. The numbers correspond to concentration indexes for the top 15 countries, computed from the multidimensional polarity measure for each corresponding five-year period (the first period was omitted because of insufficient observations).

TABLE 1.1   Multidimensional polarity index, top 15 economies, 2004–08 average

Economy	Real index	Economy	HBS index	Economy	PPP index
China	26.20	Euro area	47.34	China	63.70
United States	20.33	China	41.54	United States	51.26
Euro area	10.86	United States	30.51	Euro area	40.15
Japan	5.59	Russian Federation	25.60	Japan	28.15
United Kingdom	5.51	Canada	22.61	Russian Federation	26.02
Korea, Rep.	5.41	United Kingdom	22.49	Korea, Rep.	24.57
Russian Federation	4.79	Korea, Rep.	20.49	United Kingdom	24.01
India	4.62	Australia	20.26	India	23.38
Singapore	4.30	Brazil	19.48	Singapore	22.95
Canada	4.08	Norway	19.25	Canada	22.92
Australia	3.27	Saudi Arabia	19.18	Saudi Arabia	21.33
Malaysia	3.12	Turkey	19.17	Turkey	21.33
Turkey	3.07	India	19.14	Mexico	21.27
Mexico	2.94	Singapore	19.11	Malaysia	21.19
Saudi Arabia	2.94	Poland	18.76	Australia	21.14

Sources: World Bank staff calculations based on data from IE Singapore, IMF DOT, IMF IFS, World Bank WDI, and WIPO Patentscope databases.
Note: HBS = Harrod-Balassa-Samuelson; PPP = purchasing power parity. The shaded region indicates potential, as opposed to current, poles, with the cutoff determined by the first significant break on the index (from below). The multidimensional index was generated from the first principal component of trade-, finance-, and technology-weighted growth shares, normalized to the maximum and minimum of the 1969–2008 period. Real, HBS, and PPP-adjusted indexes indicate growth rates calculated from, respectively, GDP data in real 2000 U.S. dollars, nominal local currency converted to U.S. dollars at current exchange rates and deflated by U.S. prices, and 2005 international PPP-adjusted dollars.

China's tremendous growth spillover effects also have been documented by studies employing other approaches (Arora and Vamvakidis 2010a).

Other emerging economies that are potential growth poles include India and Russia—two of the BRIC economies—along with several other fast-growing emerging markets, such as Korea, Malaysia, Singapore, and Turkey, some of which are included in the group of Next-11 emerging countries (O'Neill et al. 2005). Although identification of these countries as potential poles is not surprising given their economic size, it is notable that several large developing economies do not feature as potential poles in the 2004–08 period—Indonesia, for example—and that countries such as Poland and Russia enter several notches higher than their economic sizes alone would suggest. Furthermore, Latin American economies—such as Brazil and Mexico—tend to appear in lower positions than would be expected by their economic size, as their patterns of international engagement means that

the spillover effects from their growth are limited. Finally, some regional economic heavyweights, such as the Arab Republic of Egypt and South Africa, do not appear in table 1.1, because they are relatively small economies at the global level, and their growth spillovers tend to be contained within their respective regions. This does not, however, rule out the possibility that such economies may serve as *regional* growth poles (box 1.2).

Also evident is the highly uneven distribution of growth polarity when measured at the global level—the top three countries (China, the euro area, and the United States) account for almost 80 percent of total global polarity, as measured by the real index for 2004–08. This metric has an interesting parallel in economic geography, where a small fraction of physical space often accounts for a disproportionately large share of economic activity. And like regional growth poles, growth polarity here appears to follow a power law relationship (a relationship that has been termed Zipf's law).

BOX 1.2   Growth poles at the regional level

The definition of growth pole used in this book focuses on the spillover effects that an economy's growth induces on the global level. One implication of such a definition is that smaller or less globally integrated economies that may well be significant drivers at a regional level—but exert a relatively marginal impact at the global level—will not generally be identified as growth poles. While this exclusion is entirely appropriate for examining the phenomenon of global multipolarity, it is nevertheless interesting to explore growth polarity within geographical regions, especially since regional poles can have a strong influence on the economic prospects of LDCs.

Table B.1.2.1 summarizes these regional indexes. As might be expected, economies that drive growth at the global level tend to appear as growth poles for their regions as well. However, since the relative importance of an economy in driving regional growth may differ from its global impact, the relative positions of economies—as measured by regional growth polarity—may not correspond to their global ones. For example, Brazil appears to be more important in Latin America than Mexico, even though Mexico places higher globally, as reported in table 1.1.

The most notable aspect of the information presented in the table below is that economies that are otherwise "crowded out" in terms of their role as *global*

growth poles can nevertheless play an important role at the *regional* level in driving growth. South Africa, for example, is far and away the most important regional growth pole in the Sub-Saharan Africa region, a finding that has been echoed in the literature (Arora and Vamvakidis 2010b). Indeed, for the 2004–08 period, South Africa's simple polarity index is one-and-a-half times more than that of the next-largest regional growth pole in Sub-Saharan Africa, Nigeria. Another factor that is important when taking into account regional considerations is how regional economic blocs may, if sufficiently integrated, serve as growth poles in their own right. While this topic is not explored in detail in this book, it is entirely conceivable that an integrated economic grouping, such as the Gulf Cooperation Council, may be a regional (or even global) growth pole.

These findings underscore the importance of understanding the distinction between a global growth pole and a regional one. Since the channels of growth spillovers may differ from one region to another, and from a regional to a global level, economies that are important at one level may be less so at another. Also important is that these differences suggest that spillovers in growth are complex and dynamic, and hence any given "ranking" of growth poles, including the ones reported here, should be treated as suggestive in the context that they are defined.

TABLE B1.2.1   Regional simple polarity index, top three countries, 2004–08 average

Country	Simple index	Country	Simple index	Country	Simple index
Sub-Saharan Africa		**East Asia and Pacific**		**Eastern Europe and Central Asia**	
South Africa	63.90	China	98.87	Russian Federation	69.44
Nigeria	41.42	Korea, Rep.	12.68	Turkey	64.18
Angola	27.57	Indonesia	5.70	Czech Republic	48.95
Latin America and the Caribbean		**Middle East and North Africa**		**South Asia**	
Brazil	45.60	Saudi Arabia	28.26	India	100.00
Argentina	33.84	Iran, Islamic Rep.	26.12	Bangladesh	10.96
Mexico	24.42	Egypt, Arab Rep.	25.71	Pakistan	8.52

Source: World Bank staff calculations based on data from World Bank WDI database.

Note: The regional multidimensional index was generated from the size-weighted growth rate calculated from GDP data in real 2000 U.S. dollars, by region, normalized to the maximum and minimum of the 1969–2008 period. To minimize distortion of the index, the normalization for ECA excludes Russian data for 1994–96. The values reported for South Asia should be interpreted with caution, since data limitations mean that the indexes are calculated only for four economies. Indexes are not comparable across regions.

BOX 1.3 **Proximate and fundamental factors related to multidimensional growth polarity**

The most natural candidates for explanatory variables to include in any regression of growth polarity are those that have been identified in the cross-country growth literature. However, there are dozens of such potential regressors, with little consensus on which variables are the most important. Such factors can be classified into two broad categories: proximate and fundamental.

As many as a quarter of all proximate factors examined in the literature have been identified as significantly and robustly related to growth, per se. The strongest evidence, as suggested by an augmented Solow growth model, comes from population growth, physical capital investment, and level of schooling (Mankiw, Romer, and Weil 1992). Other proximate factors that have been found to be relatively more important include the quality of a country's infrastructure, the health of its population, the dependency ratio, and the size of its government (Sala-i-Martin, Doppelhofer, and Miller 2004).

The set of fundamental factors, while smaller and possibly more eclectic, often are regarded as more central to explaining long-run income patterns. The case has variously (and convincingly) been made that factors such as institutional quality, economic integration, geography, ethnolinguistic fractionalization, human capital, and social capital matter (Acemoglu, Johnson, and Robinson 2005; Alesina et al. 2003; Frankel and Romer 1999; Gallup, Sachs, and Mellinger 1999; Glaeser et al. 2004; Knack and Keefer 1997; Rodrik, Subramanian, and Trebbi 2004).

By and large, econometric analysis (described in detail in annex 1.3) finds that the most reliable correlate of multidimensional growth polarity at the proximate level is educational attainment. This result is consistent with the theoretical literature that stresses the centrality of human capital for the growth process (Bils and Klenow 2000; Mankiw, Romer, and Weil 1992). Physical capital investment also appears to contribute positively to a country being a growth pole,

Like economic growth itself, growth polarity is influenced by both proximate and fundamental factors. In determining what factors are supportive of growth polarity, therefore, it is useful to disentangle these distinct classes of influences. Proximate factors include the standard ingredients that one might expect to be associated with strong economic growth, such as increased capital accumulation and population growth. Underlying these factors are "deeper" structural factors, such as the strength of the country's institutions and the extent to which a country's geography favors growth. Formal econometric analysis (reported in box 1.3) suggests that the proximate factors of importance include physical capital, education attainment, the dependency ratio, and the population's health, while institutional quality and economic integration are key fundamental factors.

Changing multipolarity in the world economy

What do the changing polarities mean for the distribution of economic influence in the global economy as a whole? To the extent that growth polarity is an accurate measure of such influence, it is possible to compute a concentration index that summarizes the degree of multipolarity in the global economy.[6] Such a *multipolarity index*—calculated from shares of growth polarity and scaled between 0 (totally diffused growth polarity) and 1 (fully concentrated growth polarity)—suggests that multipolarity increased steadily through the end of the Cold War, fell during the final decade of the 20th century, before finally rising again in the first decade of the 21st century. Indeed, over the past decade, the world has attained some of the most diverse distributions since 1968 (figure 1.4).[7,8]

BOX 1.3   (continued)

while population growth has little effect. Variables that appear to be negatively correlated with growth polarity are poor health outcomes—which can be seen as another aspect of human capital—and the need to support a nonworking population (measured by the old-age dependency ratio).

Two fundamental determinants appear to be central in influencing multidimensional growth polarity. High-quality institutions appear to be significant, both statistically and economically. Again, this result is broadly consistent with the academic literature, which finds that institutions tend to trump other fundamental factors in determining levels and growth of per capita income (Decker and Lim 2008; Rodrik, Subramaniam, and Trebbi 2004). Interestingly, economic integration appears to exert a *negative* drag on growth polarity. This is likely for two reasons. First, the polarity measure is (by construction) a function of economic size. The

negative influence of integration simply may reflect the fact that small countries—which are much more likely to exhibit greater degrees of trade openness—are less likely to be growth poles. Second, a successful growth pole is likely to rely on internal, rather than external, demand as an engine of growth.

Overall, the analysis paints a picture in which a successful growth pole is a country that possesses a relatively young, educated population and that generates internally driven growth through investment in physical and human capital. Moreover, a successful growth pole also tends to have a strong institutional framework that is supportive of economic activity. Just as important, a growth pole can consolidate its position by ensuring that key elements of its institutional environment are strong: ensuring that there is adequate respect for the rule of law, that corruption is under control, and that the government fosters social and political stability.

Since the turn of the 21st century, the world has thus become increasingly multipolar. This rising multipolarity has occurred in concert with the expansion of globalization. History tells us that successive waves of economic globalization typically have wrought periods of greater economic multipolarity, along with concomitant frictions due to changes in the global configuration of geopolitical power (Findlay and O'Rourke 2007).

Concurrent with this rising multipolarity has been a shift away from the G-7 economies as global growth drivers, and toward the economies of the developing world (figure 1.5). This shift partly explains why the post–financial crisis global environment has been marked by a renewal in international economic tensions, with heightened protectionist sentiment and talk of trade collapse and currency wars.

Yet a deeper examination of the growth polarity indexes underlying figure 1.4 suggests that the dynamics of what is captured in the figure are due not so much to a decline of developed economies (although some absolute decline, especially in the early 1970s, indeed occurred), but rather to a

FIGURE 1.4   Evolution of multipolarity, alternative indexes, 1968–2008

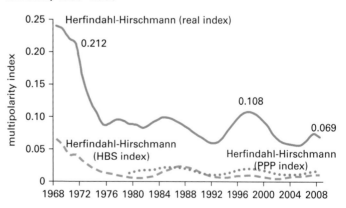

Source: World Bank staff calculations.
Note: Multipolarity index calculated as the normalized Herfindahl-Hirschman index of the respective multidimensional polarity index shares of the top 15 economies, computed over rolling 5-year averages.

rise in the growth polarities of developing economies. Moreover, while structural changes in both the advanced and emerging world may alter this dynamic, the overall trend toward a more multipolar global economic order seems unlikely to change.

FIGURE 1.5   **Global distribution of growth poles, 1994–98 and 2004–08**

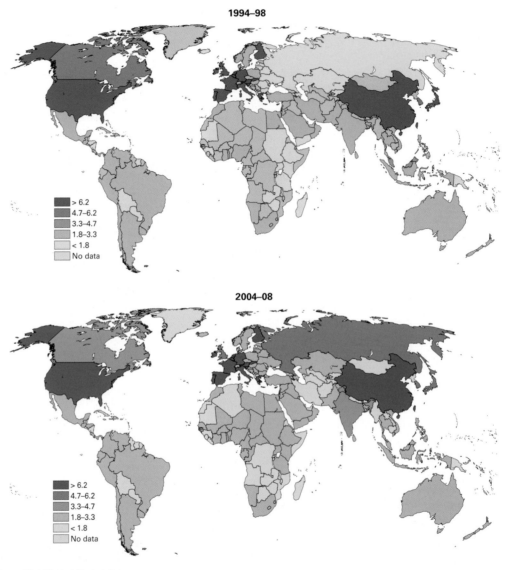

Source: World Bank staff calculations.

Note: Multipolarity index calculated as the normalized Herfindahl-Hirschman index of shares of the top 15 economies using the real multidimensional polarity index. The choice of brackets was arbitrary, but reflects the overall trend of increased distribution of growth polarity.

The Character of Growth in the Potential Emerging Economy Poles

The granularity of growth in the potential emerging economy growth poles

How potential growth poles in the emerging world will generate self-sustaining, internally driven growth is a matter of much concern. The East Asian economic "miracle" has been called a story of rapid factor accumulation premised on export-led growth strategies, with modest levels of total factor productivity (TFP) growth (Young 1995). Moreover, since the late 1990s, global growth has been heavily dependent on U.S. productivity advances and increasing consumer demand. Given the financial crisis and subsequent recession in the United States, however, U.S. consumers are unlikely to sustain this pattern of strong demand in the foreseeable future.

In the long run, an economy will continue to be a growth pole only if it is able to nurture its innovative and productive capacity—which drives its growth process—while simultaneously developing its sources of internal demand, so that its growth will also support growth elsewhere. Consequently, sustainable growth in the potential emerging economy growth poles will require both that TFP make a significant contribution to growth and that domestic consumption or investment be maintained at strong but sustainable levels. Only when growth matures in this balanced fashion can growth poles be resilient to global shocks and continue to drive the global economy forward during turbulent times.

The task ahead of the potential emerging economy poles is formidable. Between 2005 and 2009, the TFP contribution to growth in many of the newly industrialized East Asian economies has been modest at best (and negative in some cases). Demand in China, India, and Korea also appears to be more, rather than less, reliant on external sources over time; for example, the net export share of GDP in China averaged 7 percent between 2005 and 2009, compared with 2.4 percent between 2000 and 2004.

Yet the historical data suggest that shifting growth toward more domestically oriented sources is possible. In India, gross fixed capital formation was 24 percent of GDP in 1989; by 2009, that share had increased to 35 percent (moreover, the contribution of investment growth to GDP growth over 2000–09 was about one-half). In Brazil, the consumption contribution to output has been a robust 60 percent over the same period (remaining resilient through the crisis). Even in China, rapid growth did not preclude a substantial contribution of consumption to growth over certain periods: between 1990 and 1999, for example, consumption represented about 42 percent of growth, while exports represented about 46 percent.[9]

The evolution of total factor productivity in the potential emerging economy poles

The distinct trends in technological and resource utilization, efficiency, and innovation among the potential emerging economy poles belie the broad advances that have been made in terms of growth by the group as a whole. China (and, to a lesser extent, India) has seen substantial contributions from TFP to its growth since the mid-1960s, and, during their recent histories, so have Poland and Russia. Similar contributions have not prevailed in Latin American economies, however, and also have been relatively modest in emerging economies such as Indonesia, Malaysia, and South Africa (figure 1.6). In Argentina and Brazil, contributions of TFP to growth have routinely tipped into negative territory (with contributions over the entire period averaging −8 percent and −37 percent, respectively). In Indonesia and Malaysia, the *growth rate* of TFP was relatively low over most of the period.[10] The laggard contribution of TFP in many of these fast-growing emerging markets has been repeatedly pointed out in the literature (Cole et al. 2005; Young 1995).[11]

To better understand the disparate TFP performance of emerging economies, it is useful to draw a distinction between technological innovation and technological adoption. In the context of growth, innovation is probably best understood as advances in science and technology that enhance productivity and growth by moving the production possibilities frontier outward. The sort of innovation typically produced by scientists and engineers often generates spillover effects to the larger economy and, as such, is well captured by measures of research activity. In contrast, adoption of innovations involves the use of existing technologies that induce improvements in technical efficiency. Adoption generally falls within the domain of entrepreneurs and businesses, and usually has aggregate growth benefits only when it is sufficiently widespread across the economy (when diffusion is high).[12] Technological adoption and diffusion are likely better measured by the distance between the economywide deployment of a given technology to the research frontier, whether

FIGURE 1.6 Total factor productivity contribution to growth, selected potential poles

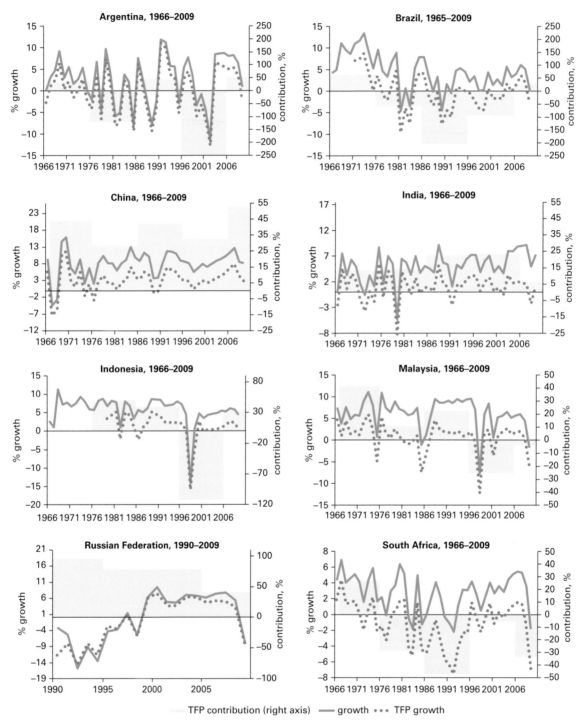

Sources: World Bank staff calculations, from IMF IFS and World Bank WDI databases.

Note: The total factor productivity contribution is defined as the share of growth not attributable to either physical capital or human capital–adjusted labor inputs, assuming a Cobb-Douglas production function with constant returns, for 10-year periods. Depreciation, returns to education, and the income share of capital are assumed to be 0.06, 0.1, and 0.33, respectively, for all countries. Growth indicates growth rates calculated from GDP data measured in constant 2000 U.S. dollars. Because of data limitations, Indonesian TFP calculations begin only in the second period. The negative contributions for Argentina (1995–2004) and South Africa (1985–94) were –2,932 percent and –479 percent, respectively, but were not fully plotted because of the severe distortion to the presentation of the axes.

measured in terms of the time to uptake or the margin of adoption.

Taking into account this distinction suggests that China's and India's relatively strong TFP contributions[13] probably are due less to pure innovative capacity than to a combination of rapid adoption and diffusion of technologies from global technological leaders, along with the gains from factor reallocation within these economies. Historically, measures of technological innovation in those two potential poles have consistently lagged those of Latin American economies (measured in per capita terms),[14] although the measures have shown a noticeable uptick since the late 1990s (figure 1.7). This trend is further corroborated by evidence that innovative activity in China and India, to the extent that it occurs, tends to be incremental in nature (Puga and Trefler 2010). If the relatively superior TFP performances in China and India are to be explained, the explanation is unlikely to be found in technological innovation alone.

A much more likely reason for the relatively superior TFP performance in China and India is catch-up growth through technology adoption, especially when accompanied by the movement of resources from less productive to more productive sectors of the economy. For many technologies, the rate of technology adoption and diffusion

in China, India, and Russia appears to be more rapid than for equivalent Latin American economies (figure 1.8). The lag of technology adoption in India relative to the United States, for example, averaged 14.1 years between 1971 and 2001, compared to lags of 16.2 years for Brazil and 20.7 years for Argentina. The relative adoption intensity of technologies within these countries can be even greater. After 1981, for instance, China saw a sharp spike in the economic size-adjusted use of technologies relative to the countries at the leading edge of the technological frontier. More generally, lags in technology usage and rates of diffusion are likely to account for much of the observed differences in cross-country TFP and, hence, in growth performances (Comin and Hobijn 2010; Comin, Hobijn, and Rovito 2008; Eaton and Kortum 1999).

However, differential rates of adoption and diffusion are insufficient to explain the relatively low TFP growth rates in Southeast Asian economies. To understand this, one needs to look to the reallocation of factors and resources stemming from structural transformation in China (since the period of economic reform beginning in the late 1970s) and India (following the economic reforms of the early 1990s), which explains the distinct historical TFP performances of these two potential emerging economy poles. Despite their

FIGURE 1.7   Technological innovation, selected potential emerging economy poles

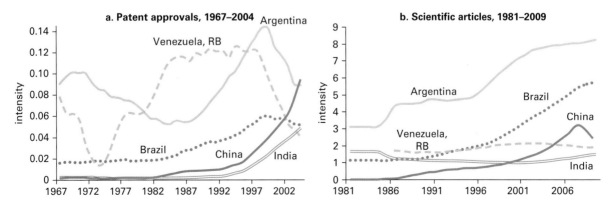

Sources: World Bank staff calculations, from World Bank WDI and WIPO Patentscope databases.
Note: Intensity of patent approvals and scientific articles published were measured as a share of 100,000 of population. Missing observations were dropped, and the series then were smoothed by taking the 5-year moving average of available annual data.

FIGURE 1.8 Technological adoption, selected potential emerging economy poles, 1971–2003

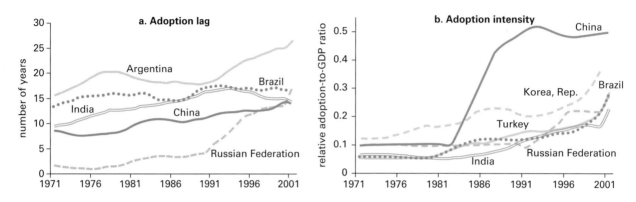

Sources: World Bank staff calculations, from *Cross-Country Historical Adoption of Technology* and the WDI database.

Note: Adoption lag is measured as the time taken for a follower country to attain the usage intensity, normalized by GDP, of the technology in a benchmark country (the United States). The total adoption lag aggregates adoption times across 12 different technologies across eight sectors, as well as three general-purpose technologies, smoothed by taking the 5-year moving average of available annual data. Relative adoption is measured as the coverage of the technology in the follower country, normalized by GDP, relative to the peak coverage in the lead country in that technology (not necessarily the United States), across 12 different technologies across eight sectors, as well as three general-purpose technologies, smoothed by taking the 5-year moving average of available annual data. Total adoption lags tend to increase over time partly because they include lags in some technologies that were invented relatively recently and, as a result, the measured lags do not have sufficient time to exceed the number of years that have elapsed since the technology's first use in the United States.

long-standing presence, these gains have not been fully exhausted; studies of the manufacturing sector suggest that TFP gains of as much as 50 percent (China) and 60 percent (India) could be attained in these countries by factor reallocations in the future (Du, Harrison, and Jefferson 2011; Hsieh and Klenow 2009). Such misallocations, more broadly, may also account for much of the differences in TFP contributions to Latin American and African growth relative to that of Asia (McMillan and Rodrik 2011).

An important factor behind TFP improvements is institutional reform that relaxes constraints on technology adoption, innovation, or resource reallocation (Parente and Prescott 2000). Some of the potential emerging economy growth poles showed statistically significant improvements in government effectiveness between 1998 and 2008, and there has been a positive, though modest, trend in governance indicators for emerging economies more generally (Kaufmann, Kraay, and Mastruzzi 2010). To the extent that trends toward institutional reform strengthen over the coming years, such trends will translate into higher TFP growth in the future.

The changing character of internal demand in the potential emerging economy poles

The patterns of consumption, absorption, and exports evident in the potential emerging economy poles appear to be conspicuously related to those countries' choice of industrialization strategies in the past. Brazil and Mexico, both of which relied on import substituting industrialization (ISI) starting in the first half of the 20th century, display consistently strong contributions from consumption growth, whereas countries such as Korea (and later China), having pursued export-oriented industrialization (EOI) from the mid-1960s have seen their consumption contribution fall in concert with their rise in export contributions (figure 1.9).[15] Indeed, as formerly closed economies such as India and Russia have opened to increased trade and export orientation, their growth patterns have shown a greater compression in the spread between consumption and export contributions (figure 1.10). China, in particular, has seen a sharp fall in the consumption-export differential in its growth performance.[16]

FIGURE 1.9 Export and consumption contribution to growth, selected potential poles

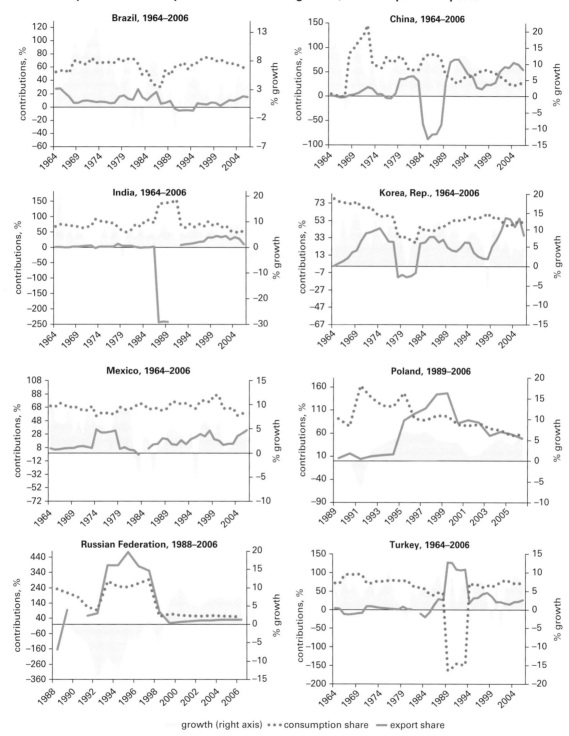

growth (right axis) •••consumption share ━ export share

Sources: World Bank staff calculations, from IMF IFS and World Bank WDI databases.

Note: The consumption (export) contribution is defined as the annual change in consumption (export) divided by the annual change in output, smoothed by taking the 5-year moving average. Observations with a positive change in the numerator and a negative change in the denominator were dropped. Growth indicates growth rates calculated from GDP data measured in constant 2000 U.S. dollars. The anomalous patterns for India (1987–91) and Turkey (1989–94) were due to negative output growth as a result of severe economic disruptions (including financial crises), before economic and financial liberalization episodes.

FIGURE 1.10   Dominance of consumption to exports in growth, selected potential emerging economy poles, 1977–2006

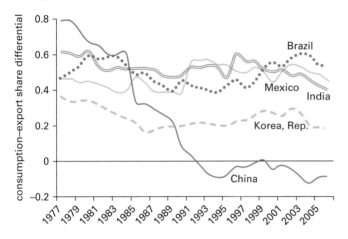

Sources: World Bank staff calculations, from IMF IFS and World Bank WDI databases.

Note: The consumption-export differential is defined as the difference between consumption and export shares of output growth. Observations with a positive change in the numerator and a negative change in the denominator were dropped, and the series then were smoothed by taking the 15-year moving average of available annual data.

Such patterns do not necessarily constitute a case for or against the use of EOI or ISI strategies,[17] and there is nothing in these historical choices that constrains an open economy from reducing its reliance on export-led growth.[18] Indeed, a case can be made for reorienting growth in the EOI countries toward higher, albeit sustainable, levels of internal demand, after these economies have sufficiently matured. This reorientation would require raising the share of consumption and investment in output growth, which would result from, respectively, a reduction in the saving rate or the user cost of capital. Thus, an understanding of the deeper, structural determinants of high saving and investment, both at the household and corporate level, is necessary.

Consumption and saving behavior in emerging economies. Consumption theory, either along the traditional lines of a permanent income life-cycle model or a more modern intertemporal consumption-leisure interpretation, suggests that factors such as disposable income and private wealth can affect household saving behavior. Moreover, for developing countries, liquidity constraints can come into play. At the macroeconomic level, these microdeterminants

of saving are likely to translate into observable macroeconomic factors, such as the real interest rate, income growth rate, and demographic structure of the economy (Attanasio and Weber 2010; Loayza, Schmidt-Hebbel, and Servén 2000; Schmidt-Hebbel, Webb, and Corsetti 1992).

In contrast to household saving, decisions about optimal corporate saving are deeply interwoven with decisions about optimal corporate financing. In a perfectly frictionless world, standard theory asserts that the capital structure of a firm is irrelevant (Modigliani and Miller 1958). In reality—and especially in developing countries—real and financial frictions are likely to be pervasive, and so the mode of financing indeed may be important (Dailami 1992). In turn, the mode of financing often is affected by the preexisting business, financial, and macroeconomic environment. The relatively immature financial structure and widespread agency problems in developing-country financial markets, for example, may induce a greater reliance on internal funding, thus increasing the incentive for firms to save (Allen et al. 2010).

Moderating the saving rate in the potential emerging economy growth poles is a nontrivial problem, especially given the steady rise in saving in these poles in recent years. China, in particular, has seen its private and public saving rise from, respectively, 33.3 percent and 5.7 percent of GDP in 1992 to an estimated 44.7 percent and 6.7 percent in 2008 (figure 1.11).[19] The causes of China's high saving rates, however, have been the subject of much debate, with literature pointing to structural concerns such as a weak social safety net and underdeveloped financial sector, life-cycle smoothing in response to the current high growth rate, industrialization policies that are biased against consumer spending, and even signaling motives as a result of its highly competitive marriage market (Bayoumi, Tong, and Wei 2010; Blanchard and Giavazzi 2006; Horioka and Wan 2007; Kuijs 2006; Modigliani and Cao 2004; Wei and Zhang 2009).

China is not alone. India also possesses high and rising levels of national saving, and since the start of the 21st century, India's growth has been accompanied by a doubling of corporate saving (from 3.1 percent of GDP in 2002 to 7.8 percent of GDP in 2008). This is somewhat worrisome,

FIGURE 1.11   **Evolution of saving, selected potential growth poles, by sector**

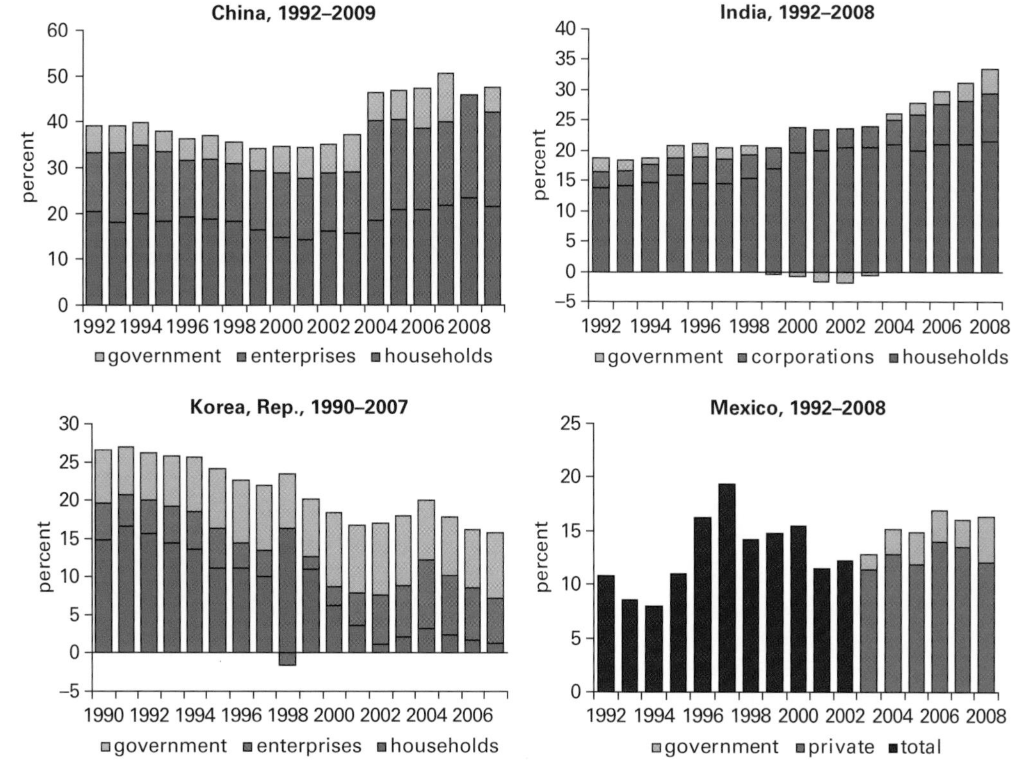

Sources: World Bank staff calculations, from All China Data Center database (China), Organisation for Economic Co-operation and Development StatExtracts database (Korea, Mexico), and Central Statistical Organisation, National Accounts Statistics (India).

Note: For China, 2009 household and enterprise saving are imputed from their respective 2008 shares of 2009 total private saving. For India, 2007 data are provisional and 2008 are estimates, and household saving is defined as the sum of household financial saving and household physical saving. For Mexico, disaggregated saving data were only available after 2002.

because India's high corporate saving is less likely to be due to optimal household responses to the introduction of new saving instruments than it is to be an indication of possible dysfunction in the development of financial markets, especially with regard to the ease of access of firms to financing. Nevertheless, higher overall saving in India may actually be optimal for its stage of development, if investment opportunities are present and financing constraints are otherwise binding.

In other potential emerging economy poles, the shares of saving in GDP are more modest and are of less concern—indeed, financing the increasing number of investment opportunities in these countries may even call for higher domestic saving, especially if access to international finance is uncertain. In Mexico, for example, saving has steadily crept up since 2001, increasing by 42 percent to top 16 percent of

GDP in 2008. Russia also has seen a rise in saving since 2002, although to a lesser extent. Much of the increase in Russia has been due to government rather than private saving, however, with the share of government saving accounting for more than half of all national saving since 2005. Korea appears to be an exception to this trend among the potential growth poles, demonstrating falling national saving over time, especially among households. This downward trend in Korea is likely due to expansion of household contributions to the social safety net, the aging population, deteriorating terms of trade, and expansion of credit available to households at low interest rates (IMF 2010d).

In China, too, demographic change in the coming decades—namely, a rising old-age dependency ratio—will affect the household saving rate. As working-age adults account for a shrinking share of the population, there should be a synchronous decline in China's household saving rate. India is experiencing a similar demographic shift, although its relatively young working-age population suggests that the country may still reap a demographic dividend in the years ahead.[20]

Investment and capital usage efficiency in emerging economies. Of course, the character of growth is affected not only by consumption and saving trends, but also by investment. Undeniably, investment trends tend to be much more volatile than consumption trends. Yet both theory (capital accumulation is at the heart of classical and endogenous growth models) and empirics (that investment is strongly pro-cyclical with output in most countries is a stylized fact) point to the central role that investment plays in the growth process.

Even so, the relationship between *changes* in investment and growth is much weaker, at least in the short run. Indeed, in some potential emerging economy growth poles, such as Korea and Mexico, such investment changes are correlated only moderately with income growth.[21] Part of

the reason for this lies in the fact, discussed in the previous section, that the TFP changes explain a much larger share of the realized growth path. Furthermore, economies also may differ in their efficiency of capital usage, as proxied by the incremental capital-output ratio (ICOR).[22] In some cases, this ratio may be even higher than in China and India, the TFP leaders among the potential emerging economy poles (figure 1.12). Indeed, this heterogeneity underscores the possibility that countries have exploited several different paths to supporting their historical growth patterns.

As a consequence, long swings in the contribution of investment to growth—as are evident for China and Malaysia, for example—generally are more difficult to reconcile with standard business cycle movements and may not always be translated into growth (figure 1.13). Nevertheless, it is important to recognize that the growth spurts in China since 1990 and in Malaysia in the 1980s and 1990s, for example, can in fact be heavily attributed to gross fixed capital formation (a phenomenon first observed by Young 1995 and more recently emphasized by Bardhan 2010). Owing to diminishing returns, however, growth reliant on capital accumulation alone ultimately is not sustainable.

Implications of different growth patterns for sustained future global growth

The differing historical nature of growth among the potential emerging economy growth poles, on both the supply and demand sides, hold differing implications for whether their growth patterns are sustainable into the future. In particular, the ability to develop indigenous innovative capacity and the ability to successfully transition toward greater internal sources of demand constitute the primary risks to strong future emerging-market growth performance.

Future TFP growth must rely more on technological innovation, not adoption. With gradual technological catch-up, the gains to TFP growth from technological adoption cannot continue indefinitely. What, then, are the prospects for the potential emerging economy poles to begin

FIGURE 1.12   Incremental capital-output ratios, selected potential emerging economy poles, 1965–2008

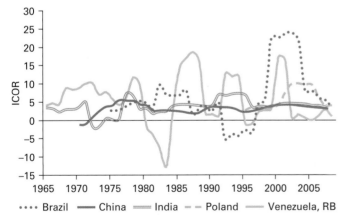

Sources: World Bank staff calculations, from IMF IFS and World Bank WDI databases.
Note: The ICOR is defined as investment in the previous period, divided by the annual change in output. Observations for which investment and growth differ by more than two orders of magnitude, and persist for only one year, were treated as outliers and dropped; the series then were smoothed by taking the 5-year moving average of available annual data. ICORs for Brazil, China, India, Mexico, Poland, and the República Bolivariana de Venezuela, for the full period are 5.69, 2.80, 3.86, 5.14, and 5.12, respectively.

innovating in the future? Enhancing innovative as well as adoptive capacity requires investment in both human capital and research and development (R&D) (Eaton and Kortum 1996; Griffith, Redding, and van Reenen 2004), coupled with enhancing the institutional environment that, among other things, supports TFP growth via these channels. Both investments are linked closely to per capita incomes, especially when countries approach high-income status (figure 1.14).[23] As incomes rise in such economies, it is very likely that their ability to develop indigenous technological advances will rise. Indeed, as discussed in chapter 2, evidence for increased innovative activity in emerging economies can already be seen at the firm level.

Investment in R&D also holds the promise of being an engine for endogenous growth (Aghion and Howitt 1997; Romer 1986, 1990). Furthermore, growth premised on such knowledge accumulation can spill over to other countries; as such, potential emerging economy growth poles that rely on such mechanisms will serve to further strengthen their positions as growth poles. This is especially true for China and India, but also for Russia; all three countries have demonstrated strengths in various aspects of R&D related to information and communications technology.

Future internal demand growth will need to be supported by a growing middle class. To the extent that there are concerns about successfully increasing the contribution of consumption to growth in developing countries excessively reliant on export-oriented growth, several medium- and long-term trends could facilitate such a switch. One important supporting trend is the rise of the so-called global middle class, which in turn could be a source of sustained growth and a strong channel for poverty reduction at the global level (Banerjee and Duflo 2008; Doepke and Zilibotti 2005; Easterly 2001; World Bank 2007).[24] Among emerging markets, this expansion of the middle class has thus far been led by China and India, which—together with the rest of East and South Asia—collectively accounted for about 970 million new entrants to the global middle class between 1990 and 2005.[25]

FIGURE 1.13   Investment shares of growth, selected potential emerging economy poles, 1972–2006

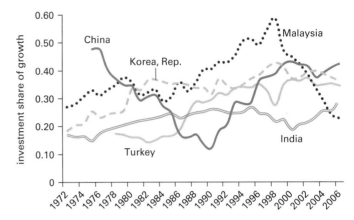

Sources: World Bank staff calculations, from IMF IFS and World Bank WDI databases.
Note: The investment share is defined as the annual change in investment divided by the annual change in output. Observations with a positive change in the numerator and a negative change in the denominator were dropped, and the series then were smoothed by taking the 10-year moving average of available annual data.

FIGURE 1.14   Global distribution of research and development expenditure and researcher shares, average over 2004–08

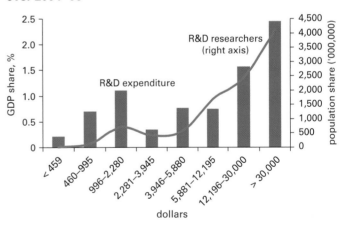

Source: World Bank staff calculations, from World Bank WDI database.
Note: The figure depicts R&D expenditure share of GDP and R&D researcher share of population, weighted respectively by GDP and population within each respective bracket. Brackets are given in gross national income (GNI) per capita, calculated using the Atlas method, and chosen to yield two groups within each of the World Bank's 2009 income categories (low income, $995 or less; lower middle income, $996–$3,945; upper middle income, $3,946–$12,195; and high income, $12,196 or more).

This trend is likely to continue, as global income inequality is generally forecast to fall in the future (Sala-i-Martin 2006; Wilson and Dragusanu 2008; World Bank 2007). Because

FIGURE 1.15   Global distribution and selected evolution of consumption share by per capita income

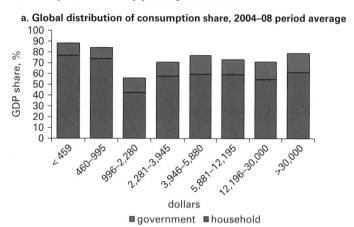

a. Global distribution of consumption share, 2004–08 period average

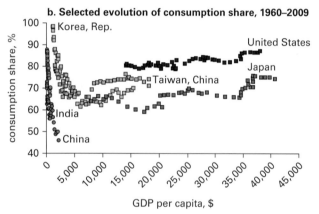

b. Selected evolution of consumption share, 1960–2009

Sources: World Bank staff calculations, from IMF IFS and World Bank WDI databases.
Note: Household and government consumption shares are measured as shares of GDP, and weighted by GDP in U.S. dollars within each respective bracket. Brackets are given in GNI per capita, calculated using the Atlas method, and chosen to yield two groups within each of the World Bank's 2009 income categories (low income, $995 or less; lower middle income, $996–$3,945; upper middle income, $3,946–$12,195; and high income, $12,196 or more). Total consumption share is the sum of household and government consumption, measured as a share of GDP, and GDP per capita is measured in constant 2000 U.S. dollars.

the middle class typically stands at the forefront of consumption demand, a larger middle class will tend to reinforce changes in consumption patterns. This, in turn, will lead to a stronger consumer in the emerging economies, thereby increasing the contribution of consumption to growth within the potential emerging economy growth poles. Multiplier effects from increases in the size of the middle class could lead to GDP levels of 8 to 15 percent higher than otherwise, as has been estimated for China (Woetzel et al. 2009). Furthermore, if rising incomes and consumption

are spent on not just domestic but also foreign goods and services, expanding middle classes in the potential emerging economy growth poles can raise demand for exports from LDCs.

Ultimately, rising levels of per capita income are likely to consolidate the transition to greater consumption-driven growth in developing countries (figure 1.15, panel a),[26] as has been the case for high-income countries on average, even in Asia (figure 1.15, panel b). Some developing countries have in fact made such successful transitions, and their experiences suggest that transitions can be stable and sustainable (box 1.4).

How long it will take for this transition to play out, however, remains unclear. In China, at least, steps are under way to address the structural challenges that may have artificially held down consumption growth.[27] But for developing countries in general, ushering in such transitions has taken on a new urgency due to the slowdown of demand in the United States and Europe as a result of the financial crisis.

The flip side of increased consumption is reduced saving and—owing to the Feldstein-Horioka observation that domestic saving and investment are highly correlated—reduced investment. Consequently, any shift toward consumption-driven growth is likely to be accompanied by a reduction in investment levels. Whether investment continues to be an important driver of growth then depends on the likelihood that, going forward, these lower levels of investment can nevertheless increase labor productivity.

This outcome, in turn, depends on whether such investments are channeled toward the appropriate sectors of the economy. While the literature has begun to explore systematic methodologies for selecting sectors that would be beneficial targets for investment (Lin 2010), considerable uncertainty remains about the growth outcomes that would result from such directed investments. Investment in green technology production, for example, could lead to productivity gains for a broader segment of the labor force, compared to investment in an economy based on knowledge products. Moreover, the implications of such investment choices for the rest of the world will also be different. This is especially important for

BOX 1.4　Suggestive evidence of successful transitions to consumption-driven growth

Many countries have experienced export-led growth in the recent decades, but very few of these have subsequently transitioned to consumption-driven growth. Even in the cases in which such a transition appears in the data, the switch to consumption-led growth has occurred because of slowdowns in growth or sharp deteriorations in export performances, or are too brief to justify a permanent structural change. Two African success stories, however, appear to provide a tantalizing glimpse of how such a transition may be realized: Botswana and Mauritius (figure B1.4.1).

Following independence in 1968, Mauritius has undergone two major transformations—first from a sugar-based economy to an industrial exporter of textiles and apparel, and then from an industrial exporter to a mainly service-based economy (services accounted for roughly 67 percent of GDP as of 2009). Sustained economic growth brought gross national income (GNI) per capita from $1,112 in 1984 to $6,340 in 2009. In the early 1980s, the export share of GDP began to rise and the consumption share began to fall, setting the stage for a period of export-driven accelerated growth from the mid-1980s through the 1990s. But in 2001 or 2002, a switch occurred, with exports falling from 64 percent to 56 percent of GDP by 2009 and private consumption

rising from 61 percent to 73 percent of GDP. This consumption-driven phase of growth occurred simultaneously with a further acceleration of economic growth and was accompanied by rapid expansion of domestic credit, development of financial markets more broadly,[a] and growth of the service sector.

In Botswana, diamond mining has played a leading role in Botswana's economy throughout its period of growth, during which GNI per capita rose from $88 at independence in 1966 to $6,280 in 2009. Between the late 1960s and the 1980s, Botswana experienced export-driven growth, driven almost exclusively by diamonds, with exports rising as a fraction of GDP and the consumption share falling. A transition began in the late 1980s, however, with Botswana's export share falling from a high of 70 percent and eventually leveling off at less than 50 percent. Meanwhile, in the 2000s, consumption rose steadily, from 26 percent in 2002 to 41 percent in 2009. As in Mauritius, this rise in Botswana's consumption occurred during a period of not only rapid economic growth, but also of significant financial market development, expansion of domestic credit, and growth of the services sector.

Outside of Africa, three economies have transitioned to consumption-driven growth in the past several decades, although the evidence in these cases is more

FIGURE B1.4.1　Evolution of consumption and export shares, Botswana and Mauritius

a. Botswana

b. Mauritius

GNI/capita (right axis)　•••　C/Y　—— X/Y

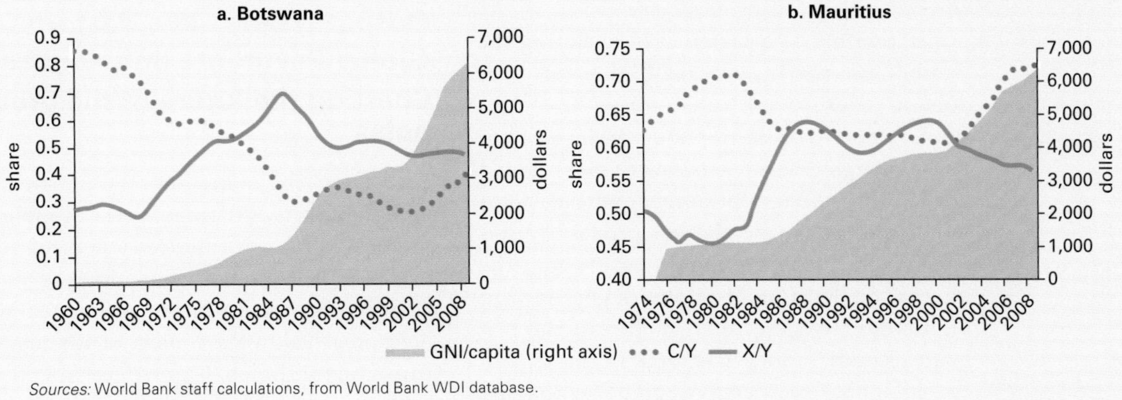

Sources: World Bank staff calculations, from World Bank WDI database.

(continued)

BOX 1.4   (continued)

tenuous. Oman and Saudi Arabia appeared to have experienced such a transition in the 1970s, although they subsequently reverted to export-reliant growth. The Syrian Arab Republic, as well, now shows some tentative signs of making a transition from export-driven to consumption-driven growth. Like Botswana and Mauritius, Syria's transition appears to have occurred alongside an expansion of domestic credit and growth of the service sector, following economic liberalization.

It would be premature to draw strong conclusions from these few cases; nonetheless, they do provide some corroborative evidence that transitions from export- to consumption-driven growth are associated with financial market development, credit expansion, and growth in the service sector. During the periods when the transition occurred, these countries' governments all undertook programs to liberalize and diversify their economies, and this has included financial market liberalization.

How might such a transition play out in the export-dependent emerging economies, especially China? If the historical evidence is anything to go by, a central part of the story would be the continued development of domestic financial markets, especially with regard to

consumer credit and financing for small and medium enterprises, both of which tend to lead to expansion of the service sector from the demand and supply sides. There is certainly room for such developments. China's consumer credit access, at 13 percent of GDP, currently lags behind other East Asian economies, such as Malaysia (48 percent) and Korea (70 percent) (Woetzel et al. 2009). Regulations surrounding access to credit for small and medium enterprises place China at 65 out of 183 economies globally, behind comparator countries such as India (32), Korea (15), and Mexico (46) (World Bank 2010a). Finally, gradual real exchange rate appreciation will also likely play a role in expanding consumers' purchasing power and will facilitate the overall transition process.

a. It is important to draw a distinction between promoting financial market *development* versus *liberalization*. While greater competition and innovation in the financial sector can certainly support its growth, liberalization should be accompanied by a strengthening of the relevant regulatory institutions and legal frameworks, so that the sector does not outrun the capacity of host governments to monitor abuse and limit excesses.

commodity-exporting LDCs, whose exports and terms of trade are critically dependent on the specific raw materials demanded.

Caution must be exercised in outlining the strategy for moving toward higher levels of domestic absorption. Importantly, the expansion of domestic consumption and investment in the emerging East Asian growth poles should not fall into the trap of purely shifting factor inputs into the (typically) less productive service sector, but rather should ensure that the internal reallocation of resources goes toward high-productivity sectors, whether at the primary, secondary, or tertiary level. In this regard, the shifts of greatest concern are those that are channeled inordinately toward construction or finance, which increases the risk of fueling asset price bubbles.

Dynamics of New Growth Poles: Implications for Domestic Output, Trade Flow Patterns, and Global Payments Imbalances

Charting the future of the growth poles

Seen from the contemporary perspective of global markets, shifting drivers of global economic growth will induce structural changes in key industries. This outcome suggests that balance-of-payments measurements will need to be approached in the context of a much-longer-run structural global growth perspective that integrates the real and financial dimensions of external account balances in a coherent way, while recognizing that persistent large imbalances inevitably will translate into a huge buildup of gross external asset and liability positions of surplus and deficit countries. Such financial account positions also will interact with growth dynamics to change the pattern of gross trade flows.

Much of the existing literature, however, either focuses on the real side aspects—trade balances, along with their domestic macroeconomic counterparts, investment-saving balances—or has taken an asset market approach, assessing the prospects for foreign financing of accumulating external debt or the opportunities for investment of accumulating assets. Different global growth scenarios, however, will imply different global macroeconomic equilibrium and external payments imbalance scenarios (Caballero, Farhi, and Gourinchas 2008). Moreover, changes in growth paths and external balances are likely to affect exchange rate outcomes (McDonald 2007), which in turn will mean changes in the flow of exports and imports. Indeed, the shift in trade toward potential emerging economy growth poles is well under way and is likely to intensify in the future with China as the hub (Wang and Whalley 2010). Keeping in mind these important interactions, the baseline scenario provided here offers a lens into the future evolution of the global economy.

The baseline scenario for the future of the global macroeconomy

In the wake of the financial crisis, the global macroeconomy seems poised to follow a two-track course in the short term, with developed countries growing at a much more sluggish pace than developing countries. Low- and middle-income countries are expected to contribute about half (49 percent) of all global growth in 2010. Owing to postcrisis drag, economic activity in the high-income economies, as well as in many of the developing economies of Eastern Europe, will remain sluggish in 2011, only reaching their long-run averages in 2012 (2.8 percent and 4.4 percent for high-income economies and Eastern Europe, respectively). In contrast, economic performance among the developing countries, which had been robust until 2010, likely will moderate as demand stimuli are retracted and output gaps trend toward zero (the developing world excluding

Eastern Europe is expected to average 6.1 percent growth for 2012) (World Bank 2011).

Whether such a two-track world persists depends, in part, on the speed of the deleveraging cycle in developed countries and the extent to which the effects of the 2007–08 financial crisis and the sovereign debt and fiscal crises in several European countries are absorbed. Avoiding an ongoing two-track global economy also depends on whether developing countries are able to manage rising inflationary pressures—originating both from pipeline commodity-related demand pressures and from the imported effects of loose monetary policy in several major advanced economies—while maintaining productivity advances, alongside a redirection of externally driven to internally generated growth.

In this book, the baseline scenario adopted is one in which (1) stabilization and restructuring policies are successfully implemented in both advanced economies and the developing economies of Eastern Europe; (2) absent further exogenous shocks, the cyclical downturn in these economies fades away by the end of 2012;[28] and (3) developing economies other than those in Eastern Europe, especially the potential emerging economy growth poles, successfully manage the surge in capital inflows and inflation in the short run. The baseline scenario also assumes that current policy tensions over exchange rates and trading arrangements do not erupt into economic conflict.

In the medium to long run—through 2025, the end of this book's modeling horizon—this book assumes a convergence of each economy toward its respective potential output in all countries. This convergence is premised on the assumption that structural reforms in advanced economies are successful in the medium term, and that institutional and structural changes occur in developing economies that lead to realignment of growth away from external to internal sources. Scenario projections from 2013–25 are generated on the assumption that economies operate on the trend path of their respective levels of potential output.

In addition to these internal adjustments, the baseline scenario also envisions external adjustments that are consistent with a likely medium-term (through 2015) path of fiscal balances, foreign asset accumulation, and energy needs.

BOX 1.5   Modeling the current account and growth process

The baseline scenario outlined in this book relies on two separate models: a current account model that generates medium-term balance of payments projections, and a growth model that generates long-term growth projections, based in part on input from the current account model.

The current account model (described in detail in annex 1.5) deployed relies on the strand of the literature concerned with the medium-term structural determinants of saving-investment differentials (Chinn and Ito 2007; Chinn and Prasad 2003; Gagnon 2010; Gruber and Kamin 2007). The main explanatory variables are the fiscal balance, official financial flows, net foreign assets, and net energy exports. Using five-year averages across 145 countries for the period 1970–2008, the current account model estimates region-specific coefficients for six country groupings: advanced economies; developing Asia, Africa, Latin America, and Middle East economies; and transition economies.

The model-predicted estimates are then compared with historical data and further adjusted to match actual 2004–08 current account balances. Initial current account projections for 2011 through 2015 then are obtained by using annual forecast data obtained from other sources, such as the International Monetary Fund's *Fiscal Monitor* (fiscal balance forecasts) and the International Energy Agency's *World Energy Outlook* (energy forecasts). Current account numbers from 2016 onward are simple linear projections of the path of

current account balances to the 2025 value implied by a given scenario. These projections were then fed into the World Bank's Linkage model (World Bank 2007) to develop the growth numbers.

The Linkage growth model (described in detail in van der Mensbrugghe 2005) was designed to capture the complex growth dynamics behind a large set of countries of interest. The model is a dynamic, global computable general equilibrium growth model that allows for this flexibility, while using the current account scenarios developed as a key input. The model includes 22 country-regions, eight sectors, and as many as eight possible factors and intermediate inputs to production. The growth process is an augmented Solow-style neoclassical production function, taking as given labor force evolution, productivity processes, and saving-investment decisions (themselves a function of demographic factors).

Finally, model-generated trade flow patterns and consumption-investment patterns are used to obtain baseline numbers corresponding to each scenario. Variations to the baseline result are obtained from changing the parameters that govern the behavior of major variables, such as the rate of growth of factor and energy productivity, population, and labor supply. Given the emphasis of this chapter on growth, however, the path taken by TFP for a given country is especially important, and alternatives to the growth baseline alter parameters that would generate meaningful variations in TFP.

The resulting medium-term fluctuations in the current account will then give way to a long-run path of external imbalances that gradually adjust toward globally sustainable levels. This (linear) 10-year glide path is one where, by 2025, non-energy-exporting countries adopt a ±3 percent surplus/deficit target if their 2015 current account balances exceed these bounds (countries within this ±3 percent band are assumed to simply maintain their 2015 levels).[29] Energy-exporting countries, owing to their generally larger export patterns, will instead target a current account surplus ceiling of 10 percent of GDP.

This baseline scenario, along with the scenario analyses to follow, relies on a combination of a medium-term current account model and a long-term global growth model (described in detail in box 1.5).

Output and growth patterns. Under the baseline scenario, emerging economies' share of global output will expand, in real terms, from 36.2 percent to 44.5 percent between 2010 and 2025 (figure 1.16). This impressive rise will be led by China. A simultaneous decline in investment and rise in consumption means that China will average a growth rate of about 7 percent throughout the period.[30] This growth rate will occur against a backdrop of a rising old-age dependency ratio—expected to almost double between 2010 and 2025—which is the primary factor behind China's rising consumption share. In spite of those demography-driven changes, China is expected to retain its strong comparative advantage in manufacturing, with labor productivity in the sector continuing to grow through 2025.

In the baseline scenario, consistent with long-term historical productivity trends, India's annual growth rates in 2011 and 2025 are 8.7 and 5.4 percent, respectively, with 8–9 percent in the earlier years and lower growth later on.[31] This growth outcome is a consequence of a combination of gradually rising consumption—in line with India's growing middle class and a lower reliance on foreign saving—and a corresponding decline in investment (of an estimated 32 to 28 percentage points of GDP). In the baseline, India's relatively favorable demographics, implying a growing labor force, is tempered in part by relatively low levels of schooling.[32] For India to be able to maintain the recently-achieved high growth rates of 9 percent, it would need to be able to mobilize domestic saving and channel saving to long-term productive investments, especially in infrastructure. Among other potential emerging economy poles, Indonesia and Singapore post strong real output growth performances, averaging 5.9 percent and 5.1 percent in this scenario, respectively.

In spite of how growth in developing economies will outpace that of advanced economies in the coming years, in the baseline scenario there is no convergence in real output between these two groups within the horizon of 15 years.[33] Nevertheless, though advanced economies will continue to account for a sizable share of the global economic output in 2025, emerging economies will be the drivers of growth. On average, advanced economies as a whole will grow at 2.3 percent over 2011–25, compared with 4.7 percent for emerging economies (figure 1.17). This growth translates, in terms of average income, to a world in which China and Brazil will share similar real GDP per capita numbers (which will be about two-thirds that of Russia and one-fifth that

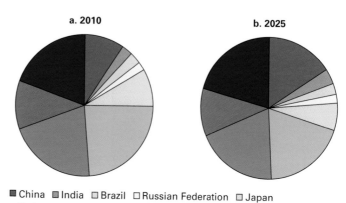

FIGURE 1.16   Global real output shares, 2010 and 2025, baseline scenario

a. 2010

b. 2025

■ China ▨ India ▢ Brazil ▢ Russian Federation ▢ Japan
▢ United States ▨ euro area ■ other industrial ■ other emerging

Source: World Bank staff calculations.

Note: Real shares are expressed in terms of constant 2009 U.S. dollar prices.

of Korea). Overall, the scenario suggests that the process of income convergence, which definitively began in the past decade, appears set to continue into the next decade (although the process need not be irreversible, and several risks that could derail the expected growth process are discussed in the final section of this chapter).

Several other studies have argued that India's real growth rate will overtake that of China by 2025 (Maddison 2007; O'Neill and Stupnytska 2009; OECD 2010; Wilson and Purushothaman 2003), whereas the baseline scenario here has China growing slightly faster than India (the actual growth rates for India in these other studies are, however, similar to the numbers in this book).[34] The difference in the baseline here is due to several reasons. The nature of the general equilibrium model employed here may capture feedback effects that are not taken into account by other modeling approaches. Moreover, the baseline scenario posits a limited increase in India's current account deficit, an outcome that is consistent with India's experience since its balance of payments crisis in 1991 (which has averaged 0.8 percent of GDP between 1991 and 2009). Unless India is able to attract substantial, stable inflows of capital that would provide the necessary international financing—at levels that would be historically unprecedented—domestic saving

FIGURE 1.17   Output growth for emerging and advanced economies, 15-year average, 1996–2010 (historical) and 2011–25 (baseline scenario)

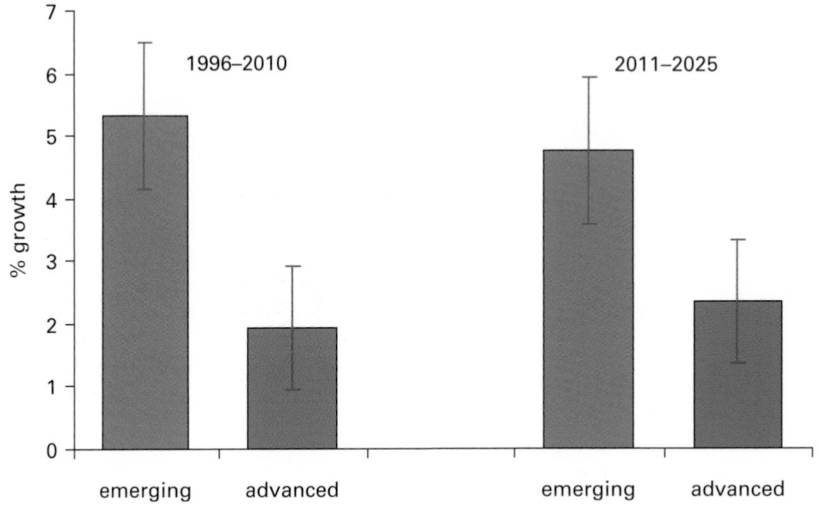

Source: World Bank staff calculations, from model projections and World Bank WDI database.
Note: Fifteen-year averages reported could significantly understate projected growth rates for any given year, with additional uncertainty from modeling errors. To emphasize the wide range of possible outcomes surrounding the baseline scenario, average growth rates are accompanied by error bars corresponding to the historical 95 percent confidence interval.

will be inadequate for achieving growth rates significantly higher than the baseline.

The baseline scenario also has a relatively slower-growing Russia over 2011–25. Thus, in spite of anticipated improvements to Russian labor productivity and expected robust global energy demand, domestic political economy concerns in Russia—including eroding confidence in the rule of law and property rights—will hold back an otherwise solid growth picture.

Consumption, investment, and current account patterns. In the baseline scenario, consumption and investment trends will demonstrate significant shifts over the 15-year modeling horizon (figure 1.18, panel a). East Asian economies, especially China, will raise their consumption shares in national output to levels close to those of the United States and India. For China, in particular, this increased consumption share will be noteworthy: a rise from 41 percent to 55 percent of GDP. Although it is presently difficult to imagine such a sharp rise in consumption by the high-saving East Asian economies, anticipated

demographic changes—especially an uptick in the old-age dependency ratio in many of these countries—will mean that increased consumption is a largely inexorable process. Indeed, the consumption-output share in the East Asian poles could even exceed that of the United States by 2022, owing in part to increasing pressure on the latter to raise savings to meet debt obligations, as well as accommodate a likely decline in its current account deficit.[35]

This increased consumption will occur alongside a fall in investment, again most notably among East Asian economies (figure 1.18, panel b). China's investment will decline modestly (from 45 percent of GDP to 39 percent). This decreasing trend is likely to be echoed by other East Asian economies; however, such declines will be somewhat more limited than the declines experienced in some other potential emerging economy poles, such as Russia (where investment will fall by more than 9 percent of GDP). The concern here is that in some emerging economies, the decline in investment may be more than is optimal, given their stage of development.

FIGURE 1.18   **Consumption and investment shares of output, current and potential growth poles, 2011–25 baseline**

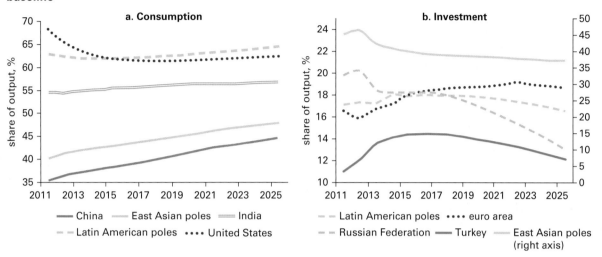

Source: World Bank staff calculations.

Note: Latin American poles refer to the potential emerging economy poles (Argentina, Brazil, Mexico, and the República Bolivariana de Venezuela) with the highest multidimensional polarity indexes in the region. East Asian poles refer to the actual (China) and potential (Indonesia, Korea, and Malaysia) emerging economy poles with the highest multidimensional polarity indexes in the region. Shares are computed from levels measured in terms of constant 2009 U.S. dollars.

Together, these long-term trends provide some reassurance that structural transformations in the potential emerging economy poles, were they to occur, can provide a solution to the current imbalances in the global economy. With emerging economies picking up a greater share of global absorptive capacity through internally driven aggregate demand, the sustainability of their growth is far more certain, and ultimately this is a boon not only to the emerging world, but also to advanced countries and, importantly, to LDCs, as demand for their exports will increase with the expansion of the middle class in the emerging world.

Such trends will start becoming evident in the medium term, during which time current account surpluses in many of the larger emerging economies will gradually soften from their recent historical highs, although the major surplus economies—the energy-exporting Middle East and Russia, and China—will maintain significant, positive current account positions (table 1.2). Although these current account positions suggest that tensions surrounding China's trade balance may persist during this period, if

TABLE 1.2   **Current account balances, current and potential growth poles, 2004–25**

Economy	2004–08	2011–15	2020	2025
Australia	–5.6	–5.9	–4.0	–3.0
Canada	1.4	–0.2	0.5	0.5
Euro area	0.3	–0.1	0.2	0.2
Japan	3.9	2.9	3.2	3.0
United Kingdom	–2.5	–2.4	–0.9	–0.9
United States	–4.5	–6.0	–4.5	–3.0
Brazil	0.6	2.0	2.8	2.8
China	8.2	8.1	5.6	3.0
India	–1.1	–1.1	–0.7	–0.7
Korea, Rep.	1.2	1.3	1.7	1.7
Mexico	–0.8	–1.4	–1.5	–1.5
Poland	–3.6	–3.2	–2.7	–2.7
Russian Federation	8.5	4.9	4.1	4.0
Saudi Arabia	26.0	17.4	12.9	10.0
Turkey	–5.2	–5.2	–3.9	–3.0

Sources: World Bank staff calculations, from IMF IFS, IMF Fiscal Monitor, USEIA International Energy Outlook (IEO), and IEA World Energy Outlook (WEO) databases.

Note: All values are percentages of GDP. The light-shaded region indicates model projections, and the dark-shaded region indicates scenario-dependent implied values. Data for 2004–08 are the historical period average and data for 2011–15 are the projected period average. Projections were performed using a current account model with the fiscal balance, official financial flows, net foreign assets, and net energy exports, with region-specific coefficients and calibrated to the actual current account balance for 2004–08. To satisfy the global adding-up constraint, residual balances were assigned to unreported regions according to GDP.

domestic rebalancing occurs more quickly than anticipated, the surplus will be even lower than projected. Unexpected policy changes in China could also have a dramatic effect. For example, a reversal in policy toward official foreign investments—the largest driver of its surplus—would rapidly bring the projected surplus closer to the 5 percent range.

The majority of advanced economies, in contrast, are projected in the baseline scenario to run current accounts that are either in deficit or flat between 2011 and 2015, with the notable exception of Japan. To the extent that there are marked deviations from historical averages, these can generally be reconciled. For example, Canada's expected deficit between 2011 and 2015 is due to the sharp expected deterioration in its fiscal balances during that time (this worsening of the government's fiscal position, in turn, resulted from cyclical worsening as a result of the mild recession it experienced in 2008–09).

The other major (nonenergy exporting) emerging economies exhibit, in the baseline scenario, either small surpluses or deficits, largely in line with their historical experience. Brazil, for example, will run a small surplus averaging 2 percent of GDP between 2011 and 2015, while India will run a small deficit averaging 1.1 percent over the same period (since 1991, India has maintained fairly small balance of payments deficits,

exceeding 2 percent only in 2008, and averaging 0.8 percent annually between 1991 and 2009).

In the long run, increasing internal demand in the emerging economy growth poles will not preclude the continued expansion of the external sector of these economies. Potential emerging economy growth poles will, in the baseline, experience significant increases in their flows of international trade, in terms of both imports and exports. Brazil and Indonesia, for example, will see their exports more than double in absolute terms, to $245 billion and $316 billion, respectively, under the baseline scenario (their respective export shares of output, however, will be approximately constant).

Emerging economies also will import more. India and Indonesia will import 109 percent and 160 percent more, respectively, in 2025 than they did in 2010, reflecting the rapid increases in the GDP of those economies. Over time, emerging economies' share of global trade gradually will converge with that of advanced economies; in the case of exports, the former will almost equalize with the latter in terms of global shares (figure 1.19). Global trade will expand, as a share of global output, from 49.9 percent to 53.6 percent in 2025.

These different possible current account paths naturally imply different prospects for countries' international investment positions—that is, these countries' external assets net of liabilities. In

FIGURE 1.19 Global import and export shares of global trade, advanced and emerging economies, 2004–25 baseline

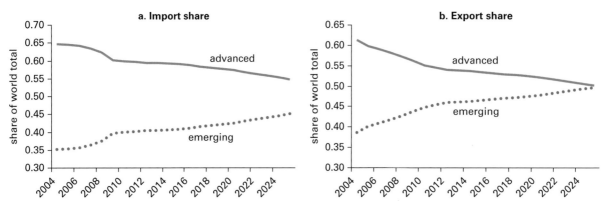

Source: World Bank staff calculations.
Note: Shares are computed from levels measured in constant 2004 prices relative to the basket of OECD exports in the same year.

FIGURE 1.20   Net international investment positions, advanced and emerging economies, and selected net asset countries, 2004–25 baseline

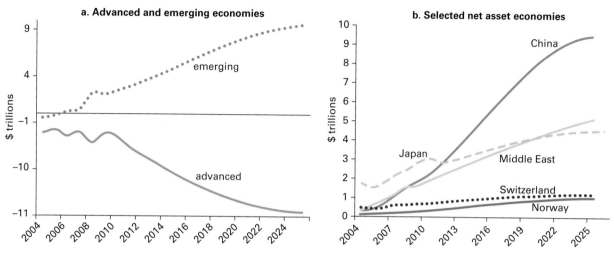

Source: World Bank staff calculations.

Note: The figures depict the baseline scenario. The net IIPs of the two groups do not net to zero because only the top 26 multidimensional polarity index economies were used in the computation. Advanced (emerging) economies thus include only the respective constituent economies within each category. The Middle East includes Mashreq Middle East and North Africa economies, of which Saudi Arabia is the largest economy. Net IIP calculations assume constant asset prices in U.S. dollars and a constant capital account–to-GDP ratio and are measured in constant 2004 prices relative to the basket of OECD exports (for emerging and advanced aggregates) and 2009 U.S. dollars (for individual countries). The net IIP for the Middle East economies was imputed from Saudi Arabia's historical current account and reserve asset positions and scaled up based on Saudi Arabia's GDP share within the group, and the net IIP for Japan reflects a 10 percent reduction as a consequence of the 2011 Tōhoku earthquake and tsunami (based on the upper bound of Japanese government estimates of reconstruction costs, assuming that all costs are borne by reductions in foreign asset positions due to repatriation, and imputing all costs to one year).

particular, the potential emerging economy poles are likely to collectively take on a large and rising net IIP (figure 1.20, panel a). This will be largely offset by the large and rising net liability position among advanced economies.

Although the contrast is dramatic, it is important to realize that these respective positive and negative positions are largely driven by the accumulation patterns of China and the United States (graphs of the two countries' net IIPs are essentially identical to figure 1.20, panel a, albeit with slightly smaller values on the axes). Japan and the Middle Eastern economies account for other large positive net IIP positions (figure 1.20, panel b).

Alternative future scenarios

Although the baseline scenario has painted a relatively sanguine picture of the future evolution of the global economy, there are clear risks that may derail this baseline. From the point of view of potential emerging economy growth poles, the most significant considerations were outlined above: the potential challenge of growth through

technological innovation rather than just adoption, uncertainty over progress on institutional reform (and its impact on productivity), and a successful transition toward growth driven by internal demand. Moreover, the path of external balances may deviate from the smooth convergence anticipated in the baseline.

Thus, it is useful to consider several alternative scenarios in addition to the baseline. Informed by the previous discussion on the changing character of growth in the potential emerging economy growth poles, this section considers three possible deviations to the baseline outcome (table 1.3).

- *Divergent productivity paths.* As discussed earlier, the strong growth performances of many potential emerging economy poles—with the exception of China, India, Poland, and Russia—have not been matched by equally impressive TFP contributions. This scenario—which can be considered a variant of the pessimistic picture painted by Krugman (1994)—considers the possibility that these four economies

TABLE 1.3   Key perturbations for alternative growth and external balance scenarios

Economy	2004–08	2020	2025	2004–08	2020	2025
	Divergent productivity (productivity growth, %)			Unbalanced growth (domestic saving, % GDP)		
Euro area	0.4	1.8	0.8	22.0	23.8	22.8
Japan	0.6	1.1	1.1	27.0	22.7	22.2
United States	−0.1	0.1	−0.1	13.0	21.3	20.5
United Kingdom	0.6	2.7	1.2	14.5	9.9	9.1
Brazil	3.1	0.7	1.2	19.1	19.0	17.3
China	6.1	4.1	6.0	49.5	46.8	47.1
India	4.2	2.0	4.4	29.0	28.9	28.1
Korea, Rep.	1.2	2.6	2.3	30.8	24.0	24.0
Malaysia	1.8	0.3	−0.5	41.1	33.4	33.4
Mexico	1.4	0.5	−0.3	20.2	17.1	14.7
Poland	5.1	4.7	5.4	16.3	10.3	8.5
Russian Federation	10.1	3.5	4.5	29.1	20.1	15.7
Singapore	6.5	2.7	1.7	44.2	35.6	35.9
Thailand	3.6	7.5	11.4	30.8	20.5	20.7
	Continued imbalances			Total rebalancing		
	(current account balance, % GDP)					
Australia	−4.6	−4.9	−4.9	−4.6	−2.5	0.0
Canada	0.4	0.5	0.5	0.4	0.3	0.0
Euro area	1.3	0.2	0.2	1.3	0.1	0.0
Japan	3.9	3.4	3.4	3.9	1.7	0.0
United Kingdom	−1.5	−0.9	−0.9	−1.5	−0.4	0.0
United States	−4.5	−5.4	−5.9	−4.5	−2.9	0.0
Brazil	0.6	2.8	2.8	0.6	1.4	0.0
China	8.2	8.2	8.2	8.2	4.0	0.0
India	−1.1	−0.7	−0.7	−1.1	−0.4	0.0
Korea, Rep.	1.2	1.7	1.7	1.2	0.8	0.0
Mexico	−0.3	−1.5	−1.5	−0.3	−0.7	0.0
Poland	−2.6	−2.7	−2.7	−2.6	−1.3	0.0
Russian Federation	8.5	4.1	4.1	8.5	2.0	0.0
Saudi Arabia	26.0	15.7	15.8	26.0	7.8	0.0
Turkey	−5.2	−4.7	−4.8	−5.2	−2.4	0.0

Source: World Bank staff calculations.

Note: Productivity is measured as the growth rate of (services) labor productivity, rather than TFP directly. This is because TFP is defined as the residual in a growth decomposition, but a computable general equilibrium model does not generally embed such residuals, so productivity changes are typically attributed to labor instead. It can be shown that there is a close link between TFP growth and labor productivity growth (Barro 1999), especially if labor quality and the return on capital do not vary much. The (baseline) unperturbed productivity growth rates for China, India, Poland, and Russia are 2.9, 0.9, 3.5, and 2.3 percent for 2020, respectively, and 3.7, 2.1, 3.1, and 2.2 percent for 2025, respectively. The (baseline) unperturbed saving shares for China, Korea, Malaysia, Singapore, and Thailand are 42.6, 22.0, 32.0, 29.0, and 16.4 percent for 2020, respectively, and 39.1, 20.0, 29.9, 20.5, and 12.0 percent for 2025, respectively.

manage to attain high levels of TFP growth (and, implicitly, make the transition from technological adoption to greater innovative capacity), whereas other emerging economies exhaust the gains from factor accumulation and reallocation, and languish in lower levels of TFP growth. In effect, the emerging world fractures into a "two-speed" world, with four economies continuing to grow rapidly in economic size and influence and the others settling into a lower growth path.

- *Unbalanced internal growth.* As mentioned previously, a transition to strong, sustainable absorption among the emerging economy potential growth poles is central to realigning these economies away from external sources of growth. This scenario considers the possibility that internal reforms designed to support higher levels of internal demand in outward-oriented economies—China, Korea, Malaysia, Singapore, and Thailand—do not result in a substantive increase in consumption shares, and the scenario explores the implications of such continued high saving on investment. To incorporate the possible effects of capital leakage, the scenario allows for external accounts to either follow the baseline path or to hold constant at 2015 levels from 2016 onward.
- *Global external balances.* A final set of scenarios traces the two polar outcomes for global imbalances. The first possibility is a situation in which imbalances persist, resulting in a continuation of current account balances along the medium-term path (the assumption imposes 2015 levels of the current account through 2025). This could be due to policy inaction, such as unwillingness to undertake major fiscal adjustments. Under this scenario, financial development in developing economies remains sluggish, while advanced economies maintain their comparative advantage in investment opportunities (Dooley, Folkerts-Landau, and Garber 2009).

Under the second external balance scenario, a major reversal in the pattern of global external balances occurs, with a total rebalancing by 2025, when all current account balances reach zero (the actual adjustment path to zero is assumed to be linear). This reversal could result from distinct improvements in the investment opportunities available in surplus emerging economies, occurring in concert with rapid financial market development, along with acute fiscal consolidation in advanced economies. Another, admittedly extreme, possibility is that international

trading relations break down, forcing external accounts toward autarky.

A detailed analysis of these scenarios is undertaken in annex 1.7. The main lessons are as follows:

- The *divergent productivity* scenario suggests that the two-track global economy may fracture even further, into a slowly divergent path for growth between advanced economies, low-productivity developing economies, and high-productivity developing economies. Whether this occurs depends on whether economies such as Argentina, Brazil, Indonesia, and Korea are able permanently to raise their TFP performances.
- The *unbalanced internal growth* scenario suggests that successfully navigating the internal realignment process toward domestic sources of growth depends not only on internal structural adjustment policies, but also on successful external accounts management. This interdependence points to the need for surplus nations to effect internal and external rebalancing efforts simultaneously.
- The *global external balances* scenarios suggest that the evolution of domestic investment, in particular, depends on the manner by which global imbalances unfold. Imposing total rebalancing on surplus economies (such as China, Russia, and the oil-exporting economies of the Middle East) tends to lead to a relatively slower rate of decline (or an actual increase) in those countries' investment shares, with the converse holding true for deficit economies such as India, Poland, and Turkey.

Growth Poles and Multipolarity in the Future World Economy

The world of 2025 truly will be multipolar. Using the baseline numbers for 2021–25, it appears that the current three growth poles will be joined by India (table 1.4). Indeed, the top seven economies—China, the euro area, the United

TABLE 1.4   Measures of growth poles, top 15 economies, 2021–25 baseline average

Economy	Output (constant 2009 $, trillions)	Contribution to global growth (%)	Simple growth polarity index	Alternate growth polarity index
China	13.9	0.94	96.46	72.96
Euro area	18.3	0.38	38.95	37.93
United States	18.8	0.24	24.36	29.56
India	3.0	0.17	17.26	13.21
Japan	6.3	0.09	9.15	10.01
United Kingdom	3.4	0.07	7.53	8.68
Indonesia	1.2	0.07	7.46	6.46
Brazil	2.4	0.06	6.21	4.57
Russian Federation	2.0	0.04	4.12	2.94
Canada	2.1	0.04	4.01	3.91
Korea, Rep.	1.4	0.04	4.00	5.55
Australia	1.5	0.03	3.50	4.55
Middle East	1.8	0.03	3.16	1.88
Sweden	0.8	0.03	3.08	3.37
Turkey	1.0	0.03	2.64	1.73

Source: World Bank staff calculations.

Note: The shaded region indicates potential poles, with the cutoff determined by the first significant break on the index (from below). The simple index was generated from size-weighted GDP growth rates normalized to the maximum and minimum of the full 1968–2025 period. The alternate index was generated from the absorption-weighted growth share and normalized to the maximum and minimum of the 2006–25 period. Both indexes use output levels calculated from data in constant 2009 U.S. dollars. The Middle East includes Mashreq Middle East and North Africa economies, of which Saudi Arabia is the largest economy. The top 15 countries in the alternate index exclude the Middle East and Turkey, but include Argentina (2.19) and South Africa (2.12).

States, India, Japan, the United Kingdom, and Indonesia—are the same whether measured by the simple polarity index (table 1.4, fourth column), or if computed from an alternative measure that better captures the trade channel of growth spillovers (table 1.4, fifth column).[36] This mix, comprising both advanced and emerging economies, underscores how different the distribution of economic power is likely to be in the future, compared to just a decade ago, or even today.

China tops both polarity indexes in 2025, a reflection of the expected continued dynamism of its economy and its increasingly large relative economic size. China will contribute about one-third of global growth at the end of the period, far more than any other economy. Nevertheless, advanced economies, especially the United States and the euro area, will continue to serve as engines for the global economy. This outcome is likely to occur even in the presence of a decline in the consumption share of the United States (and, to a lesser extent, the euro area) and modest growth rates relative to emerging economies.

Under the baseline scenario, India will join China as an emerging economy growth pole. In spite of its smaller size relative to advanced economies such as Japan and the United Kingdom, India's robust growth through the end of 2025 will mean that its contribution to global growth will surpass that of any individual advanced economy (except the United States). Together, the simple polarity indexes of China and India will be nearly twice that of the United States and the euro area by 2025.

The remainder of the potential growth poles is likely to be a mix of advanced and emerging economies. Japan and the United Kingdom, for example, will play important supporting roles in global growth dynamics, alongside Indonesia and Brazil. Indonesia's prominence in growth polarity is somewhat of a surprise, appearing higher in the indexes than Brazil, Canada, or Russia (economies that will be almost twice Indonesia's size). Depending on the index, there is some movement in and out of the top 15 countries closer to the bottom.

Current discussions often assert that the world of the future will be more multipolar. Insofar as the distribution of economic *activity* is concerned, this undoubtedly will be the case. An index of multipolarity that is based on economic size clearly points to a world that has gradually become more multipolar since 1968, and will become even more so in the future (figure 1.21): the normalized concentration index calculated from shares of GDP falls steadily by more than 40 percent from 1968 to 2025. In a significant way, then, the trend of increasing multipolarity is likely to continue.

However, a more diffused distribution of global economic activity does not in fact imply a more balanced distribution of economic growth contributions. While growth polarity in the 2021–25 period will continue to be more diffused than in the 20th century—the normalized concentration index based on the simple polarity measure in 2025 is 0.046, compared with 0.059 at the end of the 1990s and more than twice that in the early 1970s (figure 1.21)—the declining trend in the index reaches a minimum of 0.030 around 2008, pointing to the likelihood that the global economic impact of growth spillovers in 2025 may in fact emanate from fewer countries than today (at least by this measure).[37]

The notion that the postcrisis global economic environment will be fundamentally different from the environment of the past has gained considerable ground in some academic and policy circles. The reality of the multipolar world of the future is likely to be somewhat more nuanced. Advanced countries will continue to play a central role in the global economy in 2025, and while they are expected to grow more sluggishly than developing countries, the economic size of advanced countries (in real terms) will counterbalance this slower rate of growth. Still, size is not everything, and the economic influence of the large emerging economies will be increasingly palpable.[38] The financial crisis could well have marked a certain turning point in international economic relations, paving the way for a larger role for developing countries as the global economy becomes more multipolar.

Thus, in spite of the severe pain caused by the global financial crisis, the event may well have consolidated transformations in the global economy that will ensure its future resilience. A more diffuse distribution of growth poles will mean a world that better weathers shocks and is more resilient to crises; indeed, the fairly rapid recovery

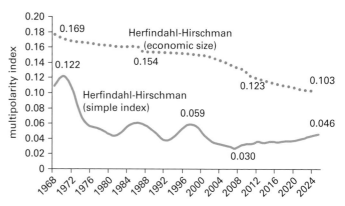

FIGURE 1.21   **Evolution of multipolarity, economic size and simple polarity index, 1968–2025 (projected)**

Source: World Bank staff calculations.

Note: Multipolarity index calculated as the normalized Herfindahl-Hirschman index of GDP and simple polarity index shares of the top 15 economies, computed over rolling 5-year averages.

of the nonindustrialized nations from the financial crisis may well attest to the start of a trend decoupling that is likely to grow stronger as the emerging world continues to mature (Canuto and Giugale 2010). Such diversification bodes well for the new multipolar world.

Policy Challenges and the Development Agenda

Challenges and risks to sustained growth in the potential emerging economy poles

The forward march of the potential emerging economy growth poles is likely to be accompanied by the continued evolution of productive capacity and internal demand, which in turn is reliant on domestic developments in these economies. The recent strong growth performance in the emerging economies may, however, mask the significant domestic development challenges of any given potential pole. These challenges are quite real and, as such, pose risks that can derail a potential growth pole's otherwise robust growth performance. Such challenges are closely related to the underlying factors that influence their growth polarities: institutions, demographics, and human capital.

The first set of challenges involves successful institutional reform in the different potential emerging economy poles. In order for these emerging economies to adapt to the changes inherent in their new global roles, domestic institutions—broadly defined to include governance structures in the economic, financial, and social sectors—will need to reflect the new economic realities. China, India, Indonesia, and Russia all face distinct institutional and governance challenges, and maintaining flexibility in terms of institutional reform is critical for establishing and consolidating their positions as growth poles.

Several of the potential emerging economy growth poles also face demographic concerns. This is especially the case for China, Korea, and Singapore, all of which will face a rising old-age dependency ratio in the years ahead. Absent productivity improvements, especially in the development of indigenous innovative capacity, the burden of older populations will likely be a drag on the vitality of their economies. This point has not been lost on policy makers in these three countries, as evidenced by the very high levels of R&D expenditure undertaken in recent years, along with national initiatives aimed at enhancing domestic innovation.

Finally, human capital is a concern in some potential growth poles, particularly in Brazil, India, and Indonesia. Reducing educational gaps and ensuring access to education is central, since promoting such an enabling environment would

further enhance human capital and stimulate domestic technological adaptation, innovative capacity, and knowledge generation. Successfully negotiating these changes also holds the potential to spur the growth of other economies—in Latin America, South Asia, and elsewhere.

Development impacts and LDCs

Although the multipolar world is ultimately about the realignment of economic poles away from advanced economies and toward developing economies, some countries nonetheless will remain in the periphery of the system. This is especially the case for LDCs, which have struggled to sustain growth in a global economy over which the LDCs have little influence or control. It is important to recognize, therefore, that the new multipolar world may raise a new set of development issues that are unique to the fact that many of the new major drivers of the world economy are also developing economies.

In and of itself, multipolarity should be positive for economies that are not growth poles. A more diffuse distribution of global growth should help mitigate volatility from idiosyncratic shocks experienced in any given pole. Consequently, economies that are not growth poles can enjoy greater stability of external demand. Moreover, some LDCs may well benefit from having new external drivers (from emerging economies) stimulating their domestic growth. Such growth will ultimately accrue to the poor living in those LDCs (Dollar and Kraay 2002), as well as to the poor within the potential emerging economy growth poles.

Such growth spillovers are likely to occur via the trade channel. The expansion of South-South trade in the future will continue the consolidation of trade-induced growth. Over the past decade, the economic complementarities between the large potential emerging economy growth poles and LDCs—the former tend to have comparative advantage in manufactures, and the latter in commodity inputs—have undergirded both rising intensity in bilateral trade (figure 1.22) and rapid growth (IMF 2011). Such complementarities, which are clearly evident from the distinct dominant categories of LDC imports and exports

FIGURE 1.22   **Shares of total LDC bilateral trade, selected advanced and emerging economies, 1991–2010**

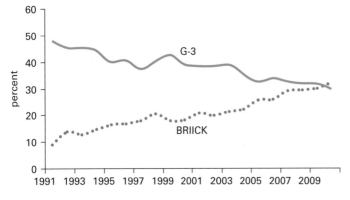

Source: World Bank staff calculations, from IMF DOT database.

Note: LDCs include all LDCs except Bhutan, Eritrea, Lesotho, and Timor-Leste (due to data limitations). G-3 economies are the euro area, Japan, and the United States; BRIICK economies are Brazil, Russia, India, Indonesia, China, and Korea.

FIGURE 1.23 **Dominant LDC merchandise exports to and imports from selected emerging economies**

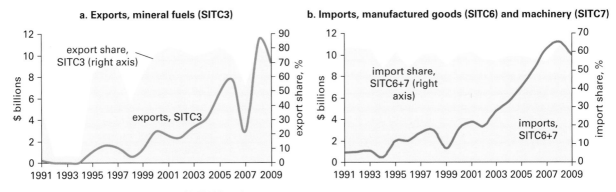

Source: World Bank staff calculations, from UN COMTRADE database.

Note: SITC = Standard International Trade Classification. The selected emerging economies are Brazil, China, India, Indonesia, Korea, and Russia. Dominant flow selected on the basis of export/import share rank for the majority of years.

vis-à-vis the major emerging economies (figure 1.23), suggest that the resulting impact on LDCs' terms of trade has been an overall improvement.

The financing channel can also be important, especially in terms of South-South FDI flows. As discussed in detail in chapter 2, merger and acquisition and greenfield activity can spur natural resource (and some manufacturing) production capacity in LDCs, stimulate local employment, and promote technology transfer. Since the sectoral composition of FDI outflows from the potential emerging economy poles is likely to differ from those of the advanced economy poles, LDCs could benefit from the diversification of their economies that results from such direct investment flows.

Multipolarity could also have a tangible impact on international foreign aid patterns. Official development assistance (ODA) to LDCs from Development Assistance Committee (DAC) countries has been fairly static since the 1980s, fluctuating between 4.5 and 8.5 percent of LDC GDP (figure 1.24). Over time, increased ODA disbursements by the potential emerging economy poles may well push ODA to greater shares. Bilateral ODA from Saudi Arabia, for example, increased by a factor of almost thirty in the decade between 1998 and 2009, rising from $107 million to $2.9 billion. Turkey's bilateral ODA has similarly increased by an order of magnitude

FIGURE 1.24 **Net ODA from DAC countries to LDCs as share of LDC GDP, 1960–2008**

Source: World Bank staff calculations, from OECD DAC and World Bank WDI databases.

Note: ODA disbursements from OECD DAC member countries to LDCs, shown as a percentage of total LDC GDP.

over the same period. China's LDC aid in 2009 constituted about 40 percent of their total disbursements, with the largest share of this destined for Sub-Saharan Africa.

However, there is considerable nuance in the actual impact for a given country. For instance, the nature of global demand for the main exports from many LDCs—typically commodities and mineral resources—could change substantially, and LDCs that are net importers of those goods may face rising global prices (box 1.6). Even when an LDC possesses a comparative advantage in the

BOX 1.6   Multipolarity and commodities

The causes of high commodities prices are multifaceted and interact in complicated ways. The combination of changes in the global climate (and associated weather-related shocks), increased financialization in commodities markets, energy policy (especially with regard to biofuels such as ethanol), and rising incomes in developing countries all play a role in inducing price spikes in commodities markets. Rising price pressures can also be compounded by government policies: food and oil subsidies, export bans, tariff barriers, precautionary hoarding, and even macroeconomic policies (such as monetary and exchange rate policies).

Historically, high prices have not been persistent across time. Most past episodes of rising commodities prices have often been relieved as geopolitical shocks fade and supply responses—such as increased exploration, technological innovation, and expanded inputs—react to high prices (figure B1.6.1, panel a). Moreover, previous cases of high commodity prices had led to

peaks for certain commodity classes that were higher, in real terms, than they are today.

However, the nature of multipolarity may mean that the traditional mechanisms that have relieved price pressure in the past may not be operative, at least for some commodity classes. The run-up in commodities prices from 2003–08 was both more sustained and much more broad-based than in the past. This may well have been due to a much more persistent demand component (especially in extractive commodities)—owing to the rise of potential emerging economy poles—and, hence, raises questions of whether supply responses can keep up.

This is especially the case for metals. While substantial yield gaps exist for agricultural outputs—especially in African economies—the ability to raise mineral extraction rates may be more limited, especially if rising energy prices render marginal extractions from the resource base economically infeasible. The commodity intensity of metal use has steadily increased since

FIGURE B1.6.1   Commodities price index, 1948–2010, and commodity intensity of demand, 1971–2010

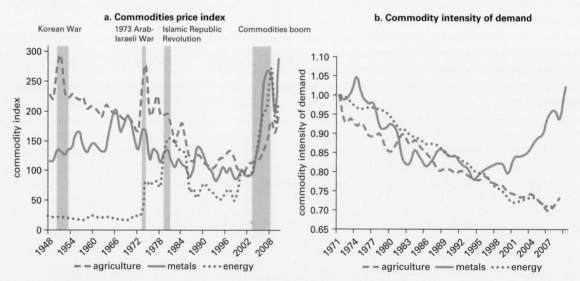

Sources: World Bank staff calculations, using FAOSTAT, IEA World Energy Outlook (WEO), and WBMS World Metal Statistics databases.
Note: The respective commodities indexes are real, manufactures unit value–deflated aggregates, with 2000 prices as the base year. The commodity intensity of demand is defined as commodity use per unit of GDP, each respectively normalized to 1971 values as the base year.

BOX 1.6   (continued)

1994 (figure B1.6.1, panel b), primarily due to demand from China (World Bank 2009a).

As economies such as India undergo structural transformations of their own, their demand for metals may well follow a similar pattern, thus maintaining upward price pressures in those commodities, even as demand from China eases as a result of moderations in both its investment rate and manufacturing capacity growth.

More generally, the rise in real metals prices may reflect a supercycle phenomenon (Cuddington and Jerrett 2008) that has occurred several times before over the past 150 years, resulting from large economies undergoing major structural transformations due to mass industrialization and urbanization. To the extent that China, India, and other potential emerging economy

poles will undergo such structural changes in the future, high metals prices may be more persistent than prices for agricultural or energy commodities (which also display more substitutability over the longer run).

The bottom line is that, in a more multipolar world, the large, fast-growing emerging economies will be more important participants in global commodity markets. Principally, this means that demand pressures from such economies may matter more at the margin. Rapid growth in emerging economies may also have secondary effects, possibly through their impact on the environment (and thus affecting supply). As a result, policy approaches of the past—such as changing government policies with respect to ethanol, or limiting hoarding behavior—may have less of an impact on future commodity prices.

---

export of a given commodity or resource in high global demand, if its future growth is export-biased, its terms of trade could deteriorate and, in the worst case, that LDC could suffer from immiserizing growth.

Moreover, the actual long-term market impact of such rising demand depends on global supply responses. If other potential emerging economy poles increase their production of these goods—for example, if Argentina, Brazil, and Russia raise their agricultural output to cater to higher demand—LDCs may find themselves unable to capitalize on the spillover effects of growth in, say, China and India. This inability is compounded by the fact that the effect of reduced growth volatility from trade openness is conditioned by the degree of export diversification (Haddad, Lim, and Saborowski 2010). Thus, economies that are relatively open but not well diversified, such as Malawi or Zambia, may in fact experience greater volatility of output as their trade with the potential emerging economy growth poles intensifies.

Annexes

Annex 1.1: Growth pole computation

The most straightforward measure of a growth pole is a given economy's contribution to global growth:

$$P_{it} = \frac{\Delta y_{it}}{Y_{t-1}},$$

where y_{it} is the GDP of country i at time t; Y_t is global GDP, which is an aggregation of GDP for all countries in the same period; and $\Delta y_{it} \equiv y_{it} - y_{it-1}$ is the change in the output of economy i. The above equation can be rewritten as follows:

$$P_{it} = s_{it-1} \cdot g_{y,it},$$

where $s_{it} \equiv y_{it}/Y_t$ is the global share of economy i at time t and $g_{y,it}$ is its GDP growth rate, which means that a growth pole as defined above is simply the size-adjusted growth rate of the economy.

Although the above definition is the most intuitive and direct approach to decomposing the relative contribution of each country to global growth, such a measure is incomplete, as it fails to embody the manner by which growth poles exert their *polarity*, in the sense of capturing the transmission and spillover mechanisms for the country's growth to others in its economic space.

The natural extension is then to allow for such alternative channels of growth transmission. This includes poles that capture trade-related spillovers:

$$P_{it}^{\mathrm{T}} = \frac{m_{it}}{X_t} \cdot g_{y,it},$$

where m_{it} is the total imports of country i at time t, and X_t is total global exports. Such a pole would not only have the direct effect of increasing their trading partners' growth through export expansion, but would also have an indirect effect of facilitating technology transfer through trade linkages. A broader measure of demand would be premised on domestic absorption:

$$P_{it}^{\mathrm{T}'} = \frac{d_{it}}{X_t} \cdot g_{y,it},$$

where absorption $d_{it} = c_{it} + i_{it} + g_{it}$ is composed of consumption c, investment i, and government spending g, all for country i at time t.

The natural counterpart to a trade-weighted growth measure is to utilize financial flows as weights instead:

$$P_{it}^{F} = \frac{fo_{it}}{FI_t} \cdot g_{y,it},$$

where fo_{it} is the capital outflows from country i at time t, and FI_t is aggregate global capital inflows. In this case, a country serves as a growth pole by sending investment capital abroad, which serves to directly ease liquidity constraints in recipient economies, while also providing indirect benefits from increased leverage along with technology transfer.

Given the importance of foreign direct investment flows in knowledge and technology transfer, however, a natural (albeit narrower) alternative measure to the above is as follows:

$$P_{it}^{F'} = \frac{fdi_{it}}{FDI_t} \cdot g_{y,it},$$

where fdi_{it} is total FDI (inflows and outflows) for country i at time t, and FDI_t is total global FDI. The use of bidirectional FDI flows is consistent with the empirical evidence that FDI promotes technology transfer, regardless of its direction.

Growth poles can have a spillover influence through labor movement, especially (but not limited to) the migration of skilled workers. The migration channel not only serves to alleviate potential labor supply shortages—while equilibrating domestic wages with global levels through factor price equalization—but also can carry valuable human capital and embedded knowledge across borders. Migration-weighted poles are defined as follows:

$$P_{it}^{M} = \frac{em_{it}}{IM_t} \cdot g_{y,it},$$

where em_{it} is the net emigration from country i at time t, and IM_t is the sum of net immigration across countries. Alternatively, it is possible to focus on only the *stock* of migrants—as a proxy for knowledge spillovers and network effects emanating from a pole country to the migrants' home country—in which case the relevant measure would use, as a weight, the country's immigrant stock share instead:

$$P_{it}^{M'} = \frac{\pi_{it}}{\Pi_t} \cdot g_{y,it},$$

where π_{it} is the immigrant stock resident in country i at time t, and Π_t is the sum of all migrants worldwide.

Finally, it is possible to attempt to directly measure the effect of technological spillovers from a pole:

$$P_{it}^{A} = \frac{a_{it}}{A_t} \cdot g_{y,it},$$

where a_{it} is a measure of technological spillovers by country i at time t, and A_t is technological spillovers for the world as a whole. By and large, a_{it} is not directly observable. Nonetheless, it can be proxied by various indicators of innovation and technology.

The simple polarity measure used in this book uses only relative GDP share as a weight, which serves as a proxy for all the different spillover channels. The benchmark multidimensional polarity measure used in this book introduces separate weights for the trade, finance, and technology channels, measured respectively by imports as a share of global exports, capital outflows as a share of global inflows, and patents as a share of global patents. The imports measure corrects for reexports for the major entrepôt economies of Hong Kong SAR, China; Singapore; and the United Arab Emirates, and also nets out intramonetary union trade using bilateral trade flows data. The capital outflows measure includes FDI and portfolio capital but excludes derivative transactions. The patents measure utilizes patent approvals to all national patent bodies reporting to the World Intellectual Property Organization. The expanded polarity measure additionally includes weights for the migration channel, as measured by immigrant stock as a share of global immigrants.

The three alternative growth measures relied on GDP data adjusted in three different ways: (1) real, (2) adjusted to account for Harrod-Balassa-Samuelson effects by removing U.S. inflation from countries' nominal growth rates, and (3) adjusted for purchasing power parity across countries. The cyclical component of the growth series then was removed by taking only the trend component after application of a Hodrik-Prescott filter ($\lambda = 6.25$).

To provide more definitiveness to the selection of growth poles (and reduce overreliance on a single dimension), the first principal component for the collection of measures described above was used to compute a composite index. This index was normalized to a scale of 0–100 for each of the three GDP variants, and is reported in table 1A.1. The bottom panel of the table shows these growth poles calculated without the inclusion of migration.[39] Here, the measure including and excluding migration is reported.

Other measures of growth spillover effects have been proposed in the literature. One class of studies incorporates third-country variables into growth regressions to identify the influence of these third countries on growth elsewhere (see, for example, Arora and Vamvakidis 2005, 2010a, 2010b). In principle, estimated coefficients can be aggregated to obtain a country's global spillover effect. Studies employing such a framework suffer from three shortcomings. First, the methodology identifies correlations; a country whose growth cycles strongly commove with that of a large, influential country may be erroneously identified as a growth driver. So while the approach is valuable for case studies motivated by a priori driver countries, it is less useful for agnostic identification of growth poles. Second, it is much more difficult to flexibly incorporate multiple spillover channels, especially when bilateral flow data are not available. Third, the methodology is more data intensive and so is less useful for forecasting purposes, in which case estimates of the future values of variables are typically much more difficult to come by.

Another class of models adopts the tools of spatial econometrics to study growth spillovers (see Rey and Janikas 2005 for a recent review). However, these studies tend to limit their focus to physical rather than economic space. Many papers (such as Keller 2002) tend to be focused mainly on one or, at most, two channels. Finally, many studies focus on negative, rather than positive, spillovers—for example, the negative economic effects of civil wars on neighboring countries (Murdoch and Sandler 2002).

Annex 1.2: Alternative measures of concentration

The fields of political science and international relations have long been interested in the study of the distribution of power. Within economics, the subfields of development, industrial relations, and international trade also have developed several measures of economic concentration and inequality, which can be applied to approximate the distribution of power as well.

There are three common measures of economic concentration, or resource-based power. The most popular of these is the Herfindahl-Hirschman index (Hirschman 1964), which is a sum of the squared market shares:

$$H_t = \sum_N s_{it}^2,$$

TABLE 1A.1   Principal components index (with and without migration subindex) for growth poles, top 10 economies, 2004–08 average

Economy	Real Index	Economy	HBS Index	Economy	PPP Index
		Without migration			
China	26.20	Euro area	47.34	China	63.70
United States	20.33	China	41.54	United States	51.26
Euro area	10.86	United States	30.51	Euro area	40.15
Japan	5.59	Russian Federation	25.60	Japan	28.15
United Kingdom	5.51	Canada	22.61	Russian Federation	26.02
Korea, Rep.	5.41	United Kingdom	22.49	Korea, Rep.	24.57
Russian Federation	4.79	Korea, Rep.	20.49	United Kingdom	24.01
India	4.62	Australia	20.26	India	23.38
Singapore	4.30	Brazil	19.48	Singapore	22.95
Canada	4.08	Norway	19.25	Canada	22.92
		With migration			
China	27.63	Euro area	49.88	China	62.94
United States	26.12	China	36.73	United States	59.41
Euro area	17.52	Russian Federation	35.89	Euro area	44.42
Russian Federation	15.11	United States	29.38	Russian Federation	32.80
India	13.61	Canada	22.11	India	25.71
United Kingdom	11.56	Ukraine	22.05	Japan	25.06
Japan	11.09	United Kingdom	20.77	United Kingdom	22.26
Korea, Rep.	11.01	Saudi Arabia	20.67	Saudi Arabia	21.44
Saudi Arabia	10.92	Australia	20.20	Canada	21.44
Singapore	10.90	India	19.78	Korea, Rep.	21.41

Sources: World Bank staff calculations, from IMF DOT, IMF IFS, World Bank WDI, and WIPO Patentscope databases.

Note: The index was generated from the share-weighted combination of the first two principal components of trade, finance, and technology-weighted growth shares, with and without migration-weighted growth shares, normalized to the maximum and minimum of the 1969–2008 period. Real, HBS, and PPP-adjusted indicate growth rates calculated, respectively, from GDP data in real 2000 U.S. dollars, nominal local currency converted to U.S. dollars at current exchange rates and deflated by U.S. prices, and 2005 international PPP-adjusted dollars.

where s_{it} is the market share of firm i at time t, and N is the total number of firms operating in the market. This index may be normalized so that the index is bound by [0, 1] by applying the following formula:

$$H_t^* = \frac{H_t - \dfrac{1}{N}}{1 - \dfrac{1}{N}},$$

The two other related concentration/distribution indexes are the Theil, which weights market shares relative to the mean market share, and the Gini, which captures the relative mean difference in shares between two firms selected randomly from the market.

In international relations, the most well-known measure of interstate power distribution

is the Ray-Singer concentration index (Ray and Singer 1973), popularized by Mansfield (1993). The index is actually an application of the normalized Herfindahl-Hirschman index to the measurement of the share of aggregate capabilities, c_{it}, held by major power i at time t:

$$C_t = \sqrt{\frac{\sum_N c_{it}^2 - \dfrac{1}{N}}{1 - \dfrac{1}{N}}},$$

where N is the total number of powers in consideration.

The technical difficulties associated with the concentration measures are well known.[40] Moreover, the share of state capabilities, c_{it}, often is not very well defined. Finally, even if reasonable proxies for economic power were chosen (such as export share in global exports, for example), concentration indexes based on power shares per se do not capture the effect of a state's relative growth rate or its influence on other states.

In positive political theory, two classical power indexes are used to measure influence over voting, or bargaining power. The Penrose-Banzhaf index (Banzhaf 1965; Penrose 1946) is the share of the total swing votes, v_{it}, held by an entity i at time t:

$$B_{it} = \frac{v_{it}}{\sum_N v_{it}},$$

where N is the total number of voting members. In contrast to the concept of swing votes, the Shapley-Shubik index (Shapley and Shubik 1954) is based on that of pivotal votes and is given by the a priori probability that a given entity is in a pivotal position:

$$S_{it} = \frac{p_{it}}{n!},$$

where p_{it} is the number of pivotal votes held by entity i at time t, and $n!$ is the number of possible permutations of voting members.

Voting indexes have technical problems of their own, which likewise are well recognized.[41] In the context of international economic relations, however, the biggest drawback is that voting indexes require a voting mechanism to be operational or relevant, which may not be the case in many forms of international interactions. Like concentration indexes, voting indexes likewise do not capture relative growth rate or spillover effects.

A third form of power distribution would involve a measure of indirect or sociocultural influence, or "soft" power (Nye 2004). However, soft power is (almost by definition) difficult to quantify. Although proxies may be available—such as the global spread of a country's language, education institutions, or national values and philosophy—no systematic measure has emerged from the literature.

Annex 1.3: Growth polarity regression details

The data set for the regressions were *country-level* data for five-year averages over the period

1971–2005. The dependent variable was the growth polarity index, measured with real GDP growth rates, excluding the migration subindex. This was rescaled with support [0, 100], using the maximum and minimum of the series, and subsequently log transformed. The independent variables were sourced variously from the World Bank's *World Development Indicators* (World Bank 2010b) and the IMF's *Direction of Trade Statistics* and *International Financial Statistics* (IMF 2010a, 2010c) databases (proximate economic variables); Barro and Lee (2010) and Lindert (2004) (education); Rodrik, Subramanian, and Trebbi (2004) (fundamental economic variables); ICRG (*International Country Risk Guide*; PRS Group 2010) (institutions); Alesina and colleagues (2003) (ethnolinguistic diversity); and WVSA (2009) (social capital). Natural logarithms were also taken for all the independent variables.

Population growth is the rate of population, investment share is investment as a share of GDP, and education attainment is the average years of schooling in the population aged 25 and older (the measure of human capital utilizes the same indicator). Infrastructure is proxied by mobile cellular subscriptions per 100 people (replacing this with the percentage of paved roads yields qualitatively similar results, but halves the sample size); poor health is proxied by the under-5 mortality rate (using life expectancy switches the sign of the coefficients on the health variable, as expected, but yields qualitatively similar results for the other variables); the dependency ratio is the population above age 65 as a share of working-age population; and government size is government consumption as a share of GDP.[42]

Trade exposure is total imports and exports as a share of GDP, geography is a country's distance from the equator, and institutional quality is an index generated from the share-weighted combination of the first three principal components of 11 institutional variables from the ICRG (excluding democratic accountability). Ethnolinguistic fractionalization is an index calculated as the simple average of ethnic and linguistic fractionalization (substituting this with ethno-linguistic-religious fractionalization yields qualitatively similar results), and democracy is the democratic accountability variable from the ICRG (using the Polity IV measure of democracy yields qualitatively similar results).

The proximate determinants regressions were performed using both error components (EC) and linear generalized method of moments (GMM). Random effects were chosen over fixed effects if justified by a Hausman test, or if fixed effect estimates were precluded due to the presence of time-invariant variables. Similarly, system GMM was chosen over difference GMM if Hansen tests suggest that the instruments are valid, otherwise difference GMM was implemented. These regressions are reported in table 1A.2, which includes the relevant key diagnostic tests.

The fundamental determinants regressions were run using instrumental variables (IV) and system GMM. The IV estimates are for the 2001–05 period; estimates for other periods were qualitatively similar. IV instruments used were settler mortality (IV-1) and fraction of European language–speaking population (IV-2) (institutions), gravity-predicted trade volume (integration), historical enrollment data from 1900 (human capital), and predicted level of democracy (democracy). These regressions are reported in table 1A.3, which includes the relevant key diagnostic tests.

Annex 1.4: Business cycle stylized facts

Table 1A.4 tabulates correlation coefficients for consumption (C), investment (I), exports (X), and output (Y), along with changes in these variables, for 15 economies with high values of the multidimensional polarity index.

TABLE 1A.2   Estimates for proximate determinants of growth polarity

	(1)		(2)		(3)		(4)		(5)	
	EC	GMM	EC	GMM	EC	GMM	EC	GMM	EC	GMM
Population growth	0.043	2.627	0.169	1.664	0.017	4.168	−0.055	2.466	−0.484	2.744
	(0.89)	(3.02)	(0.51)	(1.85)	(0.91)	(3.89)	(0.86)	(3.18)	(1.02)	(2.69)
Investment share	1.052	−0.774	0.908	−0.620	1.073	1.486	0.922	0.130	0.994	0.476
	(0.56)*	(1.00)	(0.23)***	(0.73)	(0.57)*	(0.71)**	(0.50)*	(0.80)	(0.53)*	(0.53)
Schooling	0.124	0.220	0.103	0.070	0.132	0.072	0.077	0.151	0.107	0.180
	(0.07)*	(0.14)*	(0.04)***	(0.10)	(0.07)*	(0.08)	(0.06)	(0.12)	(0.07)	(0.10)*
					Additional controls					
Infrastructure			−0.002	−0.001						
			(0.00)	(0.00)						
Poor health					0.012	−0.143				
					(0.08)	(0.06)**				
Dependency ratio							−0.401	−0.324		
							(0.17)***	(0.16)**		
Government size									−0.118	0.110
									(0.08)	(0.07)*
R^2	0.160		0.121		0.163		0.205		0.089	
F		1.69*		1.52		1.45		2.02**		1.83*
Hansen J		34.53		38.42		40.85		43.95		41.55
AR(2) z		−1.14		−1.02		−1.04		−1.28		−1.16
Observations	526	439	479	392	523	523	526	439	526	439

Sources: World Bank staff calculations, from IE Singapore, IMF DOT, IMF IFS, World Bank WDI, and WPIO Patentscope databases.

Note: GMM = generalized method of movements. Logarithms were applied to all variables. All error component models were estimated with fixed effects, except for specification (2), which was estimated with random effects. All linear GMM models were estimated as difference GMM, with the exception of specification (3), which was estimated as system GMM. Standard errors robust to heteroskedasticity (all specifications) and autocorrelation (GMM only) are reported in parentheses. A lagged dependent variable (GMM only), period dummies, and a constant term (all specifications) were included in the specifications, but not reported.

* indicates significance at the 10 percent level, ** indicates significance at the 5 percent level, and *** indicates significance at the 1 percent level.

TABLE 1A.3 Estimates for fundamental determinants of growth polarity

	(1)			(2)			(3)			(4)			(5)		
	IV-1	IV-2	GMM	IV-1	IV-2	GMM	IV-1	IV-2	GMM	IV-1	IV-2	GMM	IV-1	IV-2	GMM
Integration	−0.399	−0.522	0.098	−0.332	−0.578	0.084	−0.542	−0.857	0.050	−1.642	−0.695	−0.007	−0.944	−0.401	0.062
	(0.17)*	(0.18)***	(0.13)	(0.17)*	(0.20)***	(0.13)	(0.26)**	(0.39)**	(0.10)	(1.63)	(0.25)***	(0.14)	(0.63)	(0.20)*	(0.10)
Institutions	1.929	1.794	0.828	1.929	2.311	0.825	2.090	4.802	0.895	2.167	1.622	0.471	0.666	3.321	0.717
	(0.63)***	(1.00)*	(0.31)***	(0.61)***	(1.17)*	(0.32)**	(0.77)***	(2.85)*	(0.28)***	(2.02)	(1.20)	(0.36)	(2.36)	(3.90)	(0.25)***
Geography	−0.082	−0.083	0.013	−0.044	−0.087	0.023	−0.145	−0.338	0.011	−0.180	−0.017	−0.127	−0.479	−0.519	0.017
	(0.07)	(0.10)	(0.04)	(0.07)	(0.10)	(0.03)	(0.10)	(0.26)	(0.03)	(0.26)	(0.16)	(0.10)	(0.61)	(0.61)	(0.03)
							Additional controls								
Fractionalization				0.357	0.440	0.109									
				(0.32)	(0.43)	(0.25)									
Democracy							−0.252	−0.836	−0.050						
							(0.34)	(0.57)	(0.11)						
Social capital										0.317	0.151	0.334			
										(0.43)	(0.17)	(0.20)			
Human capital													0.990	0.105	0.099
													(0.87)	(0.99)	(0.12)
F	4.05***	4.11***	2.39**	3.33**	2.90**	2.27**	2.38*	1.59	2.14**	0.750	2.700**	1.45	1.31	2.53*	2.40**
Hansen J			70.33			69.37			73.11			45.47			73.16
AR(2) z			−0.42			−0.40			−0.60			−0.03			−0.34
Observations	42	75	359	41	74	354	39	70	359	20	47	230	15	33	357

Sources: World Bank staff calculations, from IE Singapore, IMF DOT, IMF IFS, World Bank WDI, and WIPO Patentscope databases.

Note: IV = instrumental variables. Logarithms were applied to all independent variables. Geography and social capital were always treated as exogenous. Standard errors robust to heteroskedasticity (all specifications) and autocorrelation (GMM only) are reported in parentheses. A lagged dependent variable (GMM only), period dummies, and a constant term (all specifications) were included in the specifications, but not reported.

* indicates significance at the 10 percent level, ** indicates significance at the 5 percent level, and *** indicates significance at the 1 percent level.

Annex 1.5: Current account model details

The data set for the regressions were *country-level* data for five-year averages over the period 1970–2008. The dependent variable was the current account balance, measured as a share of GDP. The independent variables were the fiscal balance, net official flows, net foreign assets, and net energy exports. The variables were sourced from the World Bank's *World Development Indicators* (World Bank 2010b) and the IMF's *International Financial Statistics* (IMF 2010c) databases, with the exception of the fiscal balance data, which were obtained from the IMF fiscal affairs department, and missing values for net foreign assets, which were complemented with data from Lane and Milesi-Ferretti (2006). Following Gagnon (2010), official flows were adjusted to include reserve assets from both the asset and liabilities side.

The regressions were performed using fixed effects regressions to obtain coefficients for each country grouping (only time, but not country,

fixed effects were included), which are reported in table 1A.5. The model-predicted estimates were then fitted to historical data from the 2004–08 period average and further calibrated to match actual 2004–08 current account balances by adding a country-specific fixed effect.

The data set for projections for the independent variables for 2011–15 were from the IMF's *Fiscal Monitor* (IMF 2010b) (fiscal balance forecasts), the IEA's (International Energy Agency) *World Energy Outlook* (IEA 2010) (energy production and consumption forecasts), and the USEIA's (U.S. Energy Information Administration) *International Energy Outlook* (USEIA 2010) (current energy profiles). Fiscal balances for 2012 and 2013 were linear projections between 2011 and 2014 (where data were available). Official flows were maintained at 2008 levels through the projection period, and net foreign assets applied the five-year lagged annual values through 2013, and maintained this value for 2014 and 2015. Net energy exports differenced production and

TABLE 1A.4   **Correlations for consumption, investment, and exports with output, and changes in consumption, investment, and exports with change in output, current and potential pole**

Economy	Correlations					
	C,Y	I,Y	X, Y	ΔC, ΔY	ΔI, ΔY	ΔX, ΔY
Euro area	0.999	0.998	0.982	0.503	0.490	0.719
United States	0.999	0.997	0.992	0.961	0.537	0.586
China	0.990	0.997	0.994	0.870	0.953	0.910
Russian Federation	0.995	0.983	0.926	0.853	0.879	0.459
United Kingdom	0.999	0.997	0.996	0.515	0.361	0.695
Japan	0.999	0.985	0.952	0.120	−0.002	0.373
Brazil	0.998	0.985	0.932	0.562	0.538	0.736
Canada	0.999	0.993	0.979	0.758	0.689	0.684
Australia	0.999	0.993	0.994	0.700	0.711	0.818
India	0.996	0.987	0.969	0.597	0.738	0.832
Korea, Rep.	0.999	0.991	0.975	0.368	0.294	0.790
Turkey	0.999	0.990	0.991	0.690	0.534	0.874
Mexico	0.999	0.996	0.984	0.541	0.556	0.727
Poland	0.999	0.986	0.992	0.865	0.858	0.926
Saudi Arabia	0.915	0.978	0.961	0.664	0.645	0.619

Sources: World Bank staff calculations, IMF IFS, and World Bank WDI databases.
Note: Cross-correlations reported for the full time period for which data are available, typically between 1965 and 2008 for most countries.

TABLE 1A.5   **Estimates for empirical current account balances model, by country group**

	Advanced economies	Developing Asia	Africa	Latin America	Middle East	Transition economies
Fiscal balance	0.400	0.240	0.300	0.430	0.640	0.340
	(0.13)***	(0.18)	(0.08)***	(0.18)**	(0.22)***	(0.27)
Official flows	0.210	0.690	0.370	0.390	0.240	0.210
	(0.37)	(0.24)***	(0.08)***	(0.12)***	(0.16)	(0.25)
Net foreign assets	0.070	0.037	0.037	0.035	0.019	0.001
	(0.01)***	(0.01)***	(0.01)***	(0.01)***	(0.01)	(0.02)
Net energy exports	0.060	0.100	0.130	0.280	0.040	0.100
	(0.10)	(0.10)	(0.03)***	(0.05)***	(0.06)	(0.06)
R^2	0.51	0.66	0.76	0.77	0.87	0.58
Observations	105	59	83	88	40	62

Sources: World Bank staff calculations, from IMF IFS, IMF Fiscal Affairs, and World Bank WDI databases.
Note: All variables are measured as percentages of GDP. All variables are in 5-year averages, with the exception of net foreign assets, which are the end-of-period values for the previous 5-year period. Standard errors robust to heteroskedasticity are reported in parentheses. Time fixed effects were included, but not reported.
* indicates significance at the 10 percent level, ** indicates significance at the 5 percent level, and *** indicates significance at the 1 percent level.

consumption of only oil and coal (due to data limitations) and scaled this upward by the ratio of total energy consumption to oil and coal consumption. Countries with no forecast energy data were imputed from regional aggregate forecasts, using their current energy profiles. Values were calculated with commodity price projection data from the World Bank's Development Prospects Group (World Bank 2011).

In addition to the 15 economies reported in table 1.2, current account balances were estimated for an additional 13 countries with high values of the multidimensional polarity index. These are reported in table 1A.6 (for projections only).

Annex 1.6: Hypothetical nominal output scenarios

The GDP projections in the main text are presented in terms of real GDP (measured by using 2009 U.S. dollars as the numeraire). Although this presentation provides an accurate depiction of the evolution of output after correcting for the possible distortionary effects arising from inflation, exchange rate valuation differences, and the ambiguity of estimating Harrod-Balassa-Samuelson effects, readers may be more accustomed to the GDP comparisons in terms of the nominal values often presented in the press. To the extent that monetary units in a common currency are an accurate representation of potential global economic power and influence, such a presentation may offer a slightly different picture from that presented in the main text.

Indeed, undertaking such an exercise suggests that, after adjusting the implied real growth rates from the growth model to account for reasonable assumptions regarding inflation and exchange rate appreciation, China potentially could overtake the United States in nominal terms by 2020 if a limited, gradual revaluation of the renminbi were to occur, and by 2024, if the exchange rate remains stable at 2009 levels (figure 1A.1, panel a). By a similar token, India could overtake both Japan and the United Kingdom in 2014 and 2020, respectively.

It is important to stress that such overtaking scenarios are meant to be illustrative, and should be interpreted with caution. The Linkage model used in the growth forecasts does not account for differential growth rates in nominal variables, nor for policy choices that could lead to changes in these nominal variables. Measurement difficulties in national price data also mean that Harrod-Balassa-Samuelson effects may be underestimated.

Annex 1.7: Detailed analysis of growth and external balance scenarios

Even under the baseline scenario, some fracturing between the growth rates among the high- and low-productivity potential growth poles is expected to occur (figure 1A.2).[43] This separation will be even more evident when compared against growth rates in the advanced economies, which not only have been historically lower, but also are facing possible headwinds from postfinancial-crisis malaise (Reinhart and Rogoff 2009). The *divergent productivity* scenario suggests that a two-track global economy is more than a possibility; indeed, if productivity differentials were to persist, a slowly divergent path for growth between advanced, low-productivity developing, and high-productivity developing economies could emerge.

The impact of this divergence on the overall shape of the multipolar world, however, will be limited, as this shape mostly depends

on the productivity paths of China and India. Furthermore, with China and India still relatively far away from the technological frontier, catch-up growth through technological adoption still may be possible within the 15-year forecast horizon. But the divergence raises a cautionary tale

TABLE 1A.6   Additional current account balances, potential poles, 2004–15

Country	2004–08	2011–15
Argentina	1.8	0.0
Indonesia	1.2	1.2
Norway	16.3	14.3
Israel	2.7	2.0
Switzerland	11.0	10.7
Malaysia	15.3	14.2
Venezuela, RB	13.5	12.9
Singapore	20.9	19.1
Thailand	0.8	1.1
South Africa	−5.7	−6.8
Ukraine	0.2	0.6
Sweden	7.7	7.1
Czech Republic	−3.1	−4.0

Sources: World Bank staff calculations, from IMF IFS, IMF Fiscal Monitor, USEIA IEO, and IEA WEO databases.

Note: All figures are percentages of GDP. The light-shaded region indicates projections; 2004–08 data are the historical period average, and 2011–15 data are the projected period average. Projections were performed using a current account model with the fiscal balance, official financial flows, net foreign assets, and net energy exports, with region-specific coefficients and calibrated to the actual current account balance for 2004–08.

FIGURE 1A.1   Nominal GDP overtaking scenarios, selected emerging and advanced economy poles, 2009–25

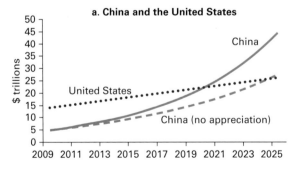

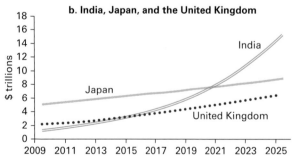

Source: World Bank staff calculations, using the World Bank WDI database.

Note: 2009 nominal GDP values are values measured in terms of U.S. dollars. Real GDP growth rates from 2010 onward are based on forecasts from the baseline scenario. Inflation is assumed to be constant at 0 percent for Japan, 2 percent for the United States, 4 percent for both China and the United Kingdom, and 7 percent for India. Exchange rate appreciation, relative to the U.S. dollar, is assumed to be constant at 0 percent for China (no appreciation case), 2 percent for Japan, and 3 percent for China (appreciation case) and India.

for other potential emerging economy growth poles, which must raise their TFP contributions to growth. By some indications, this change has already begun to occur, as exemplified by recent improvements in TFP performance in Argentina, Brazil, Indonesia, and Korea.

The messages from a possible failure to rebalance internally, as captured by the *unbalanced*

internal growth scenario, are somewhat more subtle. Continued low levels of consumption, for example, mean higher levels of domestic saving; to the extent that such saving is deployed toward productive investments, the economy may actually grow faster than with high domestic consumption. The risks here are twofold: First, that in a high-saving scenario, the surplus of domestic saving—absent a change in net capital outflows—will inevitably push the marginal productivity of capital downward. Indeed, returns to capital in this case would fall sharply, as illustrated for the case of China (figure 1A.3, panel a). Second, the material impact of such a failure to adjust domestically is affected by the size of a country's current account surplus. Running a larger surplus when the economy has not realigned would mean not only lower levels of imports compared with a high-saving scenario alone, but also a decline in import absorption exceeding that of the baseline (figure 1A.3, panel b).

The takeaway from this scenario is that navigating the internal realignment process toward domestic sources of growth depends as much on successful external accounts management as it does on internal structural adjustment policies. This interdependence can lead to counterintuitive outcomes. For example, countries that are major exporters to China may find that a China that follows an internally unbalanced growth path would

FIGURE 1A.2   Real output growth in divergent productivity scenario, advanced economies and high- versus low-productivity emerging economies, 2005–25

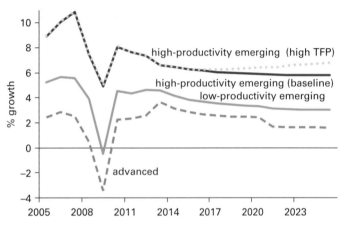

Source: World Bank staff calculations.
Note: The high-productivity emerging economies depicted are China, India, Poland, and the Russian Federation.

FIGURE 1A.3   Marginal productivity of capital and imports under various unbalanced growth scenarios, China, 2011–25

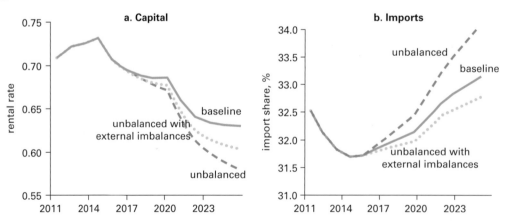

Source: World Bank staff calculations.
Note: Shares are computed from levels in terms of constant 2009 U.S. dollars.

import more, relative to the baseline. In contrast, when external imbalances are allowed to persist in tandem with internally unbalanced growth, imports are actually lower relative to the baseline.

These *global external balances* scenarios point to how the evolution of investment depends on the manner by which global imbalances unfold (figure 1A.4).[44] Several features are notable.

FIGURE 1A.4 **Investment share of output under various external balance scenarios, selected potential emerging economy poles, 2004–25**

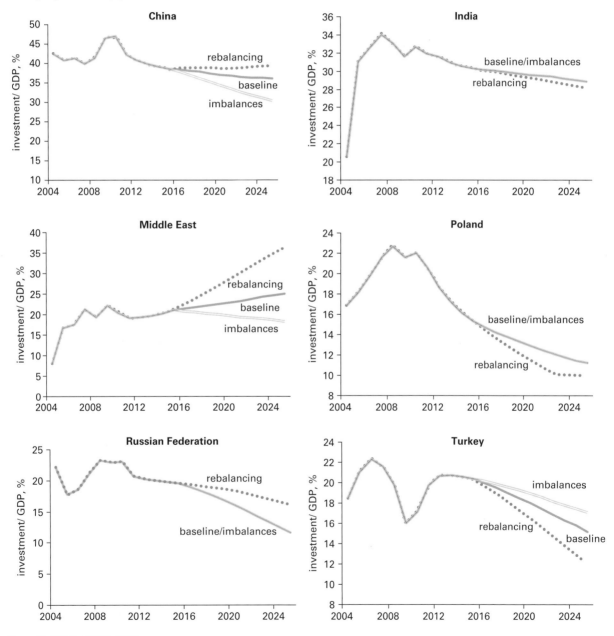

Source: World Bank staff calculations.

Note: The baseline and continued imbalances scenarios overlap (as in the case of India) if current account balances in 2015 fall within the ±3 percent band. The kink in the investment path for the rebalancing scenario in Poland is due to a model-imposed floor of 10 percent of GDP for investment (which is nonbinding if investment is below 10 percent to begin with).

First, the baseline tends to fall between the polar cases (of total rebalancing and continued imbalances). This outcome is to be expected, given that the baseline scenario adopts a compromise approach to the path of global external balances. Second, imposing a scenario of total rebalancing on surplus economies (such as China, Russia, and the oil-exporting economies of the Middle East) tends to result in a relatively slower rate of decline (or an actual increase) in the investment share. This outcome is also to be expected, as forcing a large surplus to zero, while holding saving constant, would induce reinvestment in the domestic economy. The converse holds true for deficit economies such as India, Poland, and Turkey; that is, the rebalancing scenario tends to exacerbate declines in investment. Third, while suppressing capital flight in this manner could, in principle, increase domestic investment in the surplus countries, there is a danger of also increasing either capital misallocation (into unproductive investments) or reducing consumer welfare (by limiting intertemporal consumption smoothing).

Notes

1. The formal definitions and calculations are described in detail in annex 1.1.
2. The most well known among these are the Herfindahl-Hirschman and Ray-Singer (Ray and Singer 1973) indexes, which are measures of power concentration, and the Penrose-Banzhaf (Banzhaf 1965; Penrose 1946) and Shapley-Shubik (Shapley and Shubik 1954) indexes, which are measures of voting power. These two classes of power measures present their own drawbacks. The share of economic power, which is necessary for computing concentration indexes, often is not well defined. Voting indexes require a voting mechanism, and in many international economic interactions, this institution may not be operational or relevant.
3. Although these economies accounted for a large contribution to global growth, the extremely low rates of global growth between the years 1 and 1820 mean that the polarity index, which is normalized to the full 1–2001 time period, will tend to be lower for China and India, despite their relatively large contributions.
4. More precisely, the simple polarity index is calculated as the size-weighted growth rate of an economy. This measure essentially treats a country's economic size as a proxy for its channels of influence.
5. This correction accounts for the Harrod-Balassa-Samuelson effect of rising real exchange rates as a country's income level rises over time. Hence, a country experiencing a real depreciation (as was the case of in Japan in the 2000s) will have a relatively lower real growth rate; similarly, the real appreciation of the euro in the 2000s means that the euro area's real growth was actually higher over the period.
6. The measurement of concentration has various possible approaches, and this book uses the Herfindahl-Hirschman index as its measure. The reasons for this choice, and several alternatives, are discussed in greater detail in annex 1.2.
7. The minimum for the Herfindahl-Hirschman computed from the real and purchasing power parity indexes occurred in 1992, when the G-3 economies underwent a severe recession, significantly reducing their growth influence relative to the larger economies of the emerging world.
8. The sharp decline in the early 1970s deserves some comment. This fall is a function of several factors. Most crucially, the industrial economies underwent major recessions resulting from the first oil shock in 1973 (which was reinforced by the second in 1979). This negative shock was felt worldwide by all countries (apart from oil exporters), but the slowdown was more severe for the industrial world, which had relatively larger economies at the time. This resulted in a significant reduction in their respective growth polarities, and hence, a corresponding decrease in the multipolarity index. A secondary reason is that data coverage in the earlier years was not as comprehensive, and to the extent that higher polarity countries are omitted, the polarity share calculations used to compute the Herfindahl-Hirschman would have been affected. An examination of the distribution of the polarity index during this time suggests, however, that this latter concern is likely to be less of an issue, because the decline in the Herfindahl-Hirschman appears to be driven more by a significant reduction in the polarity value for the euro area and the United States than by the introduction of high-polarity economies as the sample coverage improved.
9. The consumption contribution fell to about one third for the period 2000–08 (consumption growth was 4.1 percent while GDP growth was 10.2 percent). Moreover, a significant share of this consumption growth was from the

public sector—largely on educational and social services—and it is doubtful that such government consumption growth can be sustained indefinitely.

10. TFP contributions in Malaysia and Indonesia over the full period were 9 percent and 18 percent, respectively. It is important, however, to note that these computations apply the more standard (albeit naïve) approach of taking the residual from a Cobb-Douglas production function, assuming constant returns to scale and perfect competition. Adjustments of the form suggested by Klenow and Rodríguez-Clare (1997) raise the TFP contribution in some economies, sometimes dramatically, as does assuming a high elasticity of substitution among factors in a production function with constant elasticity of substitution. With the exception of Argentina and Indonesia, however, the corrections do not alter the *relative* performance of these economies vis-à-vis the leaders.

11. TFP measures capture not just broad technological progress but also changes in technical efficiency, which comprise, among other things, the adoption of existing technologies, resource reallocations, and institutional improvements.

12. Adoption, in turn, can be categorized according to adoption at the extensive margin (the fraction of farmers that grow hybrid corn) or the intensive margin (the amount of hybrid corn seed planted by each farmer). Both margins can generate economic gains, as the classic studies of Griliches (1957) and Clark (1987) attest.

13. It is important to recognize that even with this relatively strong TFP performance, aggregate TFP in China and India continues to lag aggregate TFP of industrial economies such as the United States.

14. Underlying this observation is the assumption that intellectual property is nonrivalrous but excludable, and so ideas and inventions generate growth, but any given innovation does not spill over perfectly to every other agent in the economy (in which case it would be the absolute, rather than per capita, number of patents and articles that matter).

15. One may object to this choice of contrasting consumption versus exports, arguing instead that *net exports* is the more relevant metric. However, this metric was not used for two reasons. First, it is just as reasonable to subtract imports from consumption (for "domestic consumption") as it is to group imports with exports. With no a priori reason to prefer one aggregation over another, the book treats each component in the national account

separately. Second, regardless of the aggregation choice, the main message—which focuses on the *gap* between the domestic and external components of growth—remains unchanged.

16. This statistic for China should, however, be interpreted with caution. While the value of exports is undoubtedly large in China, its role as a site for final assembly in many production chains means that export values would be lower, were one to account for only the domestic value-added component. Applying this correction would lower the export contribution by about half, which is nevertheless a large relative share.

17. Indeed, the use of EOI versus ISI strategies has been repeatedly revisited in the development debate (World Bank 1979, 1987, 1993). Although the empirical results remain somewhat mixed, most evidence is broadly supportive of a positive link between openness and growth (Feyrer 2009; Frankel and Romer 1999; Jones and Olken 2008; Rodríguez and Rodrik 2000), which generally favors the pursuit of EOI as a growth strategy.

18. While the export *share* of an export-oriented economy is inexorably tied to an increased outward orientation, nothing dictates that the *growth* of exports must increase after the initial trade expansion period. To see this, consider the decomposition of the GDP identity into $y \equiv c + x + z$, where $z \equiv i + g - m$, and c, g, i, x, and m are private and public consumption, investment, exports, and imports, respectively. Taking time derivatives, dividing throughout by y, and simplifying, yields $g_y = s_c g_c + s_x g_x + s_z g_z$, where for a given component a, $s_a \equiv a/y$ and $g_a \equiv (da/dt)/a$. An economy that adopts EOI can reasonably expect s_x and g_x to rise *during* the transition period away from ISI, but there is nothing that requires g_x to remain high *after* the initial transition.

19. Chinese saving rates have fluctuated but have not trended markedly up or down over the last two decades; the appearance in figure 1.11 of a discrete increase in saving in 2004 is at least partially due to a change in the approach of measuring enterprise saving (Bonham and Wiemer 2010). Regardless, both household and enterprise saving rates in China are very high, by any standard.

20. In addition to these inevitable demographic pressures, household saving rates in China and India will also be pushed down by financial market development and strengthening of public provision of health care, education, and reliable social safety nets. This outcome, of course, depends in part on policy choices.

21. Correlations between consumption, investment, and exports with output are documented in annex 1.4 for current and potential poles.

22. The ICOR is a potentially controversial concept, relying on a somewhat dated Harrod-Domar model of the growth process. Rather than relying on the concept to describe growth in its entirety, ICOR is used here in a different sense, to provide a sense of the efficiency with which capital deployment supports growth.

23. Some caution should be exercised in the interpretation of this figure. R&D expenditures are likely to be endogenous to per capita incomes. Furthermore, the nonlinear distribution of expenditure and researcher shares at the cross-section is heavily influenced by the large mass of poorer countries at the low end of the distribution, and the large weights placed on China, India, and the United States, which raises the shares in their respective income brackets.

24. It is important to recognize that there is no consensual definition for what constitutes a global middle class, and the classification of any given household as middle class often depends on the specific definition employed. One central distinction is between a middle class measured relative to the distribution of the population of the entire world versus a middle class measured relative to the population distribution within each country. Because the focus of the analysis here is on growth polarities at the global level, the discussion is premised on the former definition, with incomes between $2 and $13 a day.

25. This fairly large number stems from the assumption that the global middle class is defined in the context of what constitutes a middle class in developing countries (Ravallion 2010). A more conservative definition, using the U.S. poverty line of $13 a day as a lower bound, has 80 million people in the developing world joining the global middle class over the same time period.

26. It is important not to overstate the conclusions from this result. Analogous to the case for R&D expenditure and researcher shares, the nonlinear distribution of consumption shares at the cross-section is heavily influenced by the large mass of poorer countries at the low end of the distribution, and the large weights placed on China and the United States, which lower and raise the consumption shares in their respective income brackets.

27. This includes enabling consumer spending through policies, such as making improvements to the retail and service infrastructure, or increasing the uptake of consumer credit; these will have a direct effect via increasing the incentive to consume. Improvements to social protection and improving the efficiency of the financial system will also have an indirect effect via reducing the incentive to save.

28. Implicit in this assumption is also the fact that the current pursuit of divergent policy paths in the United States (stimulative at the expense of increased deficits and debt) and the euro area (austerity at the risk of economic malaise) do not generate wildly divergent medium and long-term economic outcomes between these two sets of economies.

29. This is consistent with the proposal for resolving global imbalances outlined in Goldstein (2010) and is similar to the ±4 percent bands proposed by the U.S. Treasury.

30. Historically, China's growth rate has fluctuated with a 3.5 percent standard deviation. It is important to recognize that these projected growth rates depend on the assumptions of the baseline scenario and, hence, should not be interpreted literally as forecasts.

31. With a historical annual standard deviation of 3.1 percent.

32. India's average years of schooling for the population aged 15 and older was 5.1 in 2010 (Barro and Lee 2010).

33. It is important to note that these level output numbers are computed in real terms (using 2009 GDP as a base). Taking into account inflation and exchange rate adjustments presents a very different alternative picture, including several overtaking possibilities. These alternatives are explored in annex 1.6.

34. The projections are, however, consistent with forecasts from other potential output-based models, such as Jorgenson and Vu (2010).

35. This secular downward shift in consumption in the industrial economies more generally, driven primarily by demographic changes, is also implied by the extended period of deleveraging that typically follows major financial crises.

36. Data limitations in the projections preclude the computation of the full multidimensional polarity index. However, as the trade channel contributes the most to the direction of the multidimensional polarity index (as measured by the eigenvector loadings corresponding to the first principal component), the alternate index presented here may nonetheless serve as a reasonable proxy.

37. Caution is advised in directly comparing these numbers to the multipolarity index computed earlier. Because data limitations in the forecasts prevent a computation using all the channels comprising the full polarity index, the multipolarity values obtained from the forecast period differ from ones calculated earlier. The analysis that follows is based on a multipolarity index calculated entirely based on the simple polarity indexes, which can be extended back to 1968.

38. One cannot also rule out the possibility of the gradual emergence of a new unipolar or bipolar world. If the trend of the Herfindahl-Hirschman using the simple index were to continue beyond 2025, such an outcome seems to be a distinct possibility.

39. Operationalizing the migration channel is problematic for three reasons, which justifies the selective inclusion. First, there are significant data limitations. Emigration flow data currently are available only for two years, 2005 and 2010, and immigration data are end-of-period stock values, rather than in-period flows. Second, measurement issues abound. Because migrant stocks are affected by depreciation (through death), these stocks may change even if actual flows remain constant. Foreign-born residents often are classified as migrants, which is especially problematic for countries that have broken up over time. Third, migration may capture not only positive spillover effects from a sending nation but also other factors. Emigration may be due to the possibility of negative shocks in the sending nation, such as war, natural disasters, or economic crises, while the immigrant stock may reflect not only contemporaneous influences, but also the cumulative effect of migration decisions over all past periods (with the major changes perhaps having occurred long ago).

40. For example, the Herfindahl (Theil) index tends to be more sensitive to changes in larger (smaller) markets, and the Gini is a unidimensional measure of inequality in distribution.

41. For example, a coalition with very few members or a very large number of members will tend to dominate in the calculation of the Shapley-Shubik index, while the Penrose-Banzhaf index is criticized on the grounds that it treats voting behavior probabilistically rather than strategically.

42. Additional robustness checks, using additional variables (the initial level of development, military expenditure share, and regional dummies) as well as alternative measures of key variables (geography with malaria incidence, and institutional quality with Worldwide Governance Indicators measures) were performed, but not reported. The results for these regressions were qualitatively similar and are available on request.

43. Undoubtedly, this is a simplification, because any aggregation inevitably introduces the possibility that there may be outliers within a group. For example, Indonesia and Singapore are both forecast to grow in excess of 5 percent over the 2011–25 period, which exceeds the equivalent growth rates of Poland and Russia at their growth peaks. Nevertheless, the message—that divergent TFP growth patterns can lead to divergent growth outcomes—remains.

44. The broader macroeconomic paths are qualitatively similar, but investment, in particular, varied according to the external balance scenario being considered. This is hardly surprising given the fact that structural factors are likely to drive growth in the long run (with external balances playing only a secondary role), whereas the current account identity, $cab \equiv s - i$, necessitates a relationship between external balances and the patterns of saving and investment. Because saving is determined mainly by the demographic structure of the economy, investment changes bear the brunt of the adjustments required by the different scenarios.

References

Acemoglu, K. Daron, Simon Johnson, and James A. Robinson. 2005. "Institutions as a Fundamental Cause of Long-Run Economic Growth." In *Handbook of Economic Growth*, vol. 1, ed. Philippe Aghion and Steven N. Durlauf, 385–472. Amsterdam: Elsevier.

Aghion, Philippe, and Peter W. Howitt. 1997. *Endogenous Growth Theory*. Cambridge, MA: MIT Press.

Alesina, Alberto F., William R. Easterly, Arnaud Devleeschauwer, Sergio Kurlat, and Romain Wacziarg. 2003. "Fractionalization." *Journal of Economic Growth* 8 (2): 155–94.

Allen, Franklin, Rajesh Chakrabarti, Sankar De, Jun Qian, and Meijun Qian. 2010. "Law, Institutions, and Finance in China and India." In *Emerging Giants: China and India in the World Economy*, ed. Barry J. Eichengreen, Poonam Gupta, and Rajiv Kumar, 135–83. Oxford, U.K.: Oxford University Press.

Arora, Vivek, and Athanasios Vamvakidis. 2005. "The Impact of U.S. Economic Growth on the Rest of the World: How Much Does It Matter?" *Journal of Economic Integration* 21 (1): 21–39.

————. 2010a. "China's Economic Growth: International Spillover." IMF Working Paper WP/10/165, International Monetary Fund, Washington, DC.

————. 2010b. "South Africa in the African Economy: Growth Spillovers." *Global Journal of Emerging Market Economies* 2 (2): 153–71.

Attanasio, Orazio P., and Guglielmo Weber. 2010. "Consumption and Saving: Models of Intertemporal Allocation and Their Implications for Public Policy." *Journal of Economic Literature* 48 (3): 693–751.

Banerjee, Abhijit V., and Esther Duflo. 2008. "What Is Middle Class about the Middle Classes around the World?" *Journal of Economic Perspectives* 22 (2): 3–28.

Banzhaf, John F. 1965. "Weighted Voting Doesn't Work: A Mathematical Analysis." *Rutgers Law Review* 19 (2): 317–43.

Bardhan, Pranab K. 2010. *Awakening Giants, Feet of Clay: Assessing the Economic Rise of China and India.* Princeton, NJ: Princeton University Press.

Barro, Robert J. 1999. "Notes on Growth Accounting." *Journal of Economic Growth* 4 (2): 119–37.

Barro, Robert J., and Jong-Wha Lee. 2010. "A New Data Set of Educational Attainment in the World, 1950–2010." NBER Working Paper 15902, National Bureau of Economic Research, Cambridge, MA.

Bayoumi, Tamim, Hui Tong, and Shang-Jin Wei. 2010. "The Chinese Corporate Savings Puzzle: A Firm-Level Cross-Country Perspective." IMF Working Paper WP/10/275, International Monetary Fund, Washington, DC.

Beck, Thorsten, and Ross Levine. 2005. "Legal Institutions and Financial Development." In *Handbook of New Institutional Economics*, eds. Claude Ménard and Mary M. Shirley, 251–80. Dordrecht, Netherlands: Springer.

Bils, Mark, and Peter J. Klenow. 2000. "Does Schooling Cause Growth?" *American Economic Review* 90 (5): 1160–83.

Blanchard, Olivier J., and Francesco Giavazzi. 2006. "Rebalancing Growth in China: A Three-Handed Approach." *China and World Economy* 14 (4): 1–20.

Bonham, Carl M., and Calla Wiemer. 2010. "Chinese Saving Dynamics: The Impact of GDP Growth and the Dependent Share." UHERO Working Paper 2010-11, University of Hawaii at Manoa, Honolulu.

Caballero, Ricardo J., Emmanuel Farhi, and Pierre-Olivier Gourinchas. 2008. "An Equilibrium Model of 'Global Imbalances' and Low Interest Rates." *American Economic Review* 98 (1): 358–93.

Canuto, Otaviano, and Marcelo Giugale, eds. 2010. *The Day after Tomorrow: A Handbook on the Future of Economic Policy in the Developing World.* Washington, DC: World Bank.

Chinn, Menzie D., and Hiro Ito. 2007. "Current Account Balances, Financial Development, and Institutions: Assaying the World 'Saving Glut.'" *Journal of International Money and Finance* 26 (4): 546–69.

Chinn, Menzie D., and Eswar S. Prasad. 2003. "Medium-Term Determinants of Current Accounts in Industrial and Developing Countries: An Empirical Exploration." *Journal of International Economics* 59 (1): 47–76.

Clark, Gregory. 1987. "Why Isn't the Whole World Developed? Lessons from the Cotton Mills." *Journal of Economic History* 47 (1): 141–73.

Cole, Harold L., Lee E. Ohanian, Alvaro J. Riascos, and James A. Schmitz Jr. 2005. "Latin America in the Rearview Mirror." *Journal of Monetary Economics* 52 (1): 69–107.

Comin, Diego A., 2010. "An Exploration of Technology Diffusion." *American Economic Review* 100 (5): 2031–59.

Comin, Diego A., Bart Hobijn, and Emilie Rovito. 2008. "Technology Usage Lags." *Journal of Economic Growth* 13 (4): 237–56.

Cuddington, John T., and Daniel Jerrett. 2008. "Super Cycles in Real Metals Prices?" *IMF Staff Papers* 55 (4): 541–65.

Dailami, Mansoor. 1992. "Optimal Corporate Debt Financing and Real Investment Decisions under Controlled Banking Systems." In *Business Finance in Less Developed Capital Markets*, ed. Klaus P. Fischer and George J. Papaioannou, 229–49. Westport, CT: Greenwood Press.

Decker, Jessica Henson, and Jamus Jerome Lim. 2008. "What Fundamentally Drives Growth? Revisiting the Institutions and Economic Performance Debate." *Journal of International Development* 20 (5): 698–725.

Doepke, Matthias, and Fabrizio Zilibotti. 2005. "Social Class and the Spirit of Capitalism." *Journal of the European Economic Association* 3 (2–3): 516–24.

Dollar, David, and Aart C. Kraay. 2002. "Growth Is Good for the Poor." *Journal of Economic Growth* 7 (3): 195–225.

Dooley, Michael P., David Folkerts-Landau, and Peter M. Garber. 2009. "Bretton Woods II Still Defines the International Monetary System." *Pacific Economic Review* 14 (3): 297–311.

Du, Luosha, Ann E. Harrison, and Gary H. Jefferson. 2011. "Do Institutions Matter for FDI Spillovers? The

Implications of China's 'Special Characteristics.'" NBER Working Paper 16767, National Bureau of Economic Research, Cambridge, MA.

Easterly, William R. 2001. "The Middle Class Consensus and Economic Development." *Journal of Economic Growth* 6 (4): 317–35.

Eaton, Jonathan, and Samuel S. Kortum. 1996. "Trade in Ideas: Patenting and Productivity in the OECD." *Journal of International Economics* 40 (3–4): 251–78.

———. 1999. "International Technology Diffusion: Theory and Measurement." *International Economic Review* 40 (3): 537–70.

———. 2002. "Technology, Geography, and Trade." *Econometrica* 70 (5): 1741–79.

El-Erian, Mohamed A. 2009. "A New Normal." *Economic Outlook, May.* Newport Beach, CA: Pacific Investment Management Company.

Ethier, Wilfred J. 1986. "The Multinational Firm." *Quarterly Journal of Economics* 101 (4): 805–33.

FAO (Food and Agriculture Organization). 2010. *FAOSTAT.* Rome: FAO.

Felsenthal, Dan S., and Moshé Machover. 1998. *The Measurement of Voting Power: Theory and Practice, Problems and Paradoxes.* Cheltenham, U.K.: Edward Elgar.

Feyrer, James D. 2009. "Trade and Income—Exploiting Time Series in Geography." NBER Working Paper 14910, National Bureau of Economic Research, Cambridge, MA.

Findlay, Ronald, and Kevin H. O'Rourke. 2007. *Power and Plenty: Trade, War, and the World Economy in the Second Millennium.* Princeton, NJ: Princeton University Press.

Fosfuri, Andrea, Massimo Motta, and Thomas Rønde. 2001. "Foreign Direct Investment and Spillovers through Workers' Mobility." *Journal of International Economics* 53 (1): 205–22.

Frankel, Jeffrey A., and David H. Romer. 1999. "Does Trade Cause Growth?" *American Economic Review* 89 (3): 379–99.

Fujita, Masahisa, Paul R. Krugman, and Anthony J. Venables. 1999. *The Spatial Economy: Cities, Regions, and International Trade.* Cambridge, MA: MIT Press.

Gagnon, Joseph E. 2010. "Current Account Imbalances in the Global Recovery: Major Policy Changes Needed." Unpublished paper, Peterson Institute for International Economics, Washington, DC.

Gallup, John Luke, Jeffrey D. Sachs, and Andrew D. Mellinger. 1999. "Geography and Economic Development." *International Regional Science Review* 22 (2): 179–232.

Glaeser, Edward L., Rafael La Porta, Florencio López-de-Silanes, and Andrei Shleifer. 2004. "Do Institutions Cause Growth?" *Journal of Economic Growth* 9 (3): 271–303.

Goldstein, Morris. 2010. "Confronting Asset Bubbles, Too Big to Fail, and Beggar-Thy-Neighbor Exchange Rate Policies." PIIE Policy Brief 10-3, Peterson Institute for International Economics, Washington, DC.

Griffith, Rachel, Stephen J. Redding, and Helen Simpson. 2004. "Foreign Ownership and Productivity: New Evidence from the Service Sector and the R&D Lab." *Oxford Review of Economic Policy* 20 (3): 440–56.

Griffith, Rachel, Stephen J. Redding, and John M. van Reenen. 2004. "Mapping the Two Faces of R&D: Productivity Growth in a Panel of OECD Industries." *Review of Economics and Statistics* 86 (4): 883–95.

Griliches, Zvi. 1957. "Hybrid Corn: An Exploration in the Economics of Technological Change." *Econometrica* 25 (4): 501–22.

Grossman, Gene M., and Elhanan Helpman. 1991a. *Innovation and Growth in the Global Economy.* Cambridge, MA: MIT Press.

———. 1991b. "Trade, Knowledge Spillovers, and Growth." *European Economic Review* 35 (2–3): 517–26.

Gruber, Joseph W., and Steven B. Kamin. 2007. "Explaining the Global Pattern of Current Account Imbalances." *Journal of International Money and Finance* 26 (4): 500–522.

Haddad, Mona E., Jamus J. Lim, and Christian Saborowski. 2010. "Trade Openness Reduces Growth Volatility When Countries Are Well Diversified." Policy Research Working Paper 5222, World Bank, Washington, DC.

Hallward-Driemeier, Mary, Giuseppe Iarossi, and Kenneth L. Sokoloff. 2002. "Exports and Manufacturing Productivity in East Asia: A Comparative Analysis with Firm-Level Data." NBER Working Paper 8894, National Bureau of Economic Research, Cambridge, MA.

Haskel, Jonathan E., Sonia C. Pereira, and Matthew J. Slaughter. 2007. "Does Inward Foreign Direct Investment Boost the Productivity of Domestic Firms?" *Review of Economics and Statistics* 89 (3): 482–96.

Hatton, Timothy J. 2010. "The Cliometrics of International Migration: A Survey." *Journal of Economic Surveys* 24 (5): 941–69.

Hirschman, Albert O. 1964. "The Paternity of an Index." *American Economic Review* 54 (5): 761.

Horioka, Charles Yuji, and Jumin Wan. 2007. "The Determinants of Household Saving in China:

A Dynamic Panel Analysis of Provincial Data." *Journal of Money, Credit, and Banking* 39 (8): 2077–96.

Hovhannisyan, Nune, and Wolfgang Keller. 2010. "International Business Travel: An Engine of Innovation?" CEPR Discussion Paper 7829, Centre for Economic Policy Research, London.

Hsieh, Chang-Tai, and Peter J. Klenow. 2009. "Misallocation and Manufacturing TFP in China and India." *Quarterly Journal of Economics* 124 (4): 1403–48.

IE (International Enterprise) Singapore. 2010. *StatLink Singapore Trade Statistics*. Singapore: IE Singapore.

IEA (International Energy Agency). 2010. *World Energy Outlook*. Paris: IEA.

IMF (International Monetary Fund). 2010a. *Direction of Trade Statistics*. Washington, DC: IMF.

———. 2010b. *Fiscal Monitor*. Washington, DC: IMF.

———. 2010c. *International Financial Statistics*. Washington, DC: IMF.

———. 2010d. *Republic of Korea: Selected Issues*. Washington, DC: IMF.

———. 2011. *New Growth Drivers for Low-Income Countries: The Role of BRICs*. Washington, DC: IMF.

Javorcik, Beata Smarzynska. 2004. "Does Foreign Direct Investment Increase the Productivity of Domestic Firms? In Search of Spillovers through Backward Linkages." *American Economic Review* 94 (3): 605–27.

Jones, Benjamin F., and Benjamin A. Olken. 2008. "The Anatomy of Start-Stop Growth." *Review of Economics and Statistics* 90 (3): 582–87.

Jorgenson, Dale W., and Khuong M. Vu. 2010. "Potential Growth of the World Economy." *Journal of Policy Modeling* 32 (5): 615–31.

Kaufmann, Daniel, Aart C. Kraay, and Massimo Mastruzzi. 2010. "The Worldwide Governance Indicators: Methodology and Analytical Issues." Policy Research Working Paper 5430, World Bank, Washington, DC.

Keller, Wolfgang. 2002. "Geographic Localization of International Technology Diffusion." *American Economic Review* 92 (1): 120–42.

Keller, Wolfgang, and Stephen R. Yeaple. 2009. "Multinational Enterprises, International Trade, and Productivity Growth: Firm-Level Evidence from the United States." *Review of Economics and Statistics* 91 (4): 821–31.

Kerr, William R. 2008. "Ethnic Scientific Communities and International Technology Diffusion." *Review of Economics and Statistics* 90 (3): 518–37.

Kerr, William R., and William F. Lincoln. 2010. "The Supply Side of Innovation: H-1B Visa Reforms and U.S. Ethnic Invention." *Journal of Labor Economics* 28 (3): 473–508.

Kim, Jinyoung, Sangjoon John Lee, and Gerald R. Marschke. 2009. "International Knowledge Flows: Evidence from an Inventor-Firm Matched Data Set." In *Science and Engineering Careers in the United States: An Analysis of Markets and Employment*, ed. Richard B. Freeman and Daniel Goroff, 321–48. Chicago: University of Chicago Press.

Klenow, Peter J., and Andrés Rodríguez-Clare. 1997. "The Neoclassical Revival in Growth Economics: Has It Gone Too Far?" In *NBER Macroeconomics Annual 1997*, vol. 12, ed. Ben S. Bernanke and Kenneth S. Rogoff, 73–114. Cambridge, MA: MIT Press.

Knack, Stephen, and Philip E. Keefer. 1997. "Does Social Capital Have an Economic Payoff? A Cross Country Investigation." *Quarterly Journal of Economics* 112 (4): 1251–88.

Krugman, Paul R. 1979. "Increasing Returns, Monopolistic Competition, and International Trade." *Journal of International Economics* 9 (4): 469–79.

———. 1994. "The Myth of Asia's Miracle." *Foreign Affairs* 73 (6): 62–78.

Kuijs, Louis. 2006. "How Will China's Saving-Investment Balance Evolve?" Policy Research Working Paper 3958, World Bank, Washington, DC.

Lane, Philip R., and Gian Maria Milesi-Ferretti. 2006. "The External Wealth of Nations Mark II: Revised and Extended Estimates of Foreign Assets and Liabilities, 1970–2004." *Journal of International Economics* 73 (2): 223–50.

Larraín, Felipe B., Luis F. López-Calva, and Andrés Rodríguez-Clare. 2001. "Intel: A Case Study of Foreign Direct Investment in Central America." In *Economic Development in Central America: Growth and Internationalization*, ed. Felipe B. Larraín, 195–250. Cambridge, MA: Harvard University Press.

Lin, Justin Yifu. 2010. "New Structural Economics: A Framework for Rethinking Development." Policy Research Working Paper 5197, World Bank, Washington, DC.

Lindert, Peter H. 2004. *Growing Public: Social Spending and Economic Growth since the Eighteenth Century*. Cambridge, U.K.: Cambridge University Press.

Loayza, Norman V., Klaus Schmidt-Hebbel, and Luis Servén. 2000. "What Drives Private Saving across the World?" *Review of Economics and Statistics* 82 (2): 165–81.

Maddison, Angus. 2003. *The World Economy: Historical Statistics*. Paris: Organisation for Economic Co-operation and Development.

———. 2007. *Contours of the World Economy 1–2030 AD: Essays in Macro-economic History*. Oxford, U.K.: Oxford University Press.

Mankiw, N. Gregory, David Romer, and David N. Weil. 1992. "A Contribution to the Empirics of Economic Growth." *Quarterly Journal of Economics* 107 (2): 407–37.

Mansfield, Edward D. 1993. "Concentration, Polarity, and the Distribution of Power." *International Studies Quarterly* 37 (1): 105–28.

Markusen, James R. 2004. *Multinational Firms and the Theory of International Trade*. Cambridge, MA: MIT Press.

McCraw, Thomas K. 2010. "Immigrant Entrepreneurs in U.S. Financial History, 1775–1914." *Capitalism and Society* 5 (1): art 3. http://www.bepress.com/cas/vol5/iss1/art3.

McDonald, Ronald. 2007. *Exchange Rate Economics: Theory and Evidence*. London: Routledge.

McMillan, Margaret S., and Dani Rodrik. 2011. "Globalization, Structural Change, and Productivity Growth." Unpublished paper, Harvard Kennedy School, Cambridge, MA.

Melitz, Marc J. 2003. "The Impact of Trade on Intra-industry Allocations and Aggregate Industry Productivity." *Econometrica* 71 (6): 1695–725.

Modigliani, Franco, and Shi Larry Cao. 2004. "The Chinese Saving Puzzle and the Life-Cycle Hypothesis." *Journal of Economic Literature* 42 (1): 145–70.

Modigliani, Franco, and Merton H. Miller. 1958. "The Cost of Capital, Corporation Finance, and the Theory of Investment." *American Economic Review* 48 (3): 261–97.

Murdoch, James C., and Todd Sandler. 2002. "Economic Growth, Civil Wars, and Spatial Spillovers." *Journal of Conflict Resolution* 46 (1): 91–110.

Nye, Joseph S. 2004. *Soft Power: The Means to Success in World Politics*. New York: PublicAffairs.

O'Neill, Jim. 2001. "Building Better Global Economic BRICs." Global Economics Paper 66, Goldman Sachs, London.

O'Neill, Jim, and Anna Stupnytska. 2009. "The Long-Term Outlook for the BRICs and N-11 Post Crisis." Global Economics Paper 192, Goldman Sachs, London.

O'Neill, Jim, Dominic Wilson, Roopa Purushothaman, and Anna Stupnytska. 2005. "How Solid Are the BRICs?" Global Economics Paper 134, Goldman Sachs, London.

OECD (Organisation for Economic Co-operation and Development). 2010. *Perspectives on Global Development 2010: Shifting Wealth*. Paris: OECD.

Oettl, Alexander, and Ajay K. Agrawal. 2008. "International Labor Mobility and Knowledge Flow Externalities." *Journal of International Business Studies* 39 (8): 1242–60.

Parente, Stephen L., and Edward C. Prescott. 2000. *Barriers to Riches*. Cambridge, MA: MIT Press.

Patentscope Database. World Intellectual Property Organization. http://www.wipro.int/pctdb/en/.

Penrose, Lionel S. 1946. "The Elementary Statistics of Majority Voting." *Journal of the Royal Statistical Society* 109 (1): 53–57.

PRS Group. 2010. *International Country Risk Guide*. East Syracuse, NY: PRS Group.

Puga, Diego, and Daniel Trefler. 2010. "Wake Up and Smell the Ginseng: International Trade and the Rise of Incremental Innovation in Low-Wage Countries." *Journal of Development Economics* 91 (1): 64–76.

Quinn, Dennis P., and A. Maria Toyoda. 2008. "Does Capital Account Liberalization Lead to Growth?" *Review of Financial Studies* 21 (3): 1403–49.

Rauch, James E. 2001. "Business and Social Networks in International Trade." *Journal of Economic Literature* 39 (4): 1177–203.

Ravallion, Martin. 2010. "The Developing World's Bulging (but Vulnerable) Middle Class." *World Development* 38 (4): 445–54.

Ray, James Lee, and J. David Singer. 1973. "Measuring the Concentration of Power in the International System." *Sociological Methods and Research* 1 (4): 403–37.

Reinhart, Carmen M., and Kenneth S. Rogoff. 2009. *This Time Is Different: Eight Centuries of Financial Folly*. Princeton, NJ: Princeton University Press.

Rey, Sergio J., and Mark V. Janikas. 2005. "Regional Convergence, Inequality, and Space." *Journal of Economic Geography* 5 (2): 155–76.

Rivera-Batiz, Luis A., and Paul M. Romer. 1991. "Economic Integration and Endogenous Growth." *Quarterly Journal of Economics* 106 (2): 531–55.

Rodríguez, Francesco R., and Dani Rodrik. 2000. "Trade Policy and Economic Growth: A Skeptic's Guide to the Cross-National Evidence." In *NBER Macroeconomics Annual*, vol. 15, ed. Ben S. Bernanke and Kenneth S. Rogoff, 261–338. Cambridge, MA: MIT Press.

Rodríguez-Clare, Andrés. 1996. "Multinationals, Linkages, and Economic Development." *American Economic Review* 86 (4): 852–73.

Rodrik, Dani, Arvind Subramanian, and Francesco Trebbi. 2004. "Institutions Rule: The Primacy of Institutions over Geography and Integration in Economic Development." *Journal of Economic Growth* 9 (2): 131–65.

Romer, Paul M. 1986. "Increasing Returns and Long-Run Growth." *Journal of Political Economy* 94 (5): 1002–37.

———. 1990. "Endogenous Technological Change." *Journal of Political Economy* 98 (5): S71–102.

Sala-i-Martin, Xavier X. 2006. "The World Distribution of Income: Falling Poverty and...Convergence, Period." *Quarterly Journal of Economics* 121 (2): 351–97.

Sala-i-Martin, Xavier X., Gernot Doppelhofer, and Ronald I. Miller. 2004. "Determinants of Long-Term Growth: A Bayesian Averaging of Classical Estimates (BACE) Approach." *American Economic Review* 94 (4): 813–35.

Schmidt-Hebbel, Klaus, Steven B. Webb, and Giancarlo Corsetti. 1992. "Household Saving in Developing Countries: First Cross-Country Evidence." *World Bank Economic Review* 6 (3): 529–47.

Shapley, Lloyd S., and Martin Shubik. 1954. "A Method for Evaluating the Distribution of Power in a Committee System." *American Political Science Review* 48 (3): 787–92.

Solow, Robert M. 1956. "A Contribution to the Theory of Economic Growth." *Quarterly Journal of Economics* 70 (1): 65–94.

USEIA (United States Energy Information Administration). 2010. *International Energy Outlook*. Washington, DC: USEIA.

van der Mensbrugghe, Dominique. 2005. *Linkage Technical Reference Document, version 6.1*. Washington, DC: World Bank.

Wang, Jing, and John Whalley. 2010. "China's Trade and Investment with the South: Pre- and Post-crisis." In *Managing Openness: Trade and Outward-Oriented Growth after the Crisis*. Ed. Mona Haddad and Ben Shepherd, 119–34. Washington, DC: World Bank.

WBMS (World Bureau of Metal Statistics). 2010. *World Metal Statistics*. Hertfordshire, U.K.: World Bureau of Metal Statistics.

Wei, Shang-Jin, and Xiaobo Zhang. 2009. "The Competitive Saving Motive: Evidence from Rising Sex Ratios and Savings Rates in China." NBER Working Paper 15093, National Bureau of Economic Research, Cambridge, MA.

Wilson, Dominic, and Raluca Dragusanu. 2008. "The Expanding Middle: The Exploding World Middle Class and Falling Global Inequality." Global Economics Paper 170, Goldman Sachs, New York.

Wilson, Dominic, and Roopa Purushothaman. 2003. "Dreaming with BRICs: The Path to 2050." Global Economics Paper 99, Goldman Sachs, New York.

Woetzel, Jonathan, Janamitra Devan, Richard Dobbs, Adam Eichner, Stefano Negri, and Micah Rowland. 2009. *If You've Got It, Spend It: Unleashing the Chinese Consumer*. Beijing: McKinsey Global Institute.

World Bank. 1979. *World Development Report 1979: Structural Change and Development Policy*. New York: Oxford University Press.

———. 1987. *World Development Report 1987: Industrialization and Foreign Trade*. New York: Oxford University Press.

———. 1993. *The East Asian Miracle: Economic Growth and Public Policy*. New York: Oxford University Press.

———. 2007. *Global Economic Prospects 2007: Managing the Next Wave of Globalization*. Washington, DC: World Bank.

———. 2009a. *Global Economic Prospects 2009: Commodities at the Crossroads*. Washington, DC: World Bank.

———. 2009b. *World Development Report 2009: Reshaping Economic Geography*. Washington, DC: World Bank.

———. 2010a. *Doing Business 2010: Reforming through Difficult Times*. Washington, DC: World Bank.

———. 2010b. *World Development Indicators*. Washington, DC: World Bank.

———. 2011. *Global Economic Prospects January 2011: Navigating Strong Currents*. Washington, DC: World Bank.

WVSA (World Values Survey Association). 2009. *World Values Survey 1981–2008 Official Aggregate v.20090901*. Madrid: WVSA.

Young, Alwyn. 1995. "The Tyranny of Numbers: Confronting the Statistical Realities of the East Asian Growth Experience." *Quarterly Journal of Economics* 110 (3): 641–80.

2

The Changing Global Corporate Landscape

THE SHIFT IN ECONOMIC AND financial power toward the developing world is having important implications for the global corporate environment. As they pursue growth opportunities outside the borders of their home countries, corporate players based in emerging markets are redefining the landscape of global investment and production. Emerging-market firms have become an important force behind new foreign direct investment (FDI) flows, in terms of both cross-border acquisitions and greenfield investments, and are growing participants in international capital markets. The transformation of firms based in Brazil, China, India, Malaysia, Mexico, the Russian Federation, and other major emerging economies into important foreign investors offers remarkable opportunities and challenges for the global economy. Moving forward, multinational firms based in emerging markets will become important agents of change on a global scale, pushing for more open policies at home and abroad and posing greater competition to advanced-country firms for natural resources, technology, and access to capital markets. At the same time, advanced economies will need to become more accustomed to receiving investments from countries with income levels and social practices very different from their own.

More than half a century of precedent defines the rise of modern multinational firms. Rapid overseas expansion of multinationals based in advanced countries in the postwar era had its origins in the technological superiority and supportive institutional environment of home countries, including ready access to financing for such expansion. In addition to technological and institutional strength, political power—whether exercised through gunboat diplomacy, as in colonial times, or through economic diplomacy—also played an important role in expanding the footprint of advanced-country multinational firms. A voluminous body of interdisciplinary literature weaving together insights from international business, economics, sociology, and international politics has documented how multinational firms strategically locate themselves to exploit the relative technological advantages of home and host countries, how the firms serve as conduits for technology transfers, and how they influence the pace of globalization. The literature—from the influential product life-cycle hypothesis (Vernon 1966) to recent advances in the context of international fragmentation of production (Antràs 2005; Harrison and Scorse 2010)—has focused on the experiences of advanced-economy firms, with little attention paid to the behavior of multinational firms from emerging markets. But with emerging-market firms progressively gaining more political power and financing ability, this focus is set to change in the future.

This chapter provides a corporate perspective on the global trajectory toward increasing multipolarity. As the growth and institutional environments facing emerging-market firms change along this trajectory, the firms' behavior—namely, their strategic investment in global expansion, their choice of foreign investment in advanced economies versus in emerging economies, and the ways in which such firms access and use cross-border financing—signals both the changing status of their home countries and their evolving business and financing strategies. The main messages of chapter 2 are as follows:

- *As they pursue growth opportunities at a global level, emerging-market firms increasingly are becoming more prominent in the international arena, and are an important force behind global FDI flows.* Between 1997 and 2003, companies based in emerging economies engaged in cross-border investment through merger and acquisition (M&A) deals worth $189 billion, or 4 percent of the value of all global M&A investment. From 2004 to 2010, that amount increased to $1.1 trillion—17 percent of the global total. Emerging-market firms made 12,516 greenfield investments worth $1.72 trillion between January 2003 and June 2010. As they expand, emerging-market firms are deepening their reach in international capital markets through an increasing number of equity cross-listings, syndicated loans, and issues on international bond markets. As of 2008, the foreign affiliates of the top 100 multinational firms based in emerging economies held foreign assets of $907 billion (of $2.68 trillion total assets) and had a foreign sales volume of $997 billion (UNCTAD 2009).

In the years ahead, emerging-market firms are likely to press for economic policies that will strengthen their investment climates at home. Emerging-market firms will serve as a force for increased integration of their home countries into the global economy, which provides additional support for open trading and investment regimes. But the firms will also serve as a growing source of competition. One illustration of this trend is that emerging-market firms are increasingly being driven by resource-seeking and efficiency-seeking motives in undertaking new cross-border investments—motives traditionally considered the preserve of advanced-country firms. Emerging-market firms will also challenge advanced-country firms' preeminence in developing new technologies and industrial processes. In some cases, leading emerging-market firms have already begun overtaking their industrial-country competitors in terms of the priority accorded

to research and development (R&D): 114 firms based in emerging economies now rank among the top 1,000 firms worldwide by R&D spending, double the number five years earlier—a particularly noteworthy change, given that the private sector traditionally has not been the main financier of R&D in developing countries. And as emerging-market firms increasingly draw on their relative advantage over their advanced-country counterparts in dealing with the often-difficult policy environments in other developing countries, the emerging-market firms are becoming a potent force for globalization in their own right.

Econometric investigations establish a statistically significant relationship between bilateral cross-border investment by emerging-market firms in countries with strong growth potential, sound institutions, and strong trade links. Moreover, the analysis confirms the hypothesis that emerging-market companies tend to expand abroad to exploit growth opportunities that are not present in their home economies, or in order to escape an unfavorable economic climate at home. Variables such as bilateral trade links and geographic distance, which represent the economic relationship between home and host countries, are also closely associated with bilateral investment flows—although the latter appear only in the case of South-South investments. Cross-border investments into advanced economies are more prevalent in the case of firms based in larger, more open economies, and in economies with more mature equity markets.

- *An increasing number of developing countries will be able to gain increased access to international bond and equity markets—and on better terms than at the present—to finance strategic investments in the global expansion of their operations.* Nearly two-thirds of emerging-market firms that have been active acquirers since the late 1990s (those that have undertaken 10 or more M&A deals) have accessed one or more forms of cross-border capital—through syndicated loans, bond issues, and equity listings. As evidence of the mutually reinforcing linkages between commercial and financial globalization, a considerable proportion of those emerging-market firms are undertaking cross-border acquisitions within two years of having raised finance on international capital markets. International bond issuance by borrowers based in emerging markets has grown dramatically since the mid-1990s and has come to represent one of the main sources of capital inflows for these companies. A comparison of borrowing trends over the past 15 years by emerging-market firms and firms based in advanced countries points to significant scope for further improvement of emerging market companies' access to international capital markets.

- *The growing importance of developing-country multinationals also could increase support for establishing an effective multilateral regulatory framework for foreign investment—a goal which has remained elusive since the 1920s.* Bilateral investment treaties (BITs), the dominant mechanism governing cross-border investment flows over the past several decades (numbering more than 2,275 in 2007, up from just 250 in the mid-1980s), have proved a suboptimal approach to the management of cross-border investment oversight, as the growing number of BITs has led to an increasingly complex web of agreements. But the rising prominence of developing countries as a source of FDI—in addition to their traditional role as a destination—soon may facilitate agreement on multilateral cross-border investment rules. Longstanding and cogent arguments suggest that an effective multilateral framework would enhance the stability and predictability of cross-border investment flows, thereby increasing the supply of productive and development-enhancing FDI.

Emerging-Market Multinationals: Agents of Change in a Multipolar World

The rise of emerging-market multinationals

Encouraged by improved regulatory treatment and steadily maturing financial systems in their home countries, corporations based in emerging markets are playing an increasingly prominent role in global business. The number of emerging-market corporations listed among the Fortune Global 500, an annual ranking, by revenues, of the world's largest corporations, rose from 47 firms in 2005 to 95 in 2010. Companies based in emerging markets have become the new engines of growth in the global M&A market, with the number of cross-border acquisitions undertaken by such companies rising from 661 acquisitions in 2001 (9 percent of global cross-border M&A transactions) to 2,447 (22 percent) in 2010 (figure 2.1). Of the total of 11,113 cross-border M&A deals announced worldwide in 2010, 5,623 deals involved emerging-market companies either as buyers or as takeover targets by advanced-country firms.

Greenfield investment by emerging-market firms, which represents internal, organic corporate

FIGURE 2.1   **Total cross-border M&A deals by firms from advanced economies and emerging-market economies, 1997–2010**

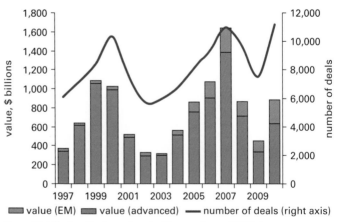

value (EM) ■ value (advanced) — number of deals (right axis)

Source: World Bank staff estimates based on Thomson-Reuters SDC Platinum.
Note: EM = emerging markets.

growth, rose from $140 billion in 2003 to almost $250 billion in 2009. The increase in emerging-market firms' share of total greenfield projects was more modest, rising from 13 percent in 2003 to 15 percent in 2009 (figure 2.2), reflecting the rapid expansion of greenfield FDI from advanced countries over this period. Overall, the relative share of greenfield activity in total cross-border investment undertaken by emerging-economy corporations fell from 80 percent in 2003 to 54 percent in 2009 (figure 2.3).

To understand how this rise in the global presence of emerging-market multinationals will translate into a multipolar world that is distinctly different from today's world, it is necessary to grasp not only the reality of this rise, but also the dimensions in which the emerging-market firms are similar—or different—as compared to developed-market corporations. Such differences will help condition not only the likely future patterns of cross-border investment, but also the impact that emerging-market multinational corporations will have on the rest of the developing world, especially in the least developed countries.

The overall cross-border investment pattern by emerging-market firms is consistent with the typical international growth strategy of individual corporations. When companies venture abroad, they often first establish a small foothold in new markets through branch or representative offices, small distribution networks, or maintenance centers. Such small greenfield investments can be the first step toward execution of a firm's globalization strategy, allowing companies with limited international exposure to gain experience and local knowledge before making a major commitment to a particular market through an outright acquisition or large-scale investment.[1] In carrying out M&A transactions, companies are often seeking more immediate access to local markets. At the same time, international M&A transactions often lead to additional cross-border investments through the necessity of the restructuring or upgrading of acquired assets, or as part of acquiring other firms' vertical- or horizontal-integration growth strategies.

Market liberalization and deregulation have been the driving forces behind recent expansion in cross-border M&A activity involving emerging-market firms. The stage was set in the 1990s by the broad trend toward privatization of public enterprises and utilities, which prompted the acceptance of foreign ownership of national assets and facilitated the significant expansion of inward FDI flows. In recent years, the policy stance has shifted, giving a strong orientation to outward investment, as many emerging-market

FIGURE 2.2 Total cross-border greenfield investment by firms from advanced economies and emerging-market economies, 2003–09

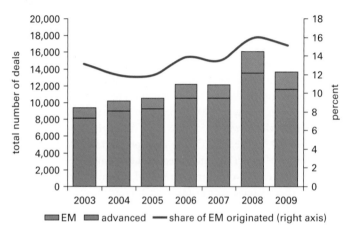

Sources: World Bank staff estimates based on UNCTAD 2010 and fDi Markets.

FIGURE 2.3 Total cross-border greenfield investment and M&A deals by emerging-market firms, 2003–10

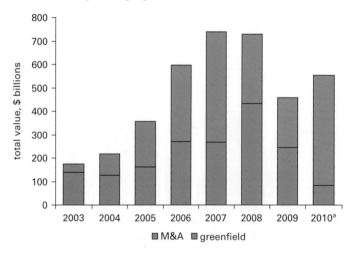

Sources: World Bank staff estimates based on Thomson-Reuters SDC Platinum and fDi Markets.
Note: M&A deal values are adjusted for missing deal value information.
a. Greenfield 2010 data are for quarter 1 and quarter 2 only.

governments have taken steps to ease restrictions on outflows of foreign investment, both to improve the ability of domestic firms to compete in global markets and to limit the accumulation of foreign exchange reserves from trade surpluses and capital inflows. For example, since the late 1990s, China has gradually reduced restrictions on outward investment by decentralizing authority for project approval and easing controls on foreign exchange outflows used for foreign investment; China has also actively promoted outward investment through loans and diplomatic support, focusing first on large state-owned enterprises and later on small and private firms. After the recent financial crisis, Argentina, Kazakhstan, the Philippines, and South Africa further boosted support to outward FDI through simplifying administrative procedures, providing business consulting service for enterprises, and relaxing exchange controls on residents. Some emerging-market governments have also helped to reduce the political risks involved in outward investment by signing BITs with host-country governments.

The rise of emerging-market firms is also apparent in their greater participation in innovation. Although the majority of corporate R&D spending still comes from G-3 economies (figure 2.4), the relative G-3 advantage is eroding, and the number of emerging-market firms included in the top 1,000 firms ranked by R&D expenditure rose from 57 firms in 2004 to 114 in 2009 (U.K. Department for Business, Innovation and Skills 2010). This is especially remarkable given that, in developing countries, the private sector traditionally has not been the main financier of local R&D efforts.[2] Even more impressive than the increased spending on R&D by emerging-market firms is the growing tendency of emerging-market residents to obtain patents from countries other than their home countries (figure 2.5).[3]

The intended technological development outcomes of increased R&D spending and the granting of additional patents can occur through innovation, absorption of existing technologies that are new to a particular market, or dissemination of technologies throughout a market (World Bank 2008). Although the creation of entirely new technologies remains an activity

FIGURE 2.4   Geographic distribution of the top 1,000 firms by R&D spending

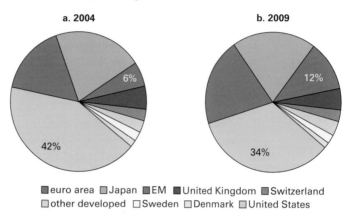

Source: U.K. Department for Business, Innovation, and Skills 2005, 2010.

FIGURE 2.5   Cross-border patents granted worldwide to residents of emerging economies, 1995–2008

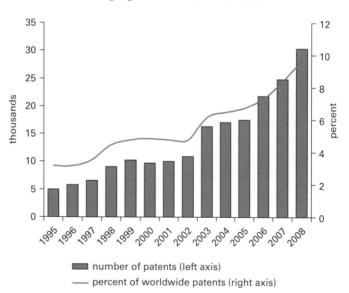

Source: World Bank staff estimates based on World Intellectual Property Organization (WIPO).

dominated by advanced economies, the pace at which developing countries absorb new technology has increased rapidly in recent years, determined by improvements in property rights and macroeconomic stability on one hand, and on the other hand, by the extent to which countries are exposed to foreign technology through FDI and trade. These same factors determine the extent to which emerging-market multinationals are able to absorb new technology and thus upgrade their capability to compete globally. Effective institutions reduce transaction costs by providing a legal framework and enforcing contracts, while simultaneously supporting societal norms that facilitate business activity without frequent recourse to adjudication.

Although the two concepts are difficult to compare in a measurable way, it is reasonable to conclude that technological progress tends to be more rapid than institutional improvements. Both concepts imply changes in the allocation of resources among individuals and firms, but it is likely that the transformations needed to improve institutions generate more opposition than introducing new technology. Firms whose profits are threatened by competition from new technology can focus on new products, while officials whose income is threatened by efforts to contain corruption typically have few alternative sources of income and thus have an incentive to be extremely resistant to change. At the same time, changes in technology can be strongly supported by individuals and firms who anticipate substantial benefits, while the impact of improvements in institutions is often more diffuse, making it

more difficult to generate support for change. Thus, the path to growth of developing-country multinationals can be viewed as a combination of improvements in institutions and technology, where at least initially the potential rate of progress (as determined by technology) is inhibited by slow institutional reform. This likely, nonlinear transition path undertaken by an economy as it develops, as represented by cross-country differences in patents and an index of the quality of the rule of law, is shown in figure 2.6.

The largest and fastest-growing emerging markets are the source of most cross-border M&A transactions. Since 2000, their firms' quest for growth opportunities outside their own borders has resulted in the largest emerging markets, particularly China, India, and the Russian Federation, being among the top 10 emerging-market source countries of cross-border M&A transactions by number of deals (figure 2.7). Other major emerging-market source countries include Brazil, Malaysia, Mexico, the Republic of Korea, Saudi Arabia, Singapore, South Africa, and the United Arab Emirates.[4] Advanced economies are the target for more than 60 percent of emerging-market firms' cross-border M&A deal value. But Brazil, China, and India, along with Indonesia, Malaysia, and Singapore, also rank among the top 15 target countries (figure 2.8).[5] Were the domestic institutional environment to continue to improve as emerging markets mature, the number of patents by emergency market firms would grow even more. This trend will be reinforced by rising educational levels in the potential emerging-economy poles, as well as by larger population sizes (in absolute terms) in many of those economies. These trends suggest that a significant share of future innovations may well originate in the emerging world.

The nature of emerging-market cross-border investments

Technology and natural resources are prominent in the sectoral composition of emerging-market cross-border investments. Firms often capitalize on technological and informational advantages in their foreign investments. Thus, firms that have expertise in a particular sector but face decreasing

FIGURE 2.6   Technology and institutional environment in developing and developed countries

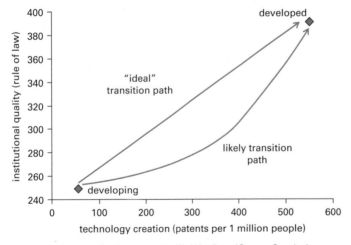

Sources: World Bank staff estimates based on World Intellectual Property Organization (WIPO) and the PRS Group.

FIGURE 2.7   Top source countries of emerging-market firms' cross-border M&A deals in emerging economies and advanced economies

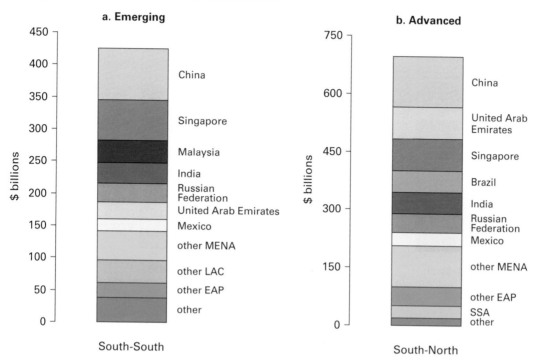

Source: World Bank staff estimates based on Thomson-Reuters SDC Platinum.

Note: EAP = East Asia and the Pacific; LAC = Latin America and the Caribbean; MENA = Middle East and North Africa; SSA = Sub-Saharan Africa.

returns as that sector matures in their home country can apply this expertise to the same industries abroad. The same concept applies to the institutional environments in which firms operate. As such, emerging-market firms with expertise overcoming the difficult institutional environment in their home countries can apply this information to similar environments in other emerging markets. This application is reflected in the prominence of mainly high-value, nontradable service sectors in emerging-market M&A transactions, where the ability to navigate political sensitivities can be a significant competitive advantage: telecommunications (the top sector for cross-border M&A transactions by emerging-market firms),[6] financial services, computer and electronic products, and professional, scientific, and technical services.

Similarly, the top sectors for greenfield investment are financial services and software and information technology. The information technology sector illustrates the importance of technological

expertise in foreign investment. Having long been important suppliers of outsourced services and contract R&D in the software and information technology industry, such emerging-market companies have become important players in their own right, establishing operations in the countries of their erstwhile partners to be close to final customers and to compete directly with their former clients. There may be a bias in emerging-market firms toward greenfield investments in knowledge-intensive sectors, in which intellectual property, process engineering, and technological innovation are key competitive advantages. Greenfield investment allows companies to protect these advantages better than does M&A investment.

The importance of technological and institutional environment advantages does not mean, however, that most firms' cross-border investments are in the predominant industry of their home operations. Indeed, nearly 60 percent of emerging-market firms' M&A deals occur outside

FIGURE 2.8   Top destination countries for emerging-market firms' cross-border M&A deals in emerging economies and advanced economies

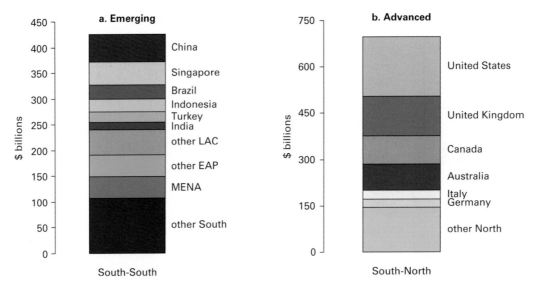

Source: World Bank staff estimates based on Thomson-Reuters SDC Platinum.

the acquirer's industry, as defined by broad three-digit North American Industry Classification System codes. This proportion has been stable over time and is similar in both advanced-country and emerging-market targets. Mining, energy, telecommunications, food and beverage production, chemical manufacturing, and credit intermediation rank among the least diversified sectors. Among the most diversified industries are computers and electronic products; primary metals manufacturing; professional, scientific, and technical services; machinery manufacturing; publishing; heavy and civil engineering construction; wholesaling; and the brokerage sector. Economies of scale and industry-specific know-how are likely determinants of the degree of diversification; the more specialized their requisite technological expertise and the larger the scope for economies of scale, the less firms tend to stray from their own sector. In terms of country of origin, East Asian firms, especially those based in China, Indonesia, Korea, Malaysia, and Singapore, are the most diversified among the economies with the most acquisitive corporate sectors (in excess of 60 percent diversifying transactions). Brazil, India, Mexico, and South Africa are home to firms with a sharper corporate focus—in those countries, diversifying deals range between 40 percent and 52 percent.

The sectoral composition of cross-border investment also reflects the rising prices of and growing competition for natural resources. Thus, oil and gas extraction is the second-largest sector, by value, of emerging-market firms' cross-border M&A transactions.[7] Mining, nonmetallic mineral production, and mining support activities also feature prominently among the top 15 target industries by value.[8] Similarly, metal, chemical, and food manufacturing activities—the downstream value-adding counterparts to the commodity-producing industries—are prominent target sectors of emerging-market firms' M&A efforts. Energy and metals also figure prominently in emerging markets' greenfield investments.[9]

South-South FDI is more likely to be greenfield, whereas South-North FDI is more likely to be acquisitive. Emerging-market firms show a distinct preference for greenfield investments over M&A transactions in other emerging markets and for M&A transactions over greenfield investments in advanced economies. Greenfield investments accounted for 72 percent of emerging-market firms' investment in other emerging markets over 2003–09, and accounted for the majority of South-South FDI flows even during the height of the expansion (figure 2.9).

Emerging-market firms have a proclivity for greenfield investments when investing in other emerging markets for several reasons. First, the parent company may have significant managerial and operational experience in coping with weak physical infrastructure and a difficult economic, regulatory, and political environment. This type of expertise is valuable for greenfield projects, which most closely resemble the initial corporate development of the parent company. Second, given the lack of markets for corporate control and suitable targets for acquisition, greenfield investments are typically the only reasonable course of action for firms seeking to establish a physical presence in emerging economies. Third, the tendency for emerging-market multinationals to invest in other emerging markets in the same region, especially in neighboring countries, encourages greenfield investment over acquisitions. Fourth, greenfield investments are often an extension of firms' domestic operation in terms of distribution, marketing, service and maintenance centers, and even offshore manufacturing, and, thus, must be established anew, rather than acquired, in new markets. Because extending existing operations to the immediate vicinity of the home base usually requires tight coordination and integration with existing facilities, greenfield investments, which allow parent companies to optimize the fit with the rest of the organization, are the preferred mode of expansion. Conversely, acquisition of existing firms often can pose integration and managerial challenges compounded by different (and often difficult) economic and legal environments. Finally, greenfield projects facilitate control over company-specific resources, such as intellectual property, process engineering, R&D, and innovation activities—some combination of which is the source of many firms' competitive advantage in emerging markets, but less so in advanced countries.

In contrast to their tendency to invest in other emerging markets through greenfield investments, emerging-market firms' expansion into advanced economies occurs predominantly through M&A transactions—85 percent of all such investments over the 2003–09 period (figure 2.10). The needs for minimizing time to market, maximizing ready availability of suitable targets, compensating for the acquirer's relative lack of

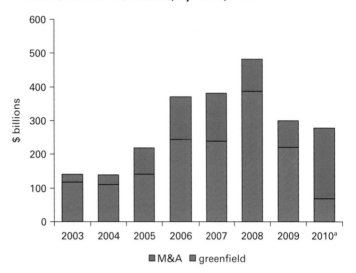

FIGURE 2.9   South-South cross-border greenfield investments and M&A deals, by value, 2003–10

Sources: World Bank staff estimates based on Thomson-Reuters SDC Platinum and fDi Markets.
Note: M&A deal values are adjusted for missing deal value information.
a. Greenfield 2010 data are for quarter 1 and quarter 2 only.

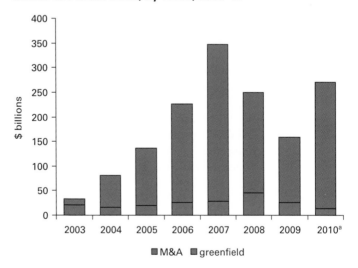

FIGURE 2.10   South-North cross-border greenfield investments and M&A deals, by value, 2003–10

Sources: World Bank staff estimates based on Thomson-Reuters SDC Platinum and fDi Markets.
Note: M&A deal values are adjusted for missing deal value information.
a. Greenfield 2010 data are for quarter 1 and quarter 2 only.

local expertise in very different business environments, and ensuring immediate access to clients and suppliers all argue for external growth rather than organic growth in the case of South-North

FDI. Thus, the amount of greenfield investment by emerging-market firms in advanced economies is very small relative to that of South-South FDI, and probably serves only as a stepping-stone for future external growth. Another reason M&A is the preferred mode of emerging-market firms' expansion into advanced economies may be that the well-developed institutional infrastructure in advanced economies typically reduces the legal, financial, and regulatory risks involved in takeovers. At the same time, the fact that the corporate and industrial environment in developed countries can be radically different from that in the acquirers' home countries means that access to local managerial and operational expertise is important.

The experience gained by firms in their home economies translates more easily to other emerging markets with often similar economic and legal structures—where it gives emerging-market firms a distinct competitive advantage over firms not used to competing in challenging institutional environments—more so than in advanced countries. Although it is possible, over time, for emerging-market companies to build up the skills required to operate efficiently and profitably in advanced economies, it often is more efficient for an emerging-market company to acquire such skills through a takeover. Nonetheless, the subsequent integration of newly acquired assets and expertise into existing operations poses its own challenges and costs, which need to be weighed against the benefits of an acquisition.

Taken together, historical trends point to the prominence of high-value-added, knowledge-intensive sectors in both greenfield and M&A investments. Thus, acquisitions such as those of the $1.4 billion stake by UAE SWF Mubadala in the Carlyle Group, and Indian software firm Satyam's multiple research-center investments in China, may well become more common in the future.

M&A deals originating in emerging markets reflect geographical proximity and economic ties. When emerging-market firms venture into other emerging-market countries, the firms prefer to acquire assets in their immediate geographic vicinity. Regional patterns show that, with the exception of deals originating in South Asia, cross-border emerging-market M&A transactions primarily target companies located in the same region, in terms of both value and number of deals (table 2.1). Similarly, emerging-market firms' expansion into advanced economies also reflects geographical proximity and economic relationships. Thus, firms based in Europe and Central Asia and in the Middle East and North Africa show a marked preference for acquisitions in European countries, while firms based in Latin America tend to acquire firms in North America. Target regions for investments by emerging-market firms in East Asia are more diversified.[10]

In devising and implementing their expansion strategies, firms face a trade-off between managerial and operational ease on one hand and diversification gains from an imperfectly correlated global business cycle on the other. Investing in countries in their own region typically has several major advantages over investing in other regions—it facilitates communication with the foreign unit, permits firms to transplant business models and operational procedures more readily, and necessitates less product adaptation and differentiation. Similarly, operational and geographic proximity allow firms greater opportunity to supervise the foreign units, to monitor local and regional competitors, and to study markets at the levels of the parent and the acquired subsidiary. Vertically integrated firms must weigh all of these operational benefits against the higher correlation in cash flows across foreign units within the same region. To the degree that business cycles are not perfectly correlated across countries, but are more correlated within regions than between regions, investing outside the home region can offer acquiring firms important gains through geographic diversification. If emerging-market firms forgo such interregional diversification opportunities, the operational benefits from intraregional integration must outweigh the greater stability of cash flows in terms of lower overall volatility.

The profile of emerging-market acquirers

Emerging-market acquirers tend to avoid bidding wars. The overwhelming majority of the

TABLE 2.1   Regional distribution of cross-border mergers and acquisitions, by number of deals and value, 1997–2010

Number of deals

TO:

FROM:		EAP	ECA	LAC	MENA	SA	SSA	Advanced Asia/Pacific	Advanced Europe	Advanced N. America	Total
	EAP	4,375	135	146	81	387	149	1,228	1,009	1,024	8,534
	ECA	54	1,174	14	19	12	13	18	624	174	2,102
	LAC	40	32	863	6	8	11	43	244	390	1,637
	MENA	153	72	20	416	116	59	55	409	220	1,520
	SA	195	62	41	58	38	82	86	452	446	1,460
	SSA	55	31	26	13	22	172	166	314	164	963
	Total	4,872	1,506	1,110	593	583	486	1,596	3,052	2,418	16,216

Value of deals, $ billions

TO:

FROM:		EAP	ECA	LAC	MENA	SA	SSA	Advanced Asia/Pacific	Advanced Europe	Advanced N. America	Total
	EAP	146	14	31	5	17	18	89	119	104	542
	ECA	1	45	—	1	1	3	3	57	28	139
	LAC	2	—	61	1	—	—	16	16	83	179
	MENA	22	11	4	45	7	4	5	119	69	285
	SA	6	6	7	2	—	13	4	35	21	94
	SSA	2	1	2	6	—	4	6	23	5	49
	Total	179	77	105	58	25	41	122	369	310	1,287

Source: World Bank staff estimates based on Thomson-Reuters SDC Platinum.
Note: — = not available, ECA = Europe and Central Asia, SA = South Asia. M&A deal volumes underestimate the actual values to the extent that values are undisclosed for some announced transactions.

cross-border acquisitions by emerging-market firms are of a friendly or neutral nature, whereby the management or board of the target company does not oppose the acquisition. Only a minute fraction of deals involve a hostile takeover bid in which the target company actively opposes advances by the acquirer. Similarly, emerging-market firms tend to avoid contested bids in which they find themselves in competition with other bidders for a particular target. Instead, emerging-market firms seem to prefer negotiated deals that minimize the risk of a costly bidding war. As Hope, Thomas, and Vyas (2011) have shown, the explanation behind this finding may lie in emerging-market firms' propensity to overpay for targets, especially those located in advanced economies. Transactions that are

important to the home country for economic or image reasons suffer even more from such a "winner's curse."[11] Hostile or contested bids typically increase the risk of overpaying for a target, leading firms to walk away from such transactions except in rare cases.

Most emerging-market acquirers pay cash. In almost 95 percent of cross-border transactions for which the type of consideration is known, emerging-market firms paid cash for the acquired assets, leaving less than 6 percent of completed deals paid for by issuance of stock in the parent company. This preference for cash, which lies in stark contrast to the payment behavior of established Western corporations, stems from two related attributes of typical developing-country acquirers. First, many emerging-market firms cannot effectively issue large amounts of stock because the firms are privately owned, are listed in equity markets lacking sufficient depth for significant secondary offerings, or are not cross-listed on any major exchange. Second, emerging-market firms tend to be privately held or controlled companies with one or more dominant shareholders (such as family-controlled firms or state-owned enterprises), which typically attach a lot of value to retaining control of the company and are reluctant to dilute that control through share issuance pursuant to acquisitions. For example, the top 20 Chinese firms undertaking foreign acquisitions are state enterprises that rely entirely on cash transactions.

The dependence on cash transactions has several implications for acquisitions by emerging-market firms. First, cash as an acquisition currency is expensive, and thus reduces the potential number and size of acquisitions. Emerging-market acquirers typically must arrange for the necessary funding upfront unless they have sufficient cash reserves available. As a result, the acquirers often negotiate standby agreements in the syndicated loan market that are contingent on approval of the acquisition by the target company. In essence, the acquirers arrange for credit facilities that the acquirers can draw down to make cash payments to incumbent shareholders. Because such credit facilities are typically expensive—they represent options on loans—acquirers often refinance the debt in global bond markets after completion of the deal. Although the cost advantage of public debt seems to argue for its extensive use in cross-border acquisitions, acquirers typically do not tap bond markets at the time of the offer because failure to complete the deal would mean a prohibitively high cost of carriage for unneeded funds. Tata Steel's cash acquisition of the Dutch steelmaker Corus, for example, was funded by syndicated loans. Given the contested nature of the deal and the uncertainty about the ultimate acquisition price, bond financing would have represented a significant financial risk to the bidders if they had been outbid by the opposition. A year after the completion of the deal, while still seeking to lower its repayment costs, Tata raised a significant portion

of the funds necessary to repay the credit facility in global bond markets.

Second, dependence on cash focuses the choice of acquisitions on low-risk transactions. In the case of a stock acquisition, the realized synergies will be shared with the incumbent shareholders of the target, who continue to have a stake in the combined company after the completion of the takeover. As a result, companies uncertain about the capture of synergies tend to opt for payment in stock to share future operational and financial risks with existing target shareholders. By contrast, incumbent shareholders cannot share in the gains from the takeover when payment is in cash because the shareholders cease to have a stake in the firm after the deal. Acquisition through cash payments requires a high degree of confidence in the existence and future realization of synergy gains by emerging-market acquirers.

Finally, the cost of cash payments means that the acquirer's management has a relatively stronger incentive to devote the necessary time, effort, and financial resources to successfully integrating the acquired assets. Several studies by management consultancies on the factors determining M&A success and failure have shown that flawed execution and lack of integration after completion of the deal are the most frequent causes for failure and the destruction of shareholder wealth. Careful target screening and selection, avoidance of a bidding war, and a high level of confidence in the existence of synergies are necessary conditions for the success of acquisitions, which then justify a cash payment. Good execution and successful integration of the acquired assets are sufficient conditions for capturing synergies. The governance structure of emerging-market firms, which often includes dominant shareholders, also helps through typically higher monitoring of acquirer management during the bidding, negotiation, and execution phases.

Implications of emerging-market FDI flows for low-income countries

Low-income countries have, in general, benefited from the growth in South-South FDI flows. Low-income countries have received $93 billion in FDI from emerging markets since 1997. In 2010 alone, FDI flows to low-income countries amounted to $13.3 billion. Throughout this period, firms located in low-income countries were the targets of 767 cross-border M&A deals (figure 2.11) that originated in a very diverse group of countries. The largest investor from 1997–2010 was the United Kingdom, with 33 percent of the total deal value, followed by China (14 percent), France (7 percent), South Africa (5 percent), and Canada (4 percent).[12] Emerging-market firms' FDI in low-income countries is on the rise, albeit from a very low initial level. Although only 1.9 percent of M&A (and 5.0 percent of greenfield) outbound transactions originating in emerging economies were directed at low-income countries, the acquisition volume significantly increased between 2003 and 2010. Furthermore, the recovery of cross-border M&A in low-income countries after the financial crisis of 2008 is primarily due to the activities of emerging-market firms, which in 2009 and 2010 were responsible for more than half of all cross-border M&A deal value. To put this contribution to FDI in low-income countries into perspective, emerging-market firms have accounted for 41 percent of cross-border deals into low-income countries since 1997, but for only 14 percent of global M&A transactions in the same period.

Besides China and South Africa, other important sources of South-South FDI into low-income countries were India and Malaysia, for M&A transactions, and for greenfield investments, India, the United Arab Emirates, and Vietnam.

Most emerging-market firms invest in low-income countries located in the same region, especially in Sub-Saharan Africa, where South Africa is the largest regional source of both cross-border M&A and greenfield transactions. In Asia, virtually all of Vietnamese greenfield investments in low-income countries went to Cambodia, the Lao People's Democratic Republic, and Myanmar.

Companies undertaking M&A and greenfield investments were predominantly in the metal and mining, oil and gas, and telecommunications sectors. However, mining companies played a larger role within North-South acquisitions than within South-South acquisitions. Telecommunications firms accounted for 20 percent of all M&A deal

FIGURE 2.11 Cross-border M&A investment to low-income countries, 1997–2010

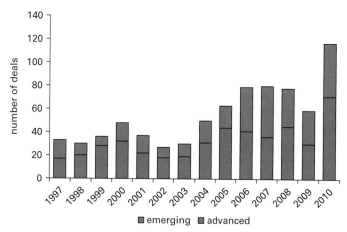

Source: World Bank staff estimates based on Thomson-Reuters SDC Platinum.

value into low-income countries; the top acquiring countries in the sector were the United Kingdom, France, the United States, Vietnam, and South Africa. Greenfield investments were dominated by the same sectors.

In spite of the continuing importance of telecommunications and the combined mining, oil, and gas sectors, the degree of sectoral concentration among companies acquiring assets in LICs has generally declined over the past decade. However, the specific concentration pattern varies widely from one destination country to the next. As the top target (by number of deals) of cross-border M&A among LICs, Tanzania provides a good example of very low concentration among the group of acquiring sectors, which has included finance, mining, professional services, food, and transportation. Investments into Bangladesh, another important low-income destination country, have also been characterized by some degree of diversification among acquiring sectors, as well as among the source countries of those investments. Such diversification is not limited to the larger LICs. Despite a much smaller aggregate deal volume, Cambodia has also attracted a diverse group of investors, both at the sectoral and source country levels.

A very different situation can be observed in countries where the majority of all value invested came from one or two big deals, as was the case in Guinea and Myanmar. In the first case, the announced $1.35 billion investment by Chinalco in the Simandou project will represent more than 90 percent of all deal value invested in Guinea since 1997. Furthermore, the second largest cross-border deal recorded—by BHP Billiton in the Guinea Alumina Project—was in the same sector. A similar pattern can be observed in Myanmar, where close to 90 percent of all inbound M&A value was concentrated in two deals, both in natural resource–related sectors.

In between these two well-defined patterns, cross-border investment into LICs can exhibit a combination of different characteristics, depending on whether one analyzes the origin of the investing firms, their industry, or the size of their investments. As a destination country, for example, Uganda combines a relatively large volume of accumulated inbound investment ($2 billion) and many deals (45) with an intermediate degree of sectoral concentration, but with a very narrow group of acquiring countries: South Africa and the United Kingdom combined were responsible for 96 percent of all deal value. But British companies engaged in acquisitions spread across very different sectors, such as food, finance, oil, and wholesale trade.

Understanding cross-border acquisitions from emerging economies

There has been little empirical analysis of the factors driving firms domiciled in developing countries to venture abroad. To fill this gap in the literature, this report undertakes an econometric investigation of the determinants of bilateral M&A flows between acquirers' home countries and their targets' countries ("host countries") (box 2.1). This analysis is guided by the existing literature, which offers several hypotheses as to why firms venture abroad.

The first set of hypotheses posit that companies seek growth opportunities abroad as they outgrow their home markets—a problem that is particularly acute in developing countries. As a result, relative growth in home and destination countries, both overall and by industry, should affect deal flow, which is tested by using

variables that measure GDP and sector growth. Companies also may pursue economies of scale or scope in their global expansion. This rationale can be investigated by examining the degree to which companies are diversifying their investments, as opposed to targeting firms within their own narrowly defined industries.

A second group of hypotheses revolves around structural economic characteristics of the home and host countries, such as economic openness, access to finance, the speed of diffusion of technological advances, and managerial and operational expertise. Indeed, one of the most frequently cited rationales for companies' global expansion is the export of innovations in the pursuit of enhancing returns to R&D activities. Given that emerging economies have become important contributors to the advancement of science and technology, one can test this group of hypotheses by including variables related to the home country's investment in science and technology, such as the number of domestic and overseas patents granted, the level of education investment, the percentage of the population attaining a tertiary education, and the number of engineering graduates.

At the same time, emerging-market firms may have specialized managerial and operational expertise, which the firms can export to markets similar to their home markets. To test this hypothesis, variables capturing operating efficiency, such as unit labor costs and capital or R&D efficiency, are investigated to determine whether the variables have a different impact on investment activity in emerging economies versus advanced economies. This class of hypotheses also includes the role of easy access to financing, for M&A activity in particular. To assess the importance of financing factors, the model includes variables capturing the cost of finance and the ease with which emerging-market firms can raise funds globally, such as through corporate bond spreads, the number of bond issues by firms from the country of origin, or the level of domestic financial development (as represented by the ratio of private credit or stock-market capitalization to GDP), among other factors.

A final set of hypotheses concern the economic relationship *between* home and host countries, which are commonly used in the bilateral trade

BOX 2.1   Empirical analysis of cross-border bilateral M&A flows from emerging economies

In analyzing the key determinants of the cross-border acquisition behavior by emerging-market-based firms (described in detail in annex 2.3), various linear and log-linear models of the bilateral M&A activity were specified for a large (unbalanced) panel of emerging economies, drawing on a comprehensive database developed for this book. The various specifications relate bilateral deal flows from 61 "home" countries to 80 "host" countries to a large range of explanatory and control variables. Throughout the analysis, the model distinguishes between deal flow to other emerging economies and deal flow to advanced countries, so that each set of estimates is allowed to take on a distinct coefficient.

The model's dependent variable is defined as the total number of cross-border M&A deals originating in emerging economies (the "home" country), for targets in either an emerging economy or advanced country, for a given year (the accompanying figure provides an example). The model controls for home- and host-country characteristics, bilateral characteristics for a given home-host pair, and global macroeconomic variables, as described in the text.

The cross-border investment database compiled for this book comprised explanatory variables drawn from a variety of sources. These sources cover macroeconomic conditions (World Bank *World Development Indicators* [WDI], IMF *International Financial Statistics*); financial factors (Dealogic DCM Analytics, U.S. Federal Reserve, MSCI, JP Morgan); commodity prices (Goldman Sachs, World Bank Development Economics Prospects Group); bilateral investment treaties (United Nations Conference on Trade and Development); country risk and institutions

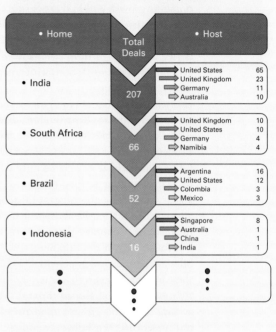

FIGURE B2.1.1   Selected bilateral M&A flows from home to host economies, 2007

indicators (PRS Group's *International Country Risk Guide*); technology and innovation (World Intellectual Property Organization); and the sectoral structure of economies (World Bank WDI). Depending on the specification, each dataset includes between 21,884 and 34,730 observations.

literature employing gravity models. Economic factors in such hypotheses include geographic determinants, such as bilateral country distances—the quality of an investor's or acquirer's knowledge and ability to obtain information about a potential acquisition target may well decrease as the distance between the two countries increases—as well as economic and policy variables, such as existing bilateral trade flows and BITs. Finally, to the extent that global macroeconomic conditions,

such as global commodity prices and interest rates, affect M&A activity, these macroeconomic conditions are included as additional controls.

The results show that firms clearly try to exploit differential growth opportunities abroad, although growth in a firm's home country is important, as well. Indeed, the effect of GDP growth is twice as large for growth in host countries compared to growth in home countries. Thus, having built up cash reserves for investment and acquisition purposes through rapid growth at home, firms pursue growth opportunities through M&A deals in the better-performing advanced economies. Another possible reason why home-country growth may be related to outbound M&A activity is that firms with higher productivity tend to be the engines of both domestic growth and FDI expansion abroad.

Acquisition activity is also influenced by economic size. The effect of home GDP levels is twice as large in transactions with developed economies as in transactions with emerging economies, which suggests that only firms from relatively large or mature emerging economies have the means to pursue expansion in advanced economies through M&A. Finally, the level of host-country development, as measured by per capita GDP, is negatively associated only with acquisitions in emerging destination countries; the variable is statistically insignificant for acquisitions in advanced countries. Firms appear to seek targets in emerging economies that have not yet attained a certain level of development, and, therefore, offer even more growth potential. Taken together, these findings suggest that emerging-market multinationals expand abroad through M&A transactions to exploit growth opportunities that are not present in their home economies, mainly by seeking out fast-growing economies—especially among industrial countries, but also in relatively less developed economies.

In terms of structural features, a country's participation in the global economy is also an important determinant of bilateral M&A flows, whether measured in terms of trade or financial integration. Firms in countries that are more integrated into the global trading system tend to be more acquisitive in other emerging markets, often because the firms' operations are more internationalized through their prior export and import activities. In the same vein, greater bilateral trade flows are associated with higher M&A activity, which further suggests that existing trade ties facilitate acquisitions.

Outbound M&A activity is also influenced by the home country's reserve holdings and capital market development. Reserve holdings are a sign of access to foreign currency which, given the propensity of emerging-market acquirers to pay in cash, facilitates the transaction. Similarly, large reserve holdings reflect a country's participation in the global economy, which allows its firms to gain prior experience in international business valuable for later M&A deals. In contrast, firms based in high-reserve economies are less likely to acquire assets in other emerging markets, presumably because they concentrate their operational and M&A efforts in the countries with which they trade, that is, predominantly advanced economies. Regarding financial development, countries with larger stock markets engage in more acquisitions in both emerging and developed countries since the countries with larger markets can more easily raise funds at home and abroad.

More generally, an acquirer's home economy needs to have attained a certain level of institutional development before its firms start to engage in cross-border M&A transactions. Economic instability in the home country, for example, will increase M&A activity in developed economies, as firms attempt to escape the vagaries of their home economy by expanding into more stable frontiers; by contrast, firms in stable emerging economies tend to be more willing to expand their M&A activities into other emerging markets. In a similar vein, emerging-economy firms actively seek to lower their political risk exposure through more acquisitions in politically stable developed economies. Similarly, more stable emerging-market home economies tend to acquire less in other emerging markets, possibly because growth opportunities remain attractive at home, thus negating the need for foreign acquisitions.

Structural factors such as technological achievements and managerial expertise do not seem to have a pronounced impact on M&A, regardless of whether the home country's economy is emerging or advanced. By contrast, geographic distance appears to have a negative effect, as expected. This negative effect implies that the cost of bilateral transactions—including the costs of communicating, coordinating, and monitoring information and maintaining a database of local knowledge—tends to matter, especially in developing countries, where informational asymmetries are particularly acute.

Taken together, the findings suggest that firms in emerging economies seek to diversify away from their local economic, financial, and political risks by making acquisitions in advanced economies, but that the firms have a greater appetite for such risks when pursuing opportunities in emerging markets. This result is likely due to differences in bilateral transactions costs faced by the firms in each type of market.

Future cross-border deals are likely to grow at a sustained, albeit slower, pace. Based on the model specified in box 2.1 (modified to include a lagged dependent variable among the regressors and grouping the host countries into advanced and emerging), it is possible to obtain projections for the number of outbound cross-border deals expected between 2010 and 2025. These projections—which also incorporate the broad macroeconomic assumptions consistent with the baseline scenario of chapter 1—suggest that the pace of cross-border deal growth is likely to slow from the 14.3 percent annual growth rate recorded between 1998 and 2008, to an average of 9.0 percent annual growth over 2010–20, and to an average of 6.7 percent annual growth between 2020 and 2025 (figure 2.12).

Consistent with the past decade, the expansion of financial globalization, as measured by the rate of growth of cross-border deals, is expected to exceed that of real economic growth. Growth in cross-border deals will outpace expected emerging-market GDP annual growth rates of 4.9 percent over 2010–20 and 4.1 percent over 2020–25. This expected growth in cross-border deals echoes a global trend of financial growth generally exceeding growth in real economic variables (box 2.2).

The Growth and Globalization of Emerging-Market Corporate Finance
Major emerging-market firms have traditionally relied on international markets for corporate finance

Given the significant informational and legal obstacles faced by emerging-market firms in

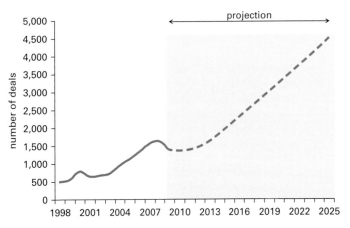

FIGURE 2.12   Projected emerging-market outbound cross-border deals through 2025

Source: World Bank staff estimates.
Note: Based on the 53 countries for which complete data are available.

the process of raising international financing, it is not surprising that firms seeking to expand their overseas operations rely, at least initially, on their own cash reserves and financing raised in their home countries (see Frost, Birkinshaw, and Ensign 2002; Del Duca 2007). Upon reaching a certain point in their life cycles, however, emerging-market firms are compelled to turn to global markets to raise capital, as financial markets in emerging-market countries often lack the depth needed to fully satisfy the financing needs of rapidly growing corporations. At the same time, global markets place the burden of proof on new borrowers, so it is important for firms to investigate the degree to which transaction and security design (and, from a broader perspective, financing procedures) can help solve the underlying financing challenges.

Corporations based in emerging markets tend to rely on three distinct sources of global financing: syndicated loans, debt securities, and foreign or cross-border equity listings. Typically, syndicated borrowing precedes foreign equity listings and international debt issuance, although this sequencing has become less strict over the past decade. Regional differences also have emerged. Eastern European corporations now often seek a foreign equity listing before they become active

BOX 2.2   The global expansion of cross-border financial transactions

The world economy is taking on an increasingly trans-national character, facilitated by a distinct increase in cross-border economic transactions and arrangements over the past two decades. On the real side, international trade flows have risen from 17.8 percent of global output in 1983 to 27.7 percent in 2007, with emerging-economy growth poles becoming increasingly active participants in this expansion. The growing presence of China in global trade has been especially conspicuous, driven by domestic reforms in the late 1970s and early 1980s and, since the country's accession to the organization in 2001, by reductions in barriers to trade made in accordance with the standards of the World Trade Organization. As a result, trade accounted for a high of 72 percent of China's GDP in 2006. Brazil and India experienced similar trade surges following their own economic liberalization efforts in the early 1990s.

Cross-border financial flows have likewise expanded dramatically in recent decades. FDI—the largest and most stable component of international financial flows—has increased as a ratio to GDP by almost an order of magnitude worldwide since the early 1980s. A significant part of this increase is due to the rise of South-North, South-South, and North-South mergers and acquisitions. But the increase in cross-border financial flows is also evident in more traditional areas of international finance, such as bonds and commercial credit (see accompanying figure). The foreign exposure of international banks, for example, rose from an average of one-quarter of GDP in the 1983–88 and 1993–98 periods to about one-third of GDP in the 2003–08 period. Similarly, foreign currency reserve accumulation by central banks almost tripled during the same period, rising from 4 percent of GDP to almost 10 percent of GDP in the 2003–08 period.

FIGURE B2.2.1   Global expansion of cross-border economic transactions, 1983–2008

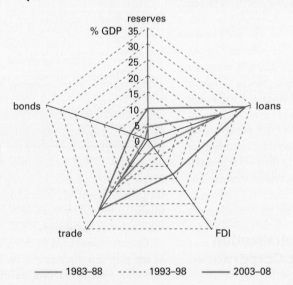

Sources: World Bank staff calculations using the Bank for International Settlements (BIS) consolidated banking statistics, World Bank WDI, and IMF IFS databases.
Note: Trade is measured as global exports, FDI is measured as net investment by foreign entities in the domestic economy, loans are measured as global foreign claims of (BIS-reporting) banks, debt is measured as global foreign bond issuance, and reserves are measured as global international reserve holdings, all as a share of global GDP. For loans, country coverage only includes those with BIS reporting banks across all three time periods, with the value of global GDP adjusted accordingly. Year ranges indicate averages of annual data for the respective period. Note that loans and reserves are stocks (as opposed to the flows of the other three dimensions) and are reported as a share of GDP mainly for analytical convenience and to provide a sense of proportion.

BOX 2.2   (continued)

By and large, the growth of internationally traded financial assets has proceeded much more rapidly than the expansion of real trade flows: indeed, financial asset accumulation grew at more than twice the rate of trade expansion, on average, between 1987 and 2008 (see accompanying figure). The same figure shows how dramatically the total value of internationally traded assets has increased over the past two decades, from $6.5 trillion in 1987 to $28.2 trillion in 2000, and to $95.3 trillion in 2008. The three main components of international financial assets—bank loans, bonds, and portfolio equity—grew in tandem from the 1980s through 2007, when all three dipped as a result of the global financial crisis. Although financial derivatives have comprised a fourth major component of international investment since about 2005, derivatives attained the same order of magnitude as portfolio equity by 2008. The dramatic expansion in the movement of financial assets across international borders over the past two decades has given rise to a massive foreign exchange market and has raised concerns about what such large foreign exchange turnovers may mean for currency volatility.

FIGURE B2.2.2   Stronger growth in international trade of financial assets than in goods trade, 1987–2008

■ internationally traded assets
— ratio of financial to trade flows (right axis)

Sources: IMF IFS database and World Bank staff calculations.
Note: The ratio of financial to trade flows was computed as the ratio of global portfolio financial flows to global imports, smoothed by taking a 3-year moving average of the series.

in global debt markets, whereas Latin American corporations increasingly issue debt on international capital markets without cross-listing their shares. Such changes in corporate financing behavior have implications for the emergence of regional financial centers and for the segment of global capital markets that they represent. Nearly two-thirds of the emerging-market firms that have been active acquirers since the late 1990s (defined as those firms that have undertaken more than 10 acquisitions over the 1997–2010 period) have accessed international capital markets; see table 2.2). Although cross-border syndicated lending predominated as the main way in which these active acquiring firms accessed cross-border financing, more than 10 percent of these firms tapped all three of the main sources of global financing.

TABLE 2.2   Top emerging-market multinationals in cross-border mergers and acquistions, by number of deals, 1997–2010

Acquirer name	Acquirer home economy	Acquirer parent home economy	Sector of the deal	Deal number	Access to international capital market		
					Foreign equity market	International bank lending market	International bond market
Flextronics International	Singapore	Singapore	Computer and Electronic Product Manufacturing	45		Yes	Yes
Temasek Holdings(Pte)Ltd	Singapore	Singapore		32			
GIC Real Estate Pte	Singapore	Singapore		31			
Investcorp Bank BSC	Bahrain	Bahrain		30	Yes		
Dimension Data Holdings PLC	South Africa	South Africa	Professional, Scientific, and Technical Services	28			
Telmex	Mexico	Mexico	Telecommunications	28		Yes	
Datatec	South Africa	South Africa	Professional, Scientific, and Technical Services	26	Yes		
CDC Software Corp	Hong Kong SAR, China	Hong Kong SAR, China	Publishing Industries (except Internet)	25	Yes		
America Movil SA de CV	Mexico	Mexico	Telecommunications	22	Yes	Yes	Yes
GIC	Singapore	Singapore		19			
Olam International	Singapore	Singapore	Merchant Wholesalers, Nondurable Goods	19		Yes	Yes
CP Foods(UK)Ltd	United Kingdom	Thailand	Food Manufacturing	17			
CEMEX SA DE CV	Mexico	Mexico	Nonmetallic Mineral Product Manufacturing	16	Yes	Yes	Yes
Evraz Group SA	Russian Federation	Russian Federation	Primary Metal Manufacturing	16		Yes	Yes
HCL Technologies	India	India	Publishing Industries (except Internet)	16		Yes	
Petrobras	Brazil	Brazil	Petroleum and Coal Products Manufacturing	16	Yes	Yes	Yes
Datacraft Asia	Singapore	South Africa	Professional, Scientific, and Technical Services	15			
ENIC PLC	United Kingdom	Costa Rica	Securities, Commodity Contracts, and Other Financial Investments and Related Activities	15			
Gazprom	Russian Federation	Russian Federation	Oil and Gas Extraction	15	Yes	Yes	Yes
Istithmar PJSC	United Arab Emirates	United Arab Emirates		15		Yes	
Vimpelkom	Russian Federation	Russian Federation	Telecommunications	15	Yes	Yes	
Asia Pacific Breweries	Singapore	Singapore	Beverage and Tobacco Product Manufacturing	14			
CEZ AS	Czech Republic	Czech Republic	Utilities	14		Yes	Yes

TABLE 2.2 (continued)

Acquirer name	Acquirer home economy	Acquirer parent home economy	Sector of the deal	Deal number	Access to international capital market		
					Foreign equity market	International bank lending market	International bond market
Fraser & Neave Holdings Bhd	Malaysia	Singapore	Beverage and Tobacco Product Manufacturing	14		Yes	
Noble Group	Hong Kong SAR, China	Hong Kong SAR, China	Merchant Wholesalers, Nondurable Goods	14			
Abu Dhabi National Energy Co	United Arab Emirates	United Arab Emirates	Utilities	13		Yes	Yes
ETISALAT	United Arab Emirates	United Arab Emirates	Telecommunications	13		Yes	
OAO Vneshtorgbank	Russian Federation	Russian Federation	Credit Intermediation and Related Activities	13			
Richter Gedeon Nyrt	Hungary	Hungary	Chemical Manufacturing	13			
Teledata Informatics	India	India	Computer and Electronic Product Manufacturing	13	Yes		
UOB	Singapore	Singapore	Securities, Commodity Contracts, and Other Financial Investments and Related Activities	13		Yes	Yes
Cobalt Holding Co	St. Lucia	El Salvador	Furniture and Related Product Manufacturing	12			
OTP Bank Nyrt	Hungary	Hungary	Credit Intermediation and Related Activities	12		Yes	Yes
PETRONAS	Malaysia	Malaysia	Oil and Gas Extraction	12			Yes
Posco Co	Korea, Rep.	Korea, Rep.	Primary Metal Manufacturing	12	Yes	Yes	Yes
SingTel	Singapore	Singapore	Telecommunications	12		Yes	
Abraaj Capital	United Arab Emirates	United Arab Emirates	Securities, Commodity Contracts, and Other Financial Investments and Related Activities	11			
Alexander Forbes	South Africa	South Africa	Securities, Commodity Contracts, and Other Financial Investments and Related Activities	11			
China Investment Corp (CIC)	China	China		11			
Grupo Bimbo SAB de CV	Mexico	Mexico	Food Manufacturing	11		Yes	Yes
Intl Microcomputer Software	United States	Hong Kong SAR, China	Computer and Electronic Product Manufacturing	11			
Jinchuan Group	China	China	Mining (except Oil and Gas)	11			
NK LUKOIL	Russian Federation	Russian Federation	Oil and Gas Extraction	11			
Nova Ljubljanska Banka dd	Slovenia	Slovenia	Credit Intermediation and Related Activities	11		Yes	Yes
OAO "Severstal"	Russian Federation	Russian Federation	Primary Metal Manufacturing	11	Yes		
Samsung Electronics Co	Korea, Rep.	Korea, Rep.	Computer and Electronic Product Manufacturing	11		Yes	Yes

(continued)

TABLE 2.2   (continued)

Acquirer name	Acquirer home economy	Acquirer parent home economy	Sector of the deal	Deal number	Access to international capital market Foreign equity market	International bank lending market	International bond market
Wilmar International	Singapore	Singapore	Food Manufacturing	11		Yes	
BIDvest Group	South Africa	South Africa	Securities, Commodity Contracts, and Other Financial Investments and Related Activities	10			
Carlos Slim Helu	Mexico	Mexico	Securities, Commodity Contracts, and Other Financial Investments and Related Activities	10			
Cia Vale do Rio Doce SA	Brazil	Brazil	Mining (except Oil and Gas)	10			
CNOOC	China	China	Oil and Gas Extraction	10		Yes	Yes
Etika Intl Hldgs	Singapore	Singapore	Food Manufacturing	10		Yes	
Gerdau SA	Brazil	Brazil	Primary Metal Manufacturing	10	Yes	Yes	Yes
Grupo Votorantim	Brazil	Brazil	Nonmetallic Mineral Product Manufacturing	10		Yes	
Harmony Gold Mining Co	South Africa	South Africa	Mining (except Oil and Gas)	10	Yes	Yes	
Hutchison Port Holdings	Hong Kong SAR, China	Hong Kong SAR, China	Support Activities for Transportation	10			
MTN Group	South Africa	South Africa	Telecommunications	10			
Mubadala Development Co	United Arab Emirates	United Arab Emirates		10		Yes	
Newbloom Pte	Singapore	Singapore	Management of Companies and Enterprises	10			
OMX AB	Sweden	United Arab Emirates	Securities, Commodity Contracts, and Other Financial Investments and Related Activities	10			
Penta Investments sro	Czech Republic	Czech Republic		10			
Petronas International	Malaysia	Malaysia	Support Activities for Mining	10			Yes
Prvni Privatizacni Fond AS	Czech Republic	Czech Republic	Securities, Commodity Contracts, and Other Financial Investments and Related Activities	10			
Ranbaxy Laboratories	India	India	Chemical Manufacturing	10			
Westcon Group Inc	United States	South Africa	Computer and Electronic Product Manufacturing	10			

Sources: World Bank staff compilation, from Dealogic, Thomson-Reuters SDC Platinum, and respective stock exchanges.
Note: Acquiring firms listed in the table are defined as such based on the home country of their parent company.

Emerging-market firms accounted for 32 percent of new cross-border equity listings by foreign companies on U.S. and European international exchanges from January 2005 to May 2010 (figure 2.13).[13] In addition, many of the companies incorporated in offshore jurisdictions have their operational base in developing countries, which means that the actual proportion of new cross-listings by firms operating in emerging markets is likely higher than 32 percent. For their part, in recent years, major international exchanges have increasingly been competing to attract firms domiciled in emerging-market countries. The New York Stock Exchange (NYSE), NASDAQ, and London Stock Exchange (LSE) all opened representative offices in Beijing in 2007–08, for example. Deutsche Börse has set up staff teams that are responsible for attracting listings from China, India, Russia, and other countries in Eastern Europe—targeting, in particular, engineering firms and companies seeking to raise capital for renewable energy projects and ventures.

As is the case for growing international firms domiciled in developed countries, one of the main motivations for emerging-market firms to list on international exchanges is to raise capital—including to finance the expansion of their cross-border operations. The LSE, in particular, has attracted a large number of cross-listings by emerging-market firms that have been active in expanding their international operations through acquisitions (figure 2.14): one-third of the emerging-market firms that have cross-listed on the LSE since 2005 acquired foreign firms over the two-year period following their listing.

The NYSE and NASDAQ also remain popular destinations for emerging-market firms seeking to raise financing through initial public offerings and subsequent issues for financing cross-border acquisitions. A total of almost $47 billion in financing has been raised since 1995 by emerging-market firms that have undertaken cross-border acquisitions and are cross-listed on the LSE, NYSE, or NASDAQ,[14] with nearly three-quarters of this financing ($33.4 billion) raised on the New York stock exchanges (figure 2.15). China and India rank as the top firm domicile countries in terms of the amount of financing raised on these exchanges,[15] with prominent

FIGURE 2.13   New cross-listings by foreign firms on U.S. and European international stock exchanges, 2005–10

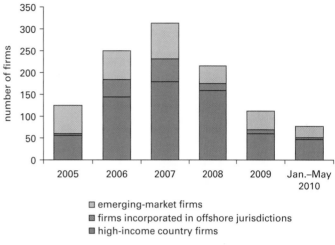

Source: World Bank staff estimates based on data from national stock exchanges.
Note: Tallies for foreign company listings on the London Stock Exchange (main list and Alternative Investment Market [AIM]), Euronext, Deutsche Börse (Regulated Official and Regulated Unofficial Markets), Luxembourg Stock Exchange; and American Depository Receipts on the New York Stock Exchange and NASDAQ. Offshore jurisdictions include firms incorporated in Barbados, Bermuda, the British Virgin Islands, the Cayman Islands, Gibraltar, Guernsey, and the U.S. Virgin Islands.

FIGURE 2.14   Share of cross-listed firms that announced acquisitions of foreign firms, 2005–Q2 2010

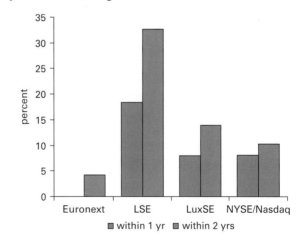

Sources: World Bank staff estimates based on data from national stock exchanges and Thompson Reuters.

sectors including media services, telecoms, financial services, renewable energy (Chinese firms), and banking and information technology (Indian firms).[16]

FIGURE 2.15   Equity financing raised on the LSE, NYSE, and NASDAQ by emerging-market acquirer firms, 1995–October 2010

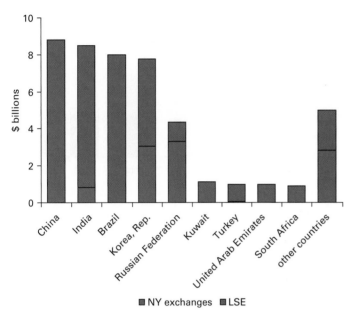

Sources: World Bank staff estimates based on data from national stock exchanges and Thompson Reuters.

Emerging-market firms increasingly will access domestic markets to raise large amounts of finance

Generally, emerging-market firms seeking to raise large amounts of financing rely on international exchanges rather than their home markets due to the access that well-capitalized international markets provide to a large, diverse investor base and high trading volume. This tendency is beginning to change, however, as firms domiciled in major emerging economies—such as China, India, and Mexico—have been able to raise large amounts of financing on their home equity markets in the past few years.[17] This trend appears set to gain momentum given the continued strong growth forecasts for these economies. But it will also be necessary for these countries to implement reforms that further develop and deepen their capital markets.

Over the next decade, it will be increasingly likely that firms from several of the high-growth emerging-market economies—that are in the process of deepening their local capital

markets—will access home markets, even when raising large amounts of financing abroad. India stands out as a high-growth economy with a large, young population that has significant potential to develop a large local investor base.[18] However, some reversal of portfolio flows—as observed, for instance, in November 2010—points to the need for India and other emerging economies that have experienced large inflows to take appropriate measures to further develop their local capital markets.

Certain emerging markets may become regional financing hubs and important sources of capital for market-seeking FDI from Northern firms

Over the next 5–10 years, capital markets in fast-growing emerging markets—especially those in Asian countries such as Korea and Singapore and, with further reforms, those in India and China—could become major regional financial hubs for firms seeking to raise capital, perhaps with individual exchanges specializing in certain industries.[19] Continually increasing trade linkages and cross-border FDI flows between Asian economies can be expected to further deepen regional stock market linkages.[20] In the several years before the onset of the global financial crisis, Singapore's stock market already had experienced rapidly increasing listings from firms domiciled in other East Asian countries, which were attracted by the well-regulated status of the exchange and the good corporate governance reputations of its listed companies.[21] Since 2007, Korea's stock market also has attracted listings from foreign companies within East Asia, mostly from China.

Before the global financial crisis, Singapore's market had begun gaining a reputation as a gateway to Asia for foreign firms from outside the region. Korea's market has been emerging more recently as a strong regional competitor in attracting firms outside the region, largely due to the exchange's high liquidity and relatively low listing costs.

Over the next decade and beyond, as local consumer demand continues to rise in the fastest-growing BRIC economies, and as these economies' capital markets continue to develop, multinational manufacturing and consumer goods firms based in Europe and the United States can be expected to increasingly cross-list on these economies' capital markets. It is only natural that cross-listings by firms from high-income countries in Europe and the United States, at first motivated solely by aims to raise their brand recognition in emerging markets, would be followed over the next 10–15 years by equity issues that tap emerging economies' capital markets for significant amounts of financing, assuming that further progress is made on financial market regulatory and institutional reforms.

India stands out among the BRICs and other fast-growing emerging-market growth poles as being likely to lead this expected trend. In 2010, the first Indian depositary receipts were issued simultaneously by the United Kingdom's Standard Chartered Bank on India's National Stock Exchange and the Bombay Stock Exchange to raise the bank's visibility in India's banking sector. In addition, the Bombay Stock Exchange struck a cooperation agreement with Deutsche Börse that paves the way for future cross-listings on India's market by German firms.[22]

Market-seeking FDI sourced from Northern manufacturing and consumer goods firms seeking closer access to potentially large new consumer markets in India could be expected to increasingly seek to raise capital locally in India to finance new subsidiaries, assuming that three developments occur. First, further progress would be needed on local capital market reforms toward a soundly functioning national financial system supported by macroeconomic policies that effectively manage private capital flows to avoid destabilizing effects of overheating and the formation of asset bubbles. Second, the Indian government's plans to double spending on transport and power infrastructure improvements to $1 trillion in the five years to 2017 would need to go forward and bear fruit. Third, market-seeking FDI in retail sectors would be able to set up new subsidiaries and finance them locally only if India's policy makers remove existing barriers to FDI in the economy's retail sectors. Notably, this Northern-sourced FDI would be distinguished from the Northern-sourced FDI of earlier decades in that the new FDI likely would be primarily market-seeking, rather than resource-seeking and efficiency-seeking.

Emerging markets are also becoming important sources of bank lending to low-income countries

Just as cross-border FDI from emerging economies is becoming more prominent in investment flows to low-income countries, there is some evidence that portfolio capital flows to low-income countries are also increasingly reflecting the growing influence of emerging economies. While overall portfolio flows from the South to LICs remain low as compared to FDI flows, international bank lending with the participation of emerging economy banks has grown significantly in absolute terms since 2004 (figure 2.16), increasing by an order of magnitude from $1.3 billion in 2003 to more than $10 billion in 2010. Overall, much of this lending activity was directed toward private corporations in LICs, comprising 78 percent of all loans in 2010.

Banks in South Africa have played an important role in bilateral and syndicated lending to LICs, especially in Sub-Saharan Africa. In 1995, for example, South African banks participated in deals valued at $305 million, and by 2010 this had increased to $2.3 billion. Chinese banks are another important source of cross-border lending to LICs. Although their involvement in the international bank loan market is relatively recent—beginning only in 2007—by 2010 they had participated in deals valued cumulatively at $7.6 billion. With the exception of China, however, most cross-border bank lending has, like cross-border FDI, reflected regional ties.

Emerging-market firms' access to international bond markets continues to expand

International bond issuance by borrowers based in emerging markets has grown dramatically since the mid-1990s (figure 2.17) and now represents a major source of capital for companies based in emerging-market countries. Between 2003 and

FIGURE 2.16   International bank lending to low-income countries, 1995–2010

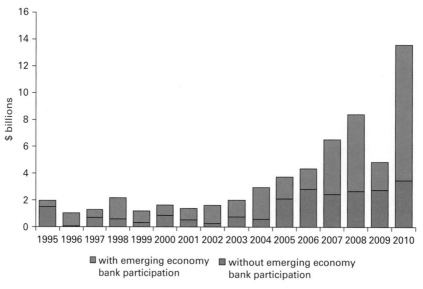

■ with emerging economy
   bank participation

■ without emerging economy
   bank participation

Source: World Bank staff calculations, from Dealogic database.

Note: Any deals with at least one emerging-economy bank listed as a lender were classified as with emerging-economy bank participation. Bank lending was calculated from all cross-border bank lending, both bilateral and syndicated, to private corporations, public corporations, and governments.

FIGURE 2.17   International bond issues emanating from emerging economies, 1998–2010

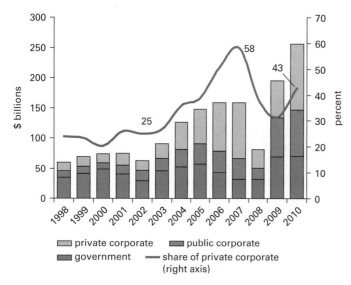

□ private corporate   ▨ public corporate
▨ government   —— share of private corporate
                              (right axis)

Source: Dealogic DCM Analytics.

September 2010, 851 privately owned emerging-market firms raised a collective $502 billion in international bond markets, while 165 state-owned emerging-market firms issued $261 billion

in debt. Even though the amount of international bond issues by these firms has grown in recent years, emerging-market private firms accounted for only 3.4 percent of the total value of global corporate bond issues between 2003 and 2009. Syndicated loans remain the primary source of financing for globally active emerging-market firms (figure 2.18).

The past decade has put a spotlight on the difficulties that emerging-market firms face in accessing international bond markets. During the global boom that preceded the 2008 financial crisis, emerging-market firms faced higher borrowing costs than their counterparts in European Union (EU) countries (figure 2.19; see box 2.3 for data calculations). For bonds issued in euros, private emerging-market firms faced average spreads over German government bonds of 110 basis points, as compared with spreads of 58 basis points for issues by firms from EU countries. For bonds issued in U.S. dollars, emerging-market firms paid a spread of 315 basis points over U.S. Treasury securities, while euro area companies paid only 55 basis points.[23]

A cross-sectional comparison of spreads on corporate bonds versus the per capita income of home countries also shows that private firms based in developed economies pay significantly lower spreads on their bonds than do private firms based in emerging economies (figure 2.20). As can be expected, firms in countries with low sovereign risk ratings (that is, with market perceptions that sovereign risk is relatively high) tend to face higher spreads (figure 2.21). This suggests that countries with high sovereign risk impose a negative externality on their corporate sector, underlining the importance of policies to enhance macroeconomic stability and improve market confidence.

Emerging-market firms also appeared to be more vulnerable to credit conditions during the global financial crisis. Although the crisis led to a widening of corporate bond spreads in both emerging and developed economies, the impact of the crisis was particularly great on investment-grade bonds issued by firms based in

FIGURE 2.18 International debt financing by emerging-market firms, 2000–10

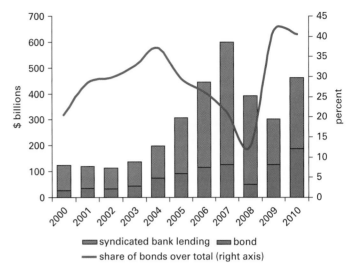

Source: Dealogic DCM Analytics and Loan Analytic s.

FIGURE 2.19 Average at-issue spreads of international private corporate bonds, by currency, 2003–07

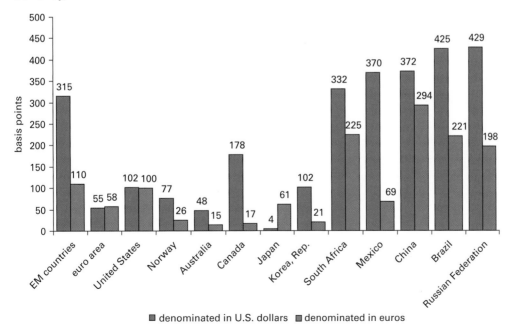

Source: World Bank staff estimates based on data from Dealogic DCM.

BOX 2.3   Data on international bond issues by firms

The analysis of factors driving international bond issuance by emerging-market firms is based on an exhaustive sample of global corporate bond offerings originating from 61 emerging-market countries (see annex 2.1 for data sources and methodology). The sample contains a total of 3,541 emerging-market corporate bonds issued between 1995 and 2009 and denominated in U.S. dollars or euros. Different currency and maturity tranches within a single bond issue are treated as separate issues because the financing raised would not be fungible across tranches.

Issuance data are drawn from Dealogic DCM Analytics and Bloomberg, which provide information on bond issues' terms, ratings, legal structure, placement and listing characteristics, pricing details, issuer attributes, among other characteristics. To ensure data integrity, pricing information and bond terms have been cross-checked between DCM and Bloomberg and incomplete data on spreads have been filled in by calculating the difference between a bond's at-issue yield-to-maturity (calculated from the terms of the issue) and the relevant benchmark yield.

FIGURE 2.20   Private bond spread versus GDP per capita

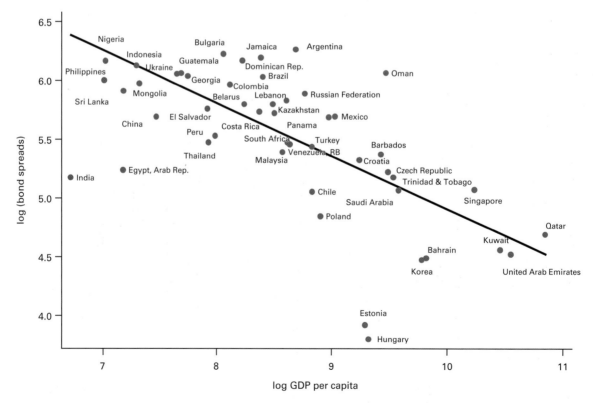

Source: World Bank staff estimates based on Dealogic DCM database and IMF IFS database.

FIGURE 2.21 Private bond spread versus sovereign risk rating

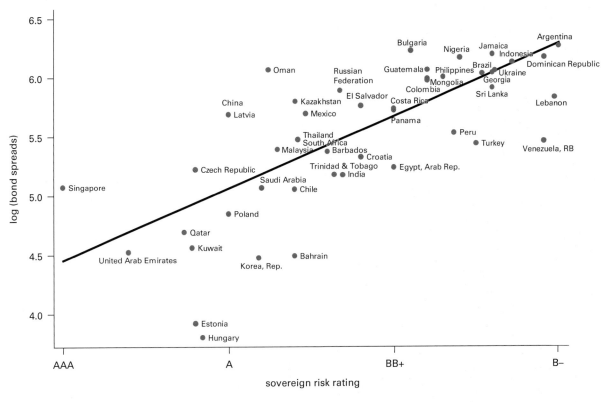

Source: World Bank staff estimates based on Dealogic DCM database.

emerging markets, for which the average spread jumped by 260 basis points from 2007 to 2009, while the spread on investment-grade bonds issued by U.S. companies rose only by 73 basis points (figure 2.22). In contrast, the average spread on non-investment-grade bonds issued by emerging-market firms rose by less than the spread on non-investment-grade bonds issued by U.S. firms, although this was most likely because the least creditworthy emerging-market borrowers tended to be shut out of the market entirely.

Although these simple comparisons of spreads on emerging-market and advanced-country bonds and economic variables are useful, econometric analysis provides deeper insights into the determinants of bond spreads (box 2.4). Because investors' risk perceptions, issue design, and placement process affect the pricing of debt securities, five groups of variables

typically determine bond offerings' at-issue credit spreads, as follows:

- Debt security terms and design attributes, including maturity, amount, seniority, coupon, offering terms and legal provisions, listing, applicable law and jurisdiction, and bond risk rating
- Macroeconomic factors for each issuer's home country[24]
- Variables capturing the degree of financial, legal, and institutional development of each issuer's home country
- Global economic and financial conditions, such as market volatility, liquidity supply and demand, global business cycle
- Industry sector of the issuers

This analysis presented in box 2.4 shows that higher GDP per capita or GDP growth in the

BOX 2.4   Econometric estimations of corporate bond spreads

The econometric analysis of corporate bond spreads relies on five groups of explanatory variables to explain the determinants of the at-issue spreads for various linear specifications. The estimation is carried out by ordinary least squares with country and sector fixed effects, and clustered standard errors adjusted for heteroskedasticity across countries. For readability, all country and sector fixed effects are suppressed from the tabulated results. The estimated system of linear equations for emerging markets is specified as follows:

$$Y_{ijt} = \alpha_j + \beta X_{jt} + \varphi I_{jt}$$
$$+ \eta Z_i + \lambda G_t + \varepsilon_{it}.$$

In this model, Y_{ijt} is the at-issue credit spread over the yield of a maturity-matched U.S. Treasury security (or, in case of a euro issue, a maturity-matched German government bond) of bond i, issued by a company domiciled in country j at time t. X_{jt} denotes macroeconomic factors of the issuer's home-country economic indicators, including the log of per capita GDP, log of inflation, real growth, and the home country's level of financial development (stock market capitalization or turnover and private credit, all as a percentage of GDP); I_{jt} denotes institutional factors, which capture the quality of the issuer's home-country legal, political, financial, and economic institutions, measured by composite indexes (constructed from principal components analysis) of the Worldwide Governance Indicators (WGI) or the *International Country Risk Guide* (ICRG) indexes of economic, financial, and political stability. Z_i denotes bond-specific features, including a set of variables relating to the issue's marketing choice, such as binary variables for the market segment (that is, Eurobond, 144A issue, or global bond), currency of denomination (U.S. dollars versus euros), the applicable law and jurisdiction (New York, United Kingdom, or other governing law), listing choice, and a set of control variables pertaining to the terms of the issue [coupon, log(amount), log(maturity), rating, seniority, call or put, common covenant provisions, and guarantees]. G_t denotes global risk factors, including market volatility (compiled by World Bank staff), the difference between 10-year and 2-year U.S. Treasury bond yields, and growth of the world industrial production index. a_j is the country dummy; e_{it} is the error term. The results are reported in table B2.4.1.

TABLE B2.4.1   Detailed econometric results for regressions on spread determinants

	ICRG model	WGI model
Bond attributes (selected variables)		
Floating-rate notes	−117.453***	−114.375***
	(0.000)	(0.000)
Euro-denominated	−3.46	0.408
	(0.799)	(0.976)
Log (maturity)	8.102	4.896
	(0.166)	(0.404)
Log (value, $ millions)	−25.682***	−25.881***
	(0.000)	(0.000)
Credit rating at launch	25.606***	25.276***
	(0.000)	(0.000)
Macroeconomic variables		
GDP growth (annual %)	−4.135*	−6.617***
	(0.026)	(0.000)
Log (GDP per capita)	52.880**	15.611
	(0.005)	(0.388)
Log (1+inflation)	304.538**	452.670***
	(0.004)	(0.000)
Stock market turnover as % of GDP	0.318*	0.492**
	(0.042)	(0.002)
Private credit as % of GDP	−1.266**	−1.265**
	(0.005)	(0.007)
Institutional factors		
ICRG composite index	−10.439***	
	(0.000)	
Worldwide Governance Indicator (WGI)		−93.138*
		(0.014)
Global factors		
Country crisis dummy	4.97	16.506
	(0.804)	(0.405)
Volatility[a]	39.232***	40.193***
	(0.000)	(0.000)
Difference between 10-year and 2-year U.S. Treasury bond yields	31.431***	34.648***
	(0.000)	(0.000)
World industry production index (%)	−9.013***	−9.442***
	(0.000)	(0.000)
Pseudo R^2	0.66	0.65
Observations	1,623	1,623

Source: World Bank staff estimates.

Note: The models are estimated with country fixed effect; sector dummies and country dummies are not reported; p-values are shown in parentheses.

a. Volatility is the monthly average of the first factor from a factor analysis using eight variables: VIX, dollar/euro, dollar/yen, dollar/sterling, agriculture commodities price index, energy price index, industrial metals price index, and the TED spread.

* $p < 0.05$, ** $p < 0.01$, *** $p < 0.001$.

FIGURE 2.22   U.S. dollar corporate bond spread to benchmarks, 2000–10, average by year

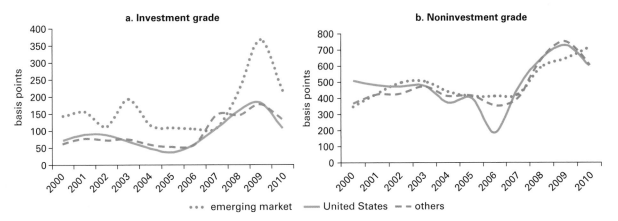

Source: World Bank staff calculations based on Dealogic database.

home country of emerging-market firms is significantly associated with lower spreads. As domestic economic conditions improve, firms' growth opportunities improve, reducing credit risk and thereby lowering borrowing costs. However, corporate borrowers from emerging markets pay a significant inflation premium. This result is consistent with the notion that international investors treat the level of home-country inflation as a signal of economic and financial stability. Since inflation distorts economic decision making and imposes significant economic costs on firms, the finding suggests that prudent monetary and fiscal policies can reduce the borrowing costs of firms in emerging markets.

The quality of institutions (as measured by the ICRG [*International Country Risk Guide*] composite country index—the higher, the better) significantly reduces credit spreads. The more developed a country's institutions are and the more reliable its legal system is, the lower international borrowing costs typically are for that country's firms. The quality of the legal system is especially important in the case of financial distress and restructuring, which often requires recourse to the home country's legal system to enforce liens, guarantees, and security interests. Analysis using the six dimensions of governance measured by the Worldwide Governance Indicators also finds a significant impact of institutional quality on bond spreads.[25] Interestingly, global investors

seem to disregard whether the issuer's home country experienced a financial or economic crisis in their pricing of emerging-market corporate debt. This result is probably due to selectivity effects: only firms with good economic prospects are able to access global debt markets, but such borrowers typically tend to have less exposure to their home economies than to the global business cycle.

Emerging-market borrowers that are willing to retain certain risks by issuing floating-rate debt appear to benefit by significantly lowering their borrowing costs. Floating-rate debt often contains a rating trigger that adjusts the spread over the reference interest rate at the next reset date in case the issue is downgraded by one of the major rating agencies, partly compensating investors for their credit exposure. For purchasers of emerging-market debt, this mechanism can be quite valuable, as emerging-market firms are often perceived as more vulnerable to changes in economic and business conditions and, hence, riskier investment propositions. Similarly, investors often are willing to pay a liquidity premium for larger issues, which are more easily traded and thus enable investors to adjust their portfolios in case of changes in the economic prospects of the issuer, the home country or region of the issuer, or global conditions. And it is not surprising that the absence of negative pledge causes, which reinforce creditor rights over collateral and provides assurances over the seniority of their claims, increase borrowing costs. Investors are willing to compensate borrowers, who will not pledge any of its assets if doing so gives the lenders less security, through lower spreads.

These findings have two important implications for emerging-market firms. First, as emerging economies continue to grow more rapidly than developed countries, and as emerging economies achieve continued improvements in their domestic institutions, their access to international bond markets will continue to improve. As time goes by, emerging-market firms will see their bond spreads fall closer to their advanced-country counterparts, and will suffer a smaller reduction in access during global recessions.

Second, this process is not automatic. Governments can play an active role in improving access to finance for their corporate sectors by investing in institutional development and providing a stable business environment. Improvements in the quality of institutions, economic stability, and the reliability of the legal system can play a critical role in reducing the spreads faced by emerging-market firms. For borrowers from advanced countries, investors typically take the existence of a stable business environment and well-functioning legal systems for granted. The goal for emerging markets is to achieve the increases in income and improvements in institutions that will provide similar levels of investor confidence.

Devising an Effective Framework for Cross-Border Investment
The proliferation of bilateral investment treaties

The rapid increase in global FDI flows since the 1970s has underlined the importance of a framework that governs cross-border investment flows. As emerging-market corporations play a growing role in global investment and finance, the need for a formal framework, especially one that provides adequate legal protection for foreign investors, has increased.[26] Unfortunately, unlike the case for international trade, efforts to agree on a multilateral framework for investment have a long history of failure (box 2.5). The reasons for

the various failures differ, of course, but largely reflect the difficulties in achieving consensus across governments at different levels of economic development, different views and interests in the definition of investor rights and protections, and disagreements over the extent to which such codes should be binding.

In the absence of a multilateral framework on cross-border investment, bilateral investment treaties have emerged as the dominant mechanism governing cross-border investment flows. The first BIT was signed between Germany and Pakistan in 1959. By the mid-1980s, the number of BITs had increased to 250, and their use continued to expand rapidly (figure 2.23). By 2007, BITs had increased to more than 2,275 in number, covering some 170 countries. Over the entire period, a majority of BITs were concluded between an advanced and a developing economy. Among advanced economies, European countries have signed more than 90 percent of all BITs, with Germany, Switzerland, the Netherlands, France and the United Kingdom leading the way (figure 2.24).

While provisions within each BIT differ, the BITs generally provide for most favored nation treatment, grant protection for investors' contractual rights, allow the repatriation of profits, restrict the use of performance requirements, and provide international arbitration in the case of a dispute between an investor and the host country (Elkins, Guzman, and Simmons 2006).

BITs indicate a credible commitment to a liberal investment regime on the part of a host country, and thus can serve as a means of attracting foreign investment. Though some econometric analysis finds that BITs have only a weak role, or no role in encouraging greater foreign investment in developing countries, on average (UNCTAD 1998b; Hallward-Driemeier 2003), others have found that BITs with stronger investment provisions, especially those that guarantee market access for FDI, have in fact been associated with stronger cross-border investment flows (Berger et al. 2010; Salacuse and Sullivan 2005). Nevertheless, it is important to recognize that BITs have important costs. BITs can require governments to restrict the scope of sovereign economic policy making in areas such

BOX 2.5 The long history of failed negotiations over a multilateral investment framework

The first attempt to design an international framework for investment was through the 1929 League of Nations conference, which was held in response to the nationalization and protectionism that increasingly characterized international economic relations through the 1920s. That conference failed to reach consensus on an international agreement on the treatment of foreign enterprises and foreigners (UNCTAD 1998a; Woolcock 2007).

Twenty years later, the Havana Charter for an International Trade Organization signed by more than 50 countries in 1948, sought to "encourage the international flow of private capital for investment" and to provide a multilateral framework for addressing the activities of foreign firms. As envisaged, the International Trade Organization would have been endowed with the role of developing and promoting the "adoption of a general agreement or statement of principles regarding the conduct, practices and treatment of foreign investment," and would have incorporated a formal mechanism for addressing violations of its charter. However, the Havana Charter never came into force, largely due to the inability of the U.S. Congress to support its ratification. Lack of provisions for protection or compensation of investors in the event of expropriation was an important reason for opposition to the treaty (Metzger 1968).

As cross-border investment flows between advanced economies surged in the 1980s and early 1990s, there was a revival of the international debate on whether an effective multilateral FDI framework should (or could) be established. Multilateral codes that dominated the debate during this era, such as the Organization for Economic Co-operation and Development (OECD) Guidelines for Multilateral Enterprises and the draft United Nations Code of Conduct for Transnational Corporations (the UN Code),

were voluntary and not enforceable. In fact, the UN Code never went into effect and was abandoned in the early 1990s after nearly two decades of unsuccessful negotiations. The OECD Guidelines were formally adopted, but they are essentially a set of recommendations governing the activities of multinational companies in OECD member countries and, like the draft UN Code of Conduct, focused mainly on the activities of the corporations rather than on the obligations and responsibilities of nation states.

Although the Uruguay Round of the GATT (1986–94) adopted an agreement that banned the imposition of Trade-Related Investment Measures (TRIMS) that were inconsistent with GATT's Article III on national treatment or Article XI on the elimination of quantitative restrictions (Salacuse and Sullivan 2005), its purpose was to avoid the imposition of local content and trade balancing requirements for approval or operation of a foreign investment project. Until the Uruguay Round, the GATT did not address cross-border investment issues at all, and the limited negotiations on cross-border investment flows within the context of the Uruguay Round did not move the international community closer to a comprehensive set of rules on FDI. The General Agreement on Trade in Services (GATS) also has some provisions that affect investment, although it is limited in scope to cover services sectors. Moreover, while governments can make commitments under the GATS concerning national treatment and the stability of the policy framework for foreign investment in particular services sectors, there is no requirement that they do so. All parties to the GATS do commit to providing most-favored-nation treatment to investors from other parties. But this implies no commitment concerning the treatment of investors in general, and also does not exclude the granting of concessions to particular investors (Molinuevo 2006).

as discriminatory taxation, performance agreements, local content requirements, and expropriation. In addition, the commitment to international arbitration means that virtually any legal or regulatory provision that affects foreign investors is potentially subject to review by a foreign tribunal.

Toward a multilateral investment framework

Building on the progress achieved in creating a multilateral legal framework for the settlement of international investment disputes under the International Center for the Settlement of

FIGURE 2.23   Total number of active bilateral investment treaties, 1980–2007

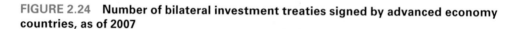

Source: International Centre for the Settlement of Investment Disputes, Database of Bilateral Investment Treaties.

FIGURE 2.24   Number of bilateral investment treaties signed by advanced economy countries, as of 2007

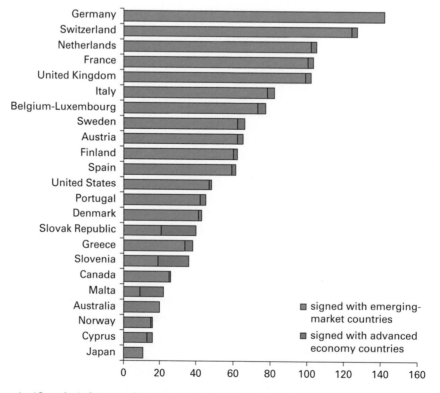

Source: International Centre for the Settlement of Investment Disputes, Database of Bilateral Investment Treaties.

Investment Disputes (ICSID) Convention, the time is ripe to move ahead with the establishment of a multilateral framework for managing cross-border investment flows. Such a framework will help improve investment climate and bring to fruition a goal that has eluded the international community since the 1920s.

The recent proliferation of BITs with relatively strong investor protection provisions is something of a puzzle, since many countries had, in earlier decades, rejected less onerous terms for investor protection when acting as a group (Guzman 1998). One possibility is that while governments are reluctant to make such concessions to all countries, governments are nonetheless willing to selectively enter into BITs that allow the governments to retain some control over the specific terms (Woolcock 2007). It is also possible that governments face considerable domestic pressures to make concessions on investor protections to a particular country that is (or could be) a major source of investment, while domestic incentives to make multilateral commitments may not be as strong (Elkins, Guzman, and Simmons 2006).[27] Another possible factor that may have given rise to the surge of BITs is competitive pressure. Countries acting in concert may block a multilateral accord, but may feel compelled to grant similar provisions in individual negotiations because of their desire to gain a competitive edge—or because of their fear of other countries doing so—in attracting FDI. Indeed, evidence suggests that host countries are more likely to sign BITs when their competitors already have done so (Elkins, Guzman, and Simmons 2006). Consequently, BITs are more common in countries that attract FDI in light manufacturing, where the investor has considerable choice in location, but less common in countries where FDI primarily targets oil and minerals sectors, where geographic choice is more restricted.

Whether this proliferation of BITs ultimately contributes to or detracts from the multilateral agenda is an open question. There is a large literature in international trade that suggests that bilateral arrangements can have trade creating or diverting effects, and therefore may be building or stumbling "blocs" for greater multilateralism.[28] Nevertheless, BITs are likely to be second-best solutions to a multilateral system,[29] as the large number of active BITs has increased the complexity of cross-border investment rules, and thus the costs of complying with those rules[30] (akin to the "spaghetti bowl" problem of an increasingly complicated global network of preferential trading arrangements). And, setting rules on a bilateral basis has eroded the negotiating position of the capital-importing countries, which bear the vast majority of obligations in these treaties but have become party to them in order to attract foreign capital (Woolcock, 2007)—despite having rejected less onerous terms for investor protection when acting as a group in earlier decades (Guzman, 1998). Moreover, constraints on policies inherent in BITs may have undermined development efforts. The evidence suggests that BITs have not only had little positive effect on economic growth and societal well-being in host countries, but may also even have had net negative effects, such as increasing uncertainty for host countries (Stiglitz 2008). In competing among themselves to sign BITs, developing host countries may have reduced the total gains to developing countries as a group.

To the extent that a multilateral mechanism could enhance the stability and predictability of cross-border investment flows, delineate clearer and more balanced lines of responsibility between host countries and investor firms (and their home countries), and provide a more fair means of resolving cross-border disputes, a multilateral investment framework would increase the supply of productive and development-enhancing foreign investment (Drabek 1998). But current trends offer a conflicting picture on the prospects for the legal framework for international investment.

Several recent studies find evidence of rising FDI protectionism in national polices, which may jeopardize even the imperfect rules-based approach to cross-border investment currently in existence, of which BITs form a core component.[31] On the other hand, in the Uruguay Round and the recent negotiations over the Doha Round, developing countries have been the major roadblocks to progress in establishing a multilateral investment framework. With developing countries having become an important source of foreign investment, opposition to a multilateral

FIGURE 2.25   The number of newly signed South-South BITs rose rapidly in the 1990s, ahead of the actual surge in South-South investment

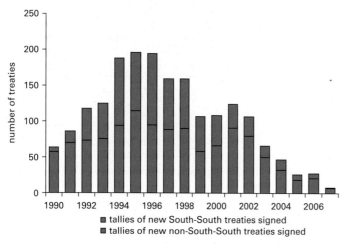

■ tallies of new South-South treaties signed
■ tallies of new non-South-South treaties signed

Source: World Bank staff estimates based on data sourced from the International Centre for the Settlement of Investment Disputes, Database of Bilateral Investment Treaties.

framework that protects investor rights may decline. The proliferation of new BITs between developing countries during the 1990s and early 2000s (figure 2.25) provides some evidence that developing countries are becoming more interested in forging rules for cross-border investment, as at least some provisions that are common across BITs could become viewed as generally accepted principles of international law (Salacuse and Sullivan 2005). This point is a controversial one, however. But as BITs with common provisions become even more widespread, and increasingly become integrated into the legal framework of participating countries, a case can be made that BITs deserve the same recognition of other principles that have become part of customary international law.

A more intriguing possibility is that BITs may themselves serve as stepping-stones to a more comprehensive multilateral investment framework. The elimination of investment restrictions via BITs may complement multilateral liberalization efforts. BITs may also facilitate the gradual building of a coalition of nations ultimately interested in a multilateral system. If BITs do indeed promote economic growth in otherwise investment-constrained economies, such growth

may reduce economic asymmetries between those nations and others, and hence make the investment-constrained economies more likely to accede to a multilateral platform. Finally, BITs may also change the domestic political economy by weakening interests arrayed against foreign investment flows. The existence of a formal multilateral institution—a world investment organization analogous to the World Trade Organization—may also be an important step forward, especially if such a multilateral forum enhances access by developing countries, especially LICs, to global investment capital.

Annexes

Annex 2.1: Database on the primary market for emerging-market international corporate bonds

The value of bonds issued by emerging countries on international markets has grown dramatically since the 1990s, making bond issuance one of the largest sources of capital inflows for developing countries. Although JP Morgan's Emerging Markets Bond Index provides dynamic information about the performance of emerging-market bonds on secondary markets, primary market information, which typically is more comprehensive, is essential for researchers to investigate the characteristics of these bonds and their implications for emerging countries and international financial markets. The World Bank's Database on the Primary Market for Emerging-Country International Corporate Bonds compiles data on 3,541 international corporate bond offerings (in tranches) issued by 61 emerging countries issued between 1995 and 2009 and denominated in either U.S. dollars or euros. Table 2A.1 shows the summary statistics of the key variables. The database offers consistent information on bond nationality, value, maturity, pricing, offer terms, legal provisions, applicable laws, credit rating, industries, and other areas (table 2A.2 contains descriptions of all the variables) obtained from Dealogic DCM Analytics and Bloomberg. Missing figures on the key spread-to-benchmark variable are carefully filled in by World Bank staff, making the database uniquely complete and consistent for studying emerging-market bond trends.

Methodology for filling in missing data. Of the universe of 3,541 emerging-country corporate bond observations included in the database, 1,413 (1,270 bonds issued in U.S. dollars and 143 bonds issued in euros) do not have spread-to-benchmark information available in the Dealogic DCM Analytics database. The missing spreads of these observations are calculated by the World Bank staff using bond pricing information from Dealogic or Bloomberg. The methodology for filling in the missing data is as follows:

Fixed-rate bonds
With yield-to-maturity available:
When an emerging bond's yield-to-maturity is available, a proper benchmark needs to be identified.

1. For bonds issued in U.S. dollars:
    U.S. Treasury bond yields with the same issue dates and terms are used as a benchmark. The bond's spread-to-benchmark is the difference between the emerging bond's yield-to-maturity rate at issuance and the benchmark Treasury bond yield-to-maturity.

    For instances in which the same terms and issuance dates for U.S. Treasury bonds are not available, the benchmark yield-to-maturity is interpolated by calculating the weighted average of closest long-term and short-term Treasury bond yields by year, as follows:

$$Y_b = x \cdot y_{g2} + (1-x) \cdot y_{g1}$$

where Y_b is the benchmark yield, Y_{g1} is the yield of closest short-term U.S. Treasury bonds, Y_{g2} is the yield of closest long-term Treasury bonds, and x is the weight of years to maturities of the closest long-term and short-term available government bond, calculated as follows:

$$M = \frac{(M - M_{g1})}{(M_{g2} - M_{g1})}$$

where M is the emerging bond's years to maturities, M_{g1} is the term of closest short-term Treasury bonds, and M_{g2} is the term of closest long-term Treasury bonds.

If no long-term or short-term Treasury bond is available, the yield of the Treasury bond with the most similar term is used as the benchmark.

2. For bonds issued in euros:
    German government bond (GGB) yields with same issue dates and terms are used as benchmarks for emerging bonds denominated in euros. The emerging bond's spread-to-benchmark is the difference between the emerging-bond yield-to-maturity at issuance and the benchmark GGB yield-to-maturity.

    The same interpolation method is used for bonds issued in euros as for bonds issued in U.S. dollars when the same issue dates and terms for GGB yields are not available. When the short-term GGBs are unavailable, one-year euro interbank rates are used for interpolation.

With yield-to-maturity not available:
When bond yield-to-maturity is not available, the yield-to-maturity is first calculated with coupon and payment information and then the same

TABLE 2A.1   Summary statistics of corporate bond issuance by emerging-market countries, 1995–2009

	Number of tranches	Total volume raised ($ billions)	Volume raised in U.S. dollars ($ billions)	Volume raised in euros ($ billions)	Average amount ($ millions)	Average spread (basis points)	Average maturity (number of years)	Average rating
Emerging countries	3,541	896.9	784.0	112.9	253.3	300.7	7.4	BBB–
Public corporate	765	290.2	239.3	50.9	379.3	220.6	7.7	BBB+
Private corporate	2,776	606.7	544.7	62.0	218.6	322.8	7.3	BBB–

Source: World Bank staff estimates.

TABLE 2A.2   Definitions of key variables included in the database

Variable name	Definition
Bond pricing variables	
Spread-to-benchmark/ discount (BP)	Spread between coupon rate of the security and government bonds or benchmark, expressed in basis points (the methodology for filling in missing data for this variable is shown in the notes)
Coupon (%)	Coupon rate of the security (%)
Offer price (%)	Percent of the face value of a tranche that is offered to public
Benchmark	The government bond spread over which the spread of the security at launch
Yield-to-maturity	Rate of return on a security assuming it is held until maturity
Basic bond characteristic variables	
Total deal value $ (face)	Total value (in $) offered of all tranches of a deal
Total deal value $ (proceeds)	Total proceeds (in $) offered of all tranches of a deal
Tranche value $ (face)	Principal amount of a tranche (in $)
Tranche value $ (proceeds)	Face value of a tranche multiplied by offer price percentage (in $)
Deal pricing date	Date the security is priced
Maturity date	Legal maturity date of a tranche
Years to maturity	Number of years from settlement date to legal maturity date
Deal type	Type of security being sold in the offering
Currency code	"USD" for a security denominated in U.S. dollars or "EUR" for a security denominated in euros
Float (Y/N)	Indicates whether coupon rate is a floating rate
Covenant and legal fields	
Governing laws	National, state, or provincial laws under which terms of a new issue are agreed
Amortization (Y/N)	For asset-backed and mortgage-backed securities, indicates whether a given tranche of a security has been amortized (gradual repayment over time)
Callable (Y/N)	Indicates whether the issue is callable by the issuer
Collateralized (Y/N)	Indicates whether a given tranche on a security is backed by collateral
Cross-default issuer (Y/N)	Indicates whether the issue contract contains a clause for cross default by the issuer
Cross-default guarantor (Y/N)	Indicates whether the issue contract contains a clause for cross default by the guarantor
Extendible (Y/N)	Identifies whether a bond's maturity can be lengthened at the option of the issuer
Rule 144A (Y/N)	Indicates whether tranche is marketed in the United States via Rule 144A
SEC registered (Y/N)	Identifies whether an issue has been sold in the United States under SEC rules
Negative pledge issuer (Y/N)	Indicates whether the issue contract contains a negative pledge issuer clause
Market type	Code of the market in which the issue is sold
Risk information	
Effective rating (current)	Calculated rating based on available ratings from Standard & Poor's, Moody's, and Fitch at time of downloading (March 2010)
Effective rating (launch)	Calculated rating based on available ratings from Standard & Poor's, Moody's, and Fitch at launch
High yield (Y/N)	Indicates if a tranche has a credit rating below investment grade
Investment grade (Y/N)	Indicates if a tranche is rated at or above investment grade
Issuer	Name of the issuing company
Issuer business description	Business description of the issuer
Issuer type	Code representing the general description of issuer
Issuer parent	Name of the parent company if the issuer is a subsidiary
Guarantor	Name of the guarantor company
Guarantor type	Code representing the general description of the guarantor
Specific industry group	Specific industry of the issuer
General industry group	General industry of the issuer
Use of proceeds	Description of the issuer's intended use for the capital raised on a tranche
Nationality information	
Deal nationality	Business nationality of the issuing entity (guarantor nationality, issuer parent nationality of operations, or nationality of risk)

Source: World Bank and Dealogic DCM database.
Note: SEC = U.S. Securities and Exchange Commission.

method described in part is applied to obtain the spread-to-benchmark.

1. If coupon and coupon frequency information is available, the following formula is used to calculate the yield-to-maturity:

$$Y = \frac{\left(\dfrac{redemption}{100} + \dfrac{coupon\ rate}{coupon\ frequency}\right) - \left(\dfrac{par}{100} + \dfrac{A}{E}\cdot\dfrac{coupon\ rate}{coupon\ frequency}\right)}{\dfrac{par}{100} + \dfrac{A}{E}\cdot\dfrac{coupon\ rate}{coupon\ frequency}}$$

$$\cdot \frac{coupon\ frequency \cdot E}{DSR}$$

where A is number of days from the beginning of the coupon period to the settlement date, DSR is number of days from the settlement date to the redemption date, and E is number of days in the coupon period.

2. For perpetual bonds, the following formula is used to calculate the yield-to-spread:

$$Y = \left[\left(1 + \frac{\dfrac{coupon\ rate}{100}}{coupon\ frequency}\right)^{coupon\ frequency} - 1\right] \cdot 100 \cdot \frac{100}{offer\ price}$$

Floating-rate bonds. For floating bonds denominated in either U.S. dollars or euros, when coupon information is available, the spread is calculated using the following formula:

$$Spread = \frac{(100 - offer\ price)}{Years\ to\ maturity} + coupon\ spread$$

Annex 2.2: Cross-border equity listings show shift in capital flows to China and other BRICs

Within an overall trend of increase in the number of listed foreign companies on international exchanges over the past few decades, a few discernible shifts in issuance activity in recent years are notable.[32] First, an increasing share of total new foreign company listings and depository receipt issuance worldwide has tended to take place on non-U.S. exchanges, due largely to less stringent listing regulatory requirements. Second,

a major shift has been occurring in capital flows, from advanced to developing countries. Foreign companies domiciled in emerging-market countries, particularly China and other BRIC countries, increasingly have been prominent in seeking new listings and raising capital on international exchanges since 2004.

The majority of new listings by Chinese-incorporated firms on international exchanges over this period have been on the U.S. exchanges, with smaller, high-growth Chinese firms particularly prominent (figure 2A.1). Chinese companies accounted for two-thirds of new American Depository Receipts (ADRs) in 2007, 40 percent of new ADRs in 2008, and more than half of all new ADRs in 2009, as signs of recovery began to emerge in global financial markets, as well as three-quarters of new issues in January through May 2010.

Taking into account the large number of firms incorporated in offshore jurisdictions that

FIGURE 2A.1   Source of ADR issues on U.S. exchanges, 2000–10

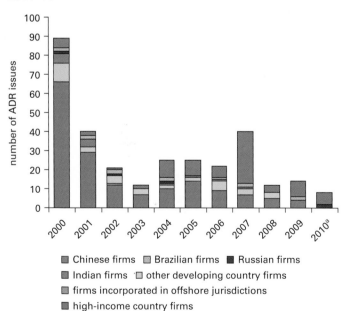

Source: BNY Mellon Depositary Receipts Division.

Note: "Offshore jurisdictions" include firms incorporated in Barbados, Bermuda, the British Virgin Islands, the Cayman Islands, Gibraltar, and the Virgin Islands (U.S.).

a. 2010 data are for the months January to May 2010.

have cross-listed on the London Stock Exchange (LSE), however, this exchange is likely to have attracted the largest total number of cross-listings by firms based in China.[33] Although no Chinese-incorporated firms have newly listed on the LSE since 2007, more than half of all new foreign company listings on the LSE Alternative Investment Market (AIM) in 2008 and two-thirds of such listings in 2009 were by firms that have incorporated in offshore jurisdictions, with many of these firms having their actual operations base in China and other developing countries (figure 2A.2).

In recent years, in continental Europe, Euronext also has been seeking to attract companies from rapidly growing emerging markets to its four market entry points in Amsterdam, Brussels, Paris, and Lisbon, and six of the eight emerging-market firms that have newly listed on Euronext since 2007 have been domiciled in China. These Chinese firms have been listing on Euronext to raise their visibility in specific European markets, as well as to raise capital to finance these market expansion plans. Newly listed Chinese companies accounted for 45 percent of the total capital raised by newly listed foreign firms on Euronext in the first five months of 2010. Germany's Deutsche Börse is actively seeking out listings by firms in China, as well as India and the Russian Federation, although high-income country firms have continued to predominate. Several notable issues in 2007–09 by Chinese firms resulted from engineering, biotech, agricultural processing, and a variety of other sectors, including at the height of the global financial crisis.

Annex 2.3: Database construction and analysis of emerging-market cross-border investment

The analysis of M&A activities of firms based in emerging-market countries draws on a new, comprehensive database that covers all publicly disclosed cross-border deals undertaken between 1997 and 2010. The database covers some 10,000 companies from 61 emerging-market economies. The data were drawn from a larger data set compiled by Thomson-Reuters SDC Platinum and cover all known transactions for which the ultimate acquiring company was based in an emerging-market country and the immediate target company was located in a country other than that of the ultimate acquirer. Those transactions involve either two or more companies pooling their assets to form a new entity (merger), or a foreign company gaining a portion of a domestic company (acquisition). The data include historical information on acquirer and target countries (both immediate and ultimate), status, sector, and consideration offered. Completed and partially completed deals were included, as well as intended and pending deals announced after September 1, 2009. When no deals were recorded for any country and year, the dependent variable was coded as zero. Selected records were corroborated with data from Bloomberg.

This list of some 10,000 emerging-market acquirer companies was then matched with data and information on their cross-border financing activities from the following sources: cross-border listings provided by major international stock exchanges (New York Stock Exchange, NASDAQ,

FIGURE 2A.2   Breakdown of tallies for new foreign company listings on the LSE AIM, 2000–10

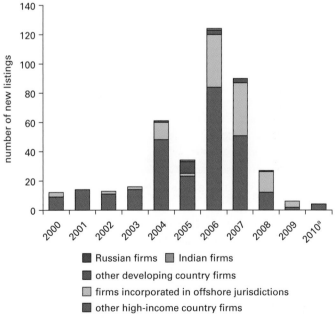

Source: World Bank staff estimates.
Note: Offshore jurisdictions include firms incorporated in Barbados, Bermuda, the British Virgin Islands, the Cayman Islands, Gibraltar, and the U.S. Virgin Islands.
a. 2010 data are for the months January to May 2010.

London Stock Exchange, Euronext, Luxembourg Stock Exchange, and Deutsche Börse); cross-border loan transactions (Dealogic Loanware); and international bond issues (Dealogic DCM). Of the emerging-market companies that undertook cross-border M&A deals, some 1,020 had directly accessed international capital markets through cross-listings of shares or depository receipts (185 companies), borrowing on international lending markets (809 companies), or bond issues on international bond markets (310 companies).

The cross-border greenfield investment data are sourced from the OCO Monitor (now fDi Markets) database (provided by the Multilateral Investment Guarantee Agency). Our data cover new outbound FDI projects and expansions of existing FDI projects by 5,000 companies from the same group of 61 emerging-market countries, undertaken between January 2003 and June 2010. Greenfield investment data include historical information on source and destination countries and on sector for each investment project. The same data sources also have been used by other researchers, including Mattoo and Subramanian (2010).

The definition used for cross-border M&A covers deals that involve an acquisition of any equity stake. This grouping includes those investments that resulted in an acquisition of less than 10 percent of a firm's voting shares. Additionally, both M&A and greenfield data include transactions with a target in any of the 35 tax-haven jurisdictions listed by the Organisation for Economic Co-operation and Development (OECD 2000). These tax-haven jurisdictions were the destination of 2.3 percent of all M&A deals and 1.4 percent of all greenfield projects. Finally, both M&A and greenfield data were cross-referenced against FDI figures from UNCTAD's 2010 issue of the *World Investment Report* for benchmarking purposes.

The econometric model distinguishes between deal flow to other emerging economies and deal flow to advanced countries by allowing for host country-specific coefficients:

$$Y_{ijt} = \alpha + \beta_k X_{it} + \gamma_k Z_{jt} + \delta_k R_{ijt} + \eta_k G_t + \varepsilon_{int}$$

The dependent variable, Y_{ijt}, is the total number of cross-border M&A deals originating in country i ("home"), defined as a country from the sample of 61 emerging countries, with targets in

country j ("host"), which is either an emerging country or an advanced country, in year t. The coefficients are allowed to vary by host-country class (developed markets, DM, or emerging markets, EM), so that $k = \{DM, EM\}$. X is the set of home-country characteristics, while Z represents host-country variables. R contains variables representing the economic relationship between home and host countries, such as bilateral investment treaties and bilateral trade. G represents global macroeconomic variables.[34] All specifications were estimated by ordinary least squares. The reported p-values are computed on the basis of standard errors that are clustered both in the country and time dimension to correct for heteroskedasticity across countries and for serial correlation within countries. Including these additional variables resulted in an unbalanced panel of between 21,884 and 34,730 observations, depending on the specification.

The results are reported in table 2A.3, for two alternative specifications: a parsimonious model with variables representing only the major hypotheses of interest, and a fully specified model with all variables of interest included. The table shows that firms clearly try to exploit differential growth opportunities abroad. The results are consistent with the first set of hypotheses: host-country GDP growth as a proxy for further growth opportunities significantly and positively influences acquisitions in advanced economies. In this case, the effect is twice as large for growth in host countries as in home countries, where the effect also matters for acquisition activities. Having attained certain growth rates at home, which allow firms to build up cash reserves for investment and acquisition purposes, the firms pursue growth opportunities through M&A deals in the better-performing advanced economies, thereby explaining the large positive growth coefficient. The size of home GDP as a proxy for economic maturity also influences acquisition activities. Interestingly, the effect is twice as large for acquisitions in developed economies as for acquisitions in emerging economies. Only firms from relatively large or mature emerging economies have the means to pursue expansion in advanced economies through M&A.

The level of host-country development, as measured by per capita GDP, negatively affects

TABLE 2A.3   Determinants of cross-border outbound M&A investments

	Emerging to emerging		Emerging to advanced	
	Fully specified	Parsimonious	Fully specified	Parsimonious
Home-country characteristics				
GDP per capita	−0.325	−0.832	−1.851	−1.066
	−0.786	−0.332	−0.267	−0.101
GDP	4.929***	2.956***	9.592***	5.121***
	−0.001	−0.003	−0.004	0.000
GDP growth	−0.654	−0.426	2.425**	0.829
	−0.273	−0.373	−0.016	−0.173
International reserves	−2.560***	−1.490***	2.711**	1.725***
	0.000	−0.004	−0.021	0.000
Economic risk rating	1.533**	0.740**	−2.664*	−0.432
	−0.019	−0.044	−0.097	−0.372
Political risk rating	−1.114*	−0.690	−0.847	−0.272
	−0.054	−0.103	−0.179	−0.332
Financial risk rating	−0.784		1.676	
	−0.123		−0.253	
Participation in global trade	5.815**	5.431**	2.539	1.947
	−0.013	−0.010	−0.369	−0.180
Market capitalization (% GDP)	2.065***	1.942***	6.895***	4.831***
	−0.002	0.000	−0.005	−0.003
Domestic credit to private sector (% GDP)	−0.836		3.558	
	−0.484		−0.221	
Private capital flows (% GDP)	0.158		−0.929	
	−0.677		−0.117	
Stocks traded, turnover ratio (%)	−0.309		−0.485	
	−0.166		−0.402	
Number of corporate bonds issued	−0.853		−5.201	
	−0.798		−0.444	
Sovereign risk rating	−9.679		−23.133	
	−0.201		−0.181	
Number of patents per million people	−5.045*		−2.217	
	−0.069		−0.339	
Host-country characteristics				
GDP per capita	−2.039***	−2.556***	0.626	0.527
	−0.007	−0.004	−0.275	−0.152
GDP	1.419	3.671*	0.380	0.781*
	−0.056		−0.484	−0.067
GDP growth	0.503	−0.093	5.698*	3.653*
	−0.566	−0.826	−0.060	−0.059
International reserves	0.648	−0.763**	−0.908**	−0.844***
	−0.572	−0.012	−0.012	−0.010
Economic risk rating	0.133	0.661	2.158	−2.590
	−0.886	−0.214	−0.377	−0.101
Political risk rating	−0.498*	−0.269	2.421***	1.375***
	−0.099	−0.251	−0.003	0.000
Financial risk rating	−0.570		−2.161*	
	−0.233		−0.087	

TABLE 2A.3   (continued)

	Emerging to emerging		Emerging to advanced	
	Fully specified	Parsimonious	Fully specified	Parsimonious
Participation in global trade	2.524**	2.864***	−11.420**	−2.237**
	−0.02	−0.007	−0.044	−0.045
Market capitalization (% GDP)	−0.489	−0.014	1.025*	0.930**
	−0.617	−0.980	−0.092	−0.050
Domestic credit to private sector (% GDP)	1.571		−0.015	
	−0.285		−0.229	
Private capital flows (% GDP)	0.104		1.633**	
	−0.603		−0.040	
Stocks traded, turnover ratio (%)	−0.910**		3.026***	
	−0.027		−0.004	
	Home-host relationship			
Distance	−1.488*	−1.602**	−1.205	0.301
	−0.088	−0.029	−0.460	−0.638
BIT dummy	1.125	0.590	1.063	0.388
	−0.126	−0.292	−0.417	−0.556
Bilateral trade (exports + imports)	3.010***	2.567***	0.464***	0.553***
	−0.003	−0.005	−0.002	−0.001
	Global variables			
U.S. 10-year Treasury rate	−3.595**	−1.189***	3.942	−2.220
	−0.026	−0.005		−0.625
Energy prices	−1.192*	−0.858***	−0.556	−1.440***
	−0.090	0.000	−0.546	−0.008
Agricultural prices	1.740*	1.208*	3.131*	−0.066
	−0.062	−0.063	−0.068	−0.948
Observations	21,884	34,730	21,884	34,730
R^2	0.298	0.280	0.298	0.280

Source: World Bank staff calculations, based on Thomson-Reuters SDC Platinum, World Bank World Development Indicators (WDI), IMF International Financial Statistics (IFS), IMF Direction of Trade Statistics, Bloomberg, Dealogic, Federal Reserve System, International Country Risk Guide, United Nations Conference on Trade and Development (UNCTAD), and World Intellectual Property Organization.

Note: Time and country-clustered *p*-values for standard errors (robust to heteroskedasticity and autocorrelation) are reported in parentheses. The fully specified specification includes only variable families with at least one statistically significant coefficient, although an even more comprehensive specification was used for exploratory purposes. * indicates significance at the 10 percent level, ** indicates significance at the 5 percent level, and *** indicates significance at the 1 percent level.

acquisitions in emerging destination countries but not in advanced countries (for which the variable is statistically insignificant). Firms only seek targets in emerging economies that have not yet attained a certain level of development, as measured by per capita GDP, and, therefore, offer even more growth potential. Taken together, these findings suggest that emerging-market multinationals expand abroad through M&A transactions to exploit growth opportunities that are not present in their home economies. Trying to escape the confines of their home markets, firms seek out fast-growing economies, especially among the advanced countries. The

effect is statistically and economically highly significant.[35]

The results also show that a country's participation in the global economy, as measured by its level of foreign currency reserves, also matters for bilateral M&A flows. Specifically, high levels of home-country reserves in emerging countries are positively associated with acquisitions in advanced countries, but negatively associated for other emerging countries. A country whose firms trade with advanced economies tends to build up foreign reserves faster, and the country's companies are more likely to engage in acquisitions in their target markets. Hence, underlying trade flows explain not only the correlation between reserves and M&A activity but also the large positive coefficient for advanced economies, whose level of economic exchange generates more reserves and acquisitions for emerging countries. At the same time, the orientation of trade and capital flows means that firms based in such countries focus on their operations in advanced countries to the detriment of acquisitions in other emerging economies, explaining the negative correlation between reserves and M&A activity in emerging countries.

The more its firms participate in global trade and, especially, in exports, the higher a country's foreign reserves, which are typically held in currencies of major importing countries, tend to be. At the same time, participation in global trade leads firms, over time, to acquire assets abroad as the logical consequence of their operations' internationalization. Hence, high foreign currency reserves are positively associated with trade with major reserve-currency countries. Having gained experience in international business through foreign trade, the next step is for firms to establish a more permanent presence abroad in order to facilitate corporate growth outside the home base. As a result, a country experiences the following positive feedback effect: a growing corporate presence of its firms abroad leads to new (intrafirm) trade and dividend remittances so that its foreign reserves rise even further. For acquisitions in other emerging countries, this pattern does not hold. As a country's foreign reserves rise with its maturing economy, with its focus often on export-led growth, its corporate sector increasingly engages in M&A in the developed world to the detriment of other emerging economies, thereby explaining the negative association between home-country reserves and acquisitions in other emerging markets. The negative coefficient of the host-country reserves in the advanced host-country equation is presumably a reflection of the structural financial account surplus (current account deficit) run by many of the most prominent target economies.

The results for a country's overall participation in the world economy, as measured by the country's ratio of trade (exports plus imports) to GDP, corroborate this interpretation. The higher a country's proportion of trade to GDP, the more

acquisitive its corporate sector tends to be, especially in pursuing targets in other emerging countries. The coefficients for host countries reveal that trade and FDI in the form of cross-border M&A may be either substitutes or complements. In the case of advanced economies, the more the host country participates in global trade, the fewer acquisitions from emerging-market firms the country tends to experience. Hence, trade and acquisitions are substitutes (negative coefficient), which is in line with the lower barriers to the movement of goods, services, and capital in advanced economies. In contrast, trade and M&A activity seem to be complements in emerging-host countries where barriers to the flow of goods and services tend to be higher. Hence, instead of exporting their products, firms export capital by establishing an operational presence in such countries, which explains the positive association between host trade and acquisitions.

Similarly, one would expect private capital flows to be associated with cross-border M&A activity. However, the results show that the variable is statistically significant only in the equation for advanced host countries. The more capital inflows an emerging-market home country receives, the less likely its firms are to engage in acquisitions in developed economies. Conversely, the more capital flows an advanced host country receives, the more likely it is to be the target of M&A activities by emerging-market firms. This finding suggests that emerging economies are either recipients or providers of global capital, but not both—in contrast to the case in many advanced economies.

A closely related effect is the positive correlation between bilateral trade and M&A flows. Trade not only signals the importance of a particular host country to firms in a given emerging economy but also serves as a stepping-stone for direct expansion of operations in the future. Firms exploit the relative expertise and the international competitive advantage which they gain through their participation in the global economy, by seeking more permanent ties with their trading partners, which the firms either integrate into their own operations or decide to serve locally through acquisitions. The quickest avenue for establishing a direct presence in an export market is therefore through the outright acquisition of assets in that country. Cross-border M&A activity therefore tends to increase with greater bilateral trade, which serves as a proxy for the importance of the host economy for a home country's corporate sector, in addition to the participation of a country's firms in the global economy. To further test this hypothesis, the specification includes the number of bilateral investment treaties that a particular home country has signed with advanced and emerging destination countries, respectively, although the variable is not statistically significant. Thus, economic ties such as trade matter more for cross-border M&A patterns than do legal ties such as treaties.

The findings regarding foreign reserves suggest that the home country's financial development also matters for its corporate sector's cross-border acquisitions. In particular, the effects are also consistent with the notion that foreign acquisitions are positively related to emerging-market firms' access to funds, for which reserve levels can also proxy. To further explore this hypothesis, the specifications include measures of stock and credit market development in acquirers' home countries. The results show that, indeed, more developed home capital markets—which facilitate raising the requisite financing, as measured by the ratio of stock-market capitalization to GDP—increase deal flow both in developed and emerging host countries. By contrast, the ratio of private credit to GDP as a measure of credit-market development is statistically not significant. The extensive funding in global markets by emerging-market firms later explored in the third section of this chapter might provide an explanation. Once a firm is sufficiently mature to contemplate expanding abroad through acquisitions, the firm typically also has access to syndicated loan markets or other forms of global funding.

To test the proposition that an acquirer's home economy needs to have attained a certain level of institutional development before its firms start to engage in cross-border M&A transactions, the analysis relies on the ICRG (*International Country Risk Guide*) indexes of political, economic, and financial risk. The results in table 2A.4 show that a home country's economic stability as measured by the ICRG economic index

positively influences M&A activity in other emerging countries but negatively influences M&A activity in advanced economies. When domestic economic conditions are risky (that is, if the ICRG index is low), firms will try to escape the vagaries of their home economy by expanding in developed countries. This finding is also consistent with the notion that cross-border acquisitions by emerging-market firms are partly driven by geographic diversification considerations. By investing in advanced economies with deep markets offering good corporate growth opportunities, firms can diversify away from their exposure to economic risks at home, while at the same time capturing scale economies.

Given that political stability is, in many respects, a prerequisite for economic and financial development, the absence of political stability stimulates cross-border M&A activity because firms strive to reduce their exposure to domestic risk factors and to diversify away from high levels of risk in their home countries. Consistent with this interpretation, the positive and significant effect of political stability on acquisitions in advanced countries seems to suggest that firms actively seek to lower their political-risk exposure through their M&A activities in developed economies. It seems counterintuitive, therefore, that lower political risk in emerging-market host economies is also associated with less cross-border acquisition activity. However, firms in stable emerging economies may see less need to acquire abroad, especially when growth opportunities are abundant at home; this likelihood may explain the negative coefficient in this case. Financial development and stability as measured by the ICRG financial risk index is not a factor, presumably because the direct measures of financial development in home and host economies capture the associated effects. All in all, the findings suggest that political, economic, and financial development significantly affect M&A activity in other emerging economies but not in advanced countries. Given the insufficient legal and economic infrastructure in many emerging countries, such stability is particularly important for acquisitions in other emerging economies. In contrast, advanced economies, with their vast markets and well-developed legal systems, are worthwhile destinations regardless of an originating country's level of institutional developThe models also include the distance between countries' capitals as a proxy for transaction costs,[36] as prior research has shown that the quality of an investor's or acquirer's information about a potential acquisition target decreases as the distance between the two countries increases, whereas the costs of communication, coordination, and monitoring all increase with distance. At the same time, firms tend to be more knowledgeable about the political, legal, and financial environments of economies in close geographical proximity to their own. Better information should reduce the cost of acquiring and operating subsidiaries. Hence, one would expect that the greater the physical distance between home and host country, the less bilateral M&A activity will occur. In fact, results of the analysis show that acquisition activity decreases in distance, but only for deal flow to other emerging countries. The transaction-cost conjecture is not borne out for advanced host countries for which the distance variable is statistically insignificant.

This finding also suggests that emerging-market firms investing in other emerging markets do so only in the vicinity of their home base. The difficulties of acquiring, integrating, and operating foreign assets in other emerging economies are such that any additional complications arising from obstacles to information acquisition or transmission reduce the attractiveness of acquisitions farther away. In contrast, acquisitions in advanced economies do not seem to be influenced by distance-related effects such as information or transaction costs. Not only are the legal and economic environment sufficiently developed, but managerial expertise also tends to be related to the operation of complex international business, and the requisite information is readily available in advanced markets. All these factors make it easier to overcome obstacles to acquiring and integrating firms located in advanced host countries. Taken together, the institutional and distance-related findings suggest that investment in economic, legal, and financial infrastructure—in itself a sign of a rapidly maturing economy—significantly enhances the internationalization of an emerging country's corporate

sector, which can lead to the important positive feedback effects further enhancing growth prospects at home.

Finally, technological achievements—as measured by the number of patents granted to a particular originating country—do not seem to have a pronounced impact on M&A, regardless of whether the home country is emerging or advanced. Acquisitions of firms located in advanced economies tend to aim at vertical integration; that is, the deals involve acquisition of either upstream or downstream assets. As a result, firms typically master the technologies so that innovation activities and the diffusion of technological advances have little impact on emerging M&A patterns, thus explaining the statistical insignificance of the patents variable in the advanced-country equation. In fact, technological achievement has a negative impact on acquisitions in emerging markets. This finding suggests that firms venture abroad for reasons other than their technological ability, such as to gain operational and managerial skills required to run large, vertically integrated operations on a global scale.

Notes

1. The literature on globalization strategy emphasizes the real-option aspects of such staged investments. The initial greenfield investment is a stepping-stone to understanding a local economy. Assuming demand, technological, geological, and other uncertainties are positively resolved over time, follow-up investments then create a permanent presence in the foreign market by extending the scope and reach of the initial unit. Lukas and Gilroy (2006) provide theoretical analysis on this phenomenon, while Brouthers and Dikova (2010) establish empirical evidence.

2. In member countries of the Organisation for Economic Co-operation and Development (OECD), by contrast, the private sector has funded 51 to 63 percent of R&D in each year since the early 1980s (OECD Stats).

3. "Residents" are broadly defined here as businesses, individuals, universities, and governments.

4. The picture is very similar for greenfield investments, with minor variations in the composition of the top 10 countries.

5. Unlike the data on the country of origin, the destinations of greenfield investments differ considerably from destinations of M&A transactions. Given that investments in developing countries dominate this type of FDI, it is unsurprising to find that BRIC countries (Brazil, Russia, India, and China) also are prominent destinations. Other emerging economies that have attracted a lot of greenfield investments in recent years, as measured by either value or number of investments, are the Arab Republic of Egypt, Indonesia, Kazakhstan, Libya, Malaysia, Nigeria, Saudi Arabia, Thailand, Tunisia, Ukraine, and Vietnam.

6. Recent representative deals in this sector include India's Bharti Airtel purchasing Zain Africa from the Kuwait Investment Authority, its largest shareholder; the Russian government buying a stake in Sistema Shyam TeleServices of India; and state-owned China Mobile Communications acquiring Pakistan's Paktel.

7. In 2010, state-owned Korea National Oil Corp launched the country's first cross-border hostile takeover, of U.K. oil group Dana Petroleum, with financing provided by five local banks. Similarly, CNOOC, a state-owned Chinese energy company, recently purchased 50 percent of Argentina's Bridas.

8. For instance, as of July 2010, Chinalco of China had plans to purchase a 50 percent stake in Rio Tinto's Simandou iron ore project in Guinea for $1.35 billion, while Vale, Brazil's iron and steel company, is paying $2.5 billion for 51 percent of another portion of the same Guinean deposit.

9. By category, the major divergence between greenfield and M&A transactions is the importance of real estate, which represents 25 percent of the total value of greenfield investments and a negligible amount of the value of M&A deals. The prominence of the sector is a reflection of real estate investments by Middle Eastern and Asian companies in emerging economies—particularly in economies in their own regions.

10. Greenfield investments by emerging-market firms also occur primarily within the same geographic region, although most greenfield investments go to other emerging markets.

11. When Tata Steel acquired Dutch steelmaker Corus in a hotly contested bidding war against Brazil's CSN Ratan Tata, the chairman of Tata group, explained, "We all felt that to lose would go beyond the group and it would be an issue of great disappointment in the country. So on the one hand, you want to do the right thing by your shareholders and on the other hand, you did not want to lose." (Leahy 2007)

12. Historically, most M&A investment into LICs has come from advanced economies. Many relatively large targets of M&A investment (the Democratic Republic of the Congo, Ghana, Kenya, Tanzania, and Uganda) have typically relied on flows originating mostly in the North. In contrast, regional sources have played a greater role in smaller markets (such as Malawi, Myanmar, Kyrgyzstan, and Zimbabwe).

13. This shift is documented in more detail in annex 2.2.

14. A total of 352 of the nearly 9,000 emerging-market firms or their affiliates that undertook acquisitions in the period between 1997 and the first half of 2010 are currently cross-listed on major international exchanges in the United States and Europe.

15. Brazil and Korea rank third and fourth, respectively, but the financing was raised by just a few firms in each country's case.

16. Russia has been the most common domicile country for firms raising financing on the LSE since 1995, with iron and steel manufacturing and mining (a sector in which the LSE has a longstanding international reputation as a market for raising finance) as the two most popular sectors in which the firms operate.

17. Some $172 billion was raised on China's exchanges by Chinese firms in the first 10 months of 2010, up from $100 billion in all of 2008.

18. In 2007, according to the World Federation of Exchanges, India's National Stock Exchange was the second-fastest-growing stock exchange worldwide, albeit starting from a low base, as it was established in 1993.

19. Stock exchanges in India and Singapore signed a memorandum of understanding in 2010 under which the exchanges will explore future areas for collaboration including ways to promote cross-border investment on their exchanges.

20. A number of new and expanded free trade agreements between Asian economies (including India and China) in recent years point to increased trade linkages between countries in the region.

21. In October 2010, SGX (Singapore Exchange) made an approved bid to acquire ASX (Australian Securities Exchange). The bid was motivated, on the part of both exchanges, by a desire to compete against HKEx (the stock exchange of Hong Kong SAR, China), and was based on their mutual intentions to benefit from synergies in revenue generation (drawing on the ASX's relative strength

in bonds and the SGX's wide range of derivative products) and to encourage currently listed firms to cross-list on the partner exchange.

22. The German and Indian stock exchanges agreed in 2008 to simplify access to their exchanges for companies in their respective markets. The links between the two exchanges were also tightened via Deutsche Börse's purchase of 5 percent stakes in the Bombay Stock Exchange.

23. The wider divergence between emerging-market corporates and euro area corporates in the U.S. market could in part reflect the impact of investor preferences on the composition of borrowers. If U.S. investors weight return more heavily than quality compared to European investors, then U.S. investors may be willing to lend to more risky companies, albeit at higher spreads.

24. The data are collected from a variety of sources and match the bond issuance by month, quarter, or year based on the available frequency. Note that the home country of a bond issuance is defined as the nationality of the issuer's parents or the nationality of the guarantor for guaranteed bonds.

25. The WGI, constructed by the World Bank Institute, includes indicators of six dimensions of governance: voice and accountability, political stability and absence of violence, government effectiveness, regulatory quality, rule of law, and control of corruption. The six indicators are measured in units ranging from about –2.5 to 2.5, with higher values corresponding to better governance performance.

26. Cross-border portfolio capital flows and banking flows raise other issues not considered here, such as the long-standing proposal to discourage short-term speculative flows by imposing a "Tobin tax" and whether capital controls should be imposed in a crisis situation.

27. In either case, it is clear that negotiating a BIT with a single country, or a treaty with a similar format with several countries, is less complicated than participating in multilateral negotiations.

28. Whether such arrangements enhance or undermine multilateralism depends on a host of factors, including the chosen structure of protection (Aghion, Antràs, and Helpman 2007; Kemp and Wan 1976), country asymmetries (Goyal and Joshi 2006; Saggi and Yildiz 2010), multilateral institutional support (Maggi 1999), and political economy considerations (Ornelas 2005). The empirical evidence finds that concerns that preferential liberalization may undermine multilateralism are generally unwarranted (Estevadeordal, Freund, and Ornelas 2008).

29. Alternatively, a world where BITs are widespread may actually be the only politically feasible form of multilateralism, and a second-best outcome that is welfare-superior to financial autarky (Ornelas [2008] makes the analogous case for trade). While this is certainly a possibility, the discussion here concentrates on the economically efficient first-best outcome (which may or may not be politically efficient).

30. Two decades ago, Salacuse (1990) referred to what was already an "increasingly dense network of treaty relationships," albeit, at the time, between capital-exporting industrial countries and developing countries. Efforts to standardize BITs have largely been unsuccessful.

31. Sauvant (2009) finds that countries that revised their national rules governing inbound FDI in such a way as to render the overall set of international regulations for investment less welcoming were the destination of some 40 percent of FDI inflows worldwide.

32. The overall trend of increase in foreign company listings on major exchanges over the past few decades reflects advances in trading technology, competition among exchanges, and companies' desire to list on major exchanges to boost international recognition and fund future M&A transactions.

33. One-third of the 285 foreign firms that cross-listed from 2005 to the second quarter of 2010 on the LSE's AIM, a market with less stringent regulatory and disclosure requirements for small-cap, growing companies, were incorporated offshore.

34. To address, albeit in a limited fashion, endogeneity concerns, the specification was also performed with one-period lagged explanatory variables. The results were qualitatively similar for almost all coefficients and are available on request.

35. To assess the findings' robustness, the model was also estimated with growth rates for specific sectors rather than GDP, but the results are not statistically significant and therefore not tabulated.

36. For country pairs involving dependent territories, the analysis uses the capital of the territory.

References

Aghion, Philippe, Pol Antràs, and Elhanan Helpman. 2007. "Negotiating Free Trade." *Journal of International Economics* 73 (1): 1–30.

Antràs, Pol. 2005. "Incomplete Contracts and the Product Cycle." *American Economic Review* 95 (4): 1054–73.

Berger, Axel, Matthias Busse, Peter Nunnenkamp, and Martin Roy. 2010. "More Stringent BITs, Less Ambiguous Effects on FDI? Not a Bit!" Working Paper 1621, Kiel Institute for the World Economy, Kiel, Germany.

Brouthers, Keith D., and Desislava Dikova. 2010. "Acquisitions and Real Options: The Greenfield Alternative." *Journal of Management Studies* 47 (6): 1048–71.

Del Duca, Louis F. 2007. "Developing Global Transnational Harmonization Procedures for the Twenty-First Century: The Accelerating Pace of Common and Civil Law Convergence." *Texas International Law Journal* 42 (3): 625–60.

Drabek, Zdenek. 1998. "A Multilateral Agreement on Investment: Convincing the Skeptics." WTO Staff Working Paper, ERAD-98-05, World Trade Organization, Geneva.

Elkins, Zachary, Andrew T. Guzman, and Beth Simmons. 2006. "Competing for Capital: Diffusion of Bilateral Investment Treaties, 1960–2000." *International Organization* 60 (3): 811–46.

Estevadeordal, Antoni, Caroline L. Freund, and Emanuel Ornelas. 2008. "Does Regionalism Affect Trade Liberalization toward Nonmembers?" *Quarterly Journal of Economics* 123 (4): 1531–75.

Frost, Tony S., Julian M. Birkinshaw, and Prescott C. Ensign. 2002. "Centers of Excellence in Multinational Corporations." *Strategic Management Journal* 23 (11): 997–1018.

Goyal, Sanjeev, and Sumit Joshi. 2006. "Bilateralism and Free Trade." *International Economic Review* 47 (3): 749–78.

Guzman, Andrew T. 1998. "Why LDCs Sign Treaties That Hurt Them: Explaining the Popularity of Lateral Investment Treaties." *Virginia Journal of International Law* 38 (Summer): 639–88.

Hallward-Driemeier, Mary. 2003. "Do Bilateral Investment Treaties Attract FDI? Only a Bit and They Could Bite Back." Working Paper 3121, World Bank, Washington, DC.

Harrison, Ann, and Jason Scorse. 2010. "Multinationals and Anti-sweatshop Activism." *American Economic Review* 100 (1): 247–73.

"Havana Charter for an International Trade Organization." Final act of the United Nations Conference on Trade and Employment held at Havana, Cuba. November 21, 1947–March 24, 1948.

Hope, Ole-Kristian, Wayne B. Thomas, and Dushyantkumar Vyas. 2011. "The Cost of Pride: Why Do Firms from Developing Countries Bid Higher?" *Journal of International Business Studies* 42 (1): 128–51.

Kemp, Murray C., and Henry Y. Wan Jr. 1976. "An Elementary Proposition Concerning the Formation of Customs Unions." *Journal of International Economics* 6 (1): 95–97.

Leahy, Joe. 2007. "Tata Warns Corus Jobs Not Guaranteed." *Financial Times*, Febrauary 2.

Lukas, Elmar, and Bernard Michael Gilroy. 2006. "The Choice between Greenfield Investment and Cross-Border Acquisition: A Real Option Approach." Quarterly Review of Economics and Finance 46 (3): 447–65.

Maggi, Giovanni. 1999. "The Role of Multilateral Institutions in International Trade Cooperation." *American Economic Review* 89 (1): 190–214.

Mattoo, Aaditya, and Arvind Subramanian. 2010. "Crisscrossing Globalization: The Phenomenon of Uphill Skill Flows." *Annual World Bank Conference on Development Economics 2009, Gobal: People Politics, and Globalization*. Ed. Justin Lin and Boris Pleskovic. Washington, DC: World Bank.

Metzger, Stanley. 1968. "Private Foreign Investment and International Organizations." *International Organization* 22 (1): 288–309.

Molinuevo, Martin. 2006. "WTO Disciplines on Foreign Investment: Wasn't the GATS about Trade in Services?" Universidad de Bolonia, Buenos Aires. http://phase1.nccr-trade.org/images/stories/publications/Molinuevo.Tesis%20UniBo.Wasnt%20the%20GATS%20about%20trade.pdf.

OECD (Organisation for Co-operation and Development). 2000. "Towards Global Tax Co-operation: Report to the 2000 Ministerial Council Meeting and Recommendations by the Committee on Fiscal Affairs—Progress in Identifying and Eliminating Harmful Tax Practices." OECD, Paris.

Ornelas, Emanuel. 2005. "Trade Creating Free Trade Areas and the Undermining of Multilateralism." *European Economic Review* 49 (7): 1717–35.

———. 2008. "Feasible Multilateralism and the Effects of Regionalism," *Journal of International Economics* 74 (1): 202–24.

Saggi, Kamal, and Halis Murat Yildiz. 2010. "Bilateralism, Multilateralism, and the Quest for Global Free Trade." *Journal of International Economics* 81 (1): 26–37.

Salacuse, Jeswald W. 1990. "BIT by BIT: The Growth of Bilateral Investment Treaties and Their Impact on Foreign Investment in Developing Countries." *International Lawyer* 24 (3): 655–75.

Salacuse, Jeswald W., and Nicholas P. Sullivan. 2005. "Do BITS Really Work? An Evaluation of Bilateral Investment Treaties and their Grand Bargain." *Harvard International Law Journal* 46 (1):68–129.

Sauvant, Karl P. 2009. "Driving and Countervailing Forces: A Rebalancing of National FDI Policies?" In *Yearbook on International Investment Law and Policy 2008–2009*, ed. Karl P. Sauvant, 215–72. New York: Oxford University Press.

Stiglitz, Joseph E. 2008. "Regulating Multinational Corporations: Towards Principles of Cross-Border Legal Frameworks in a Globalized World Balancing Rights with Responsibilities" (The Ninth Annual Grotius Lecture). *American University International Law Review* 23 (3): 451–558.

U.K. Department for Business, Innovation, and Skills. 2005. *R&D Scoreboard*. London: U.K. Department for Business, Innovation, and Skills.

———. 2010. *R&D Scoreboard*. London: U.K. Department for Business, Innovation and Skills.

UNCTAD (United Nations Conference on Trade and Development). 1998a. *Bilateral Investment Treaties in the Mid-1990s*. New York: United Nations.

———. 1998b. "Existing Regional and Multilateral Investment Agreements and Their Relevance to a Possible Multilateral Framework on Investment: Issues and Questions." United Nations, New York.

———. 2009. *World Investment Report: Transnational Corporations, Agricultural Production, and Development*. Geneva: United Nations.

———. 2010. *World Investment Report: Investing in a Low-Carbon Economy*. Geneva: United Nations.

Vernon, Raymond. 1966. "International Investment and International Trade in the Product Cycle." *Quarterly Journal of Economics* 80 (2): 190–207.

Woolcock, Stephen. 2007. "Multi-level Economic Diplomacy: The Case of Investment." In *The New Economic Diplomacy*, ed. Nicholas Bayne and Stephen Woolcock, 141–61. Aldershot, Hampshire, U.K.: Ashgate.

World Bank. 2008. *Global Economic Prospects 2008: Technology Diffusion in the Developing World*. Washington, DC: World Bank.

3

Multipolarity in International Finance

THE MANNER IN WHICH THE international monetary system evolves matters crucially for development policy and practice. It has direct implications for developing countries' access to international capital and the stability of their currencies. The 2008–09 financial crises exposed some of the structural weaknesses of the current international monetary system and underscored the need for reform.

Big issues are on the table, ranging from capital account convertibility and a choice of exchange rate regime in major emerging-market economies to methods of governance of the international monetary system, including the mechanisms for global liquidity creation, balance-of-payments adjustment, and decisions regarding the types of international reserve assets. At the core of these issues is the question of whether the current international monetary system will remain intact with periodic tweaking, or whether it will be fundamentally overhauled to accommodate the new realities of multiple growth centers, the growing role of transnational actors, and the increasing assertiveness by leading emerging-market economies on the global stage. With such transformations in the making, calls for "cooperative incrementalism" (Cooper 1976), as were common in the past, may not suffice in addressing the monetary challenges of a multipolar world economic order.

As the second decade of the 21st century unfolds, three fundamental considerations are emerging as central to the debate on the future shape of the international monetary system: first, the system's capacity to accommodate the growing economic power and active participation of leading emerging-market economies, including a possible global role for their currencies; second, the system's embodiment of the necessary institutional mechanisms to advance international cooperation, while reducing the risks of protectionism, currency wars, and political conflict; and third, distributional equity in promoting the particular developmental needs and objectives of low-income developing countries. Though all of these elements have long been intrinsic to international monetary policy making and discourse, the significance of these elements has increased in recent years as globalization of markets and industries has deepened policy linkages among countries.

This chapter maps out the implications of ongoing changes in the dynamics of global growth and wealth for the future course of international monetary and financial arrangements. In anticipating future trends, the chapter focuses on how and why currencies other than the U.S. dollar may become international reserve, invoicing, payment, and intervention currencies in the decades ahead. Although the hurdles that policy makers and markets must clear for a currency to gain international status are high, overcoming such challenges is increasingly within the realm of possibilities for selected economies in the emerging world. At present, the euro is a growing source of international competition to the U.S. dollar. Among emerging economies, China's renminbi is likely to take on a more important international role in the long term as part of a multicurrency international currency system, given the size and dynamism of China's economy and the rapid globalization of its corporations and banks into global trade and finance.

The main messages of the analysis presented in this chapter are as follows:

- *Looking ahead, the most likely scenario for the international monetary system is a multicurrency system centered around the U.S. dollar, the euro, and the renminbi.* Under that scenario, the dollar would lose its position as the unquestioned principal international currency by 2025, making way for an expanded international role for the euro and a burgeoning international role for the renminbi. The probability of this scenario playing out is buttressed by the likelihood, as outlined in chapter 1, that the United States, the euro area, and China will constitute the three major growth poles by 2025, providing stimulus to other countries through trade, finance, and technology channels, and thereby creating international demand for the U.S., European, and Chinese currencies. This scenario is contingent upon China and the euro area successfully implementing financial and structural reforms and managing their fiscal and monetary policies in a way consistent with the international status of their currencies. For euro area authorities, the incentive to undertake such reforms will be the desire to safeguard the gains of the long-running single-market project, while China will be motivated by the need to mitigate the significant risk of currency mismatch to which the country is currently exposed, as China's transactions with the rest of the world are denominated predominantly in dollars.

An international monetary regime anchored to three national currencies may offer the prospect of greater stability than does the present dollar-centered system, through better distribution of lender-of-last-resort responsibility and better provision of liquidity during times of distressed market conditions. In addition, diversifying the source of foreign exchange reserve supply may permit developing countries to meet their reserve accumulation objectives more easily, making their stocks of reserves less exposed to the risk of depreciation by any one of the reserve currencies. A multicurrency regime would also have the potential to command great legitimacy, but only if certain conditions were satisfied—namely, that countries issuing the main international

currencies manage global liquidity consistently with global growth and investment, that the same countries stabilize their bilateral exchange rates, and that those countries devise mechanisms for sharing the benefits of international currency status with other countries. Such benefits, including seigniorage income, lower costs of international borrowing, macroeconomic autonomy, and the privilege of running current account deficits with limited restraint, are potent. Estimates of seigniorage income for the United States arising from foreign residents' holdings of dollar notes alone have averaged around $15 billion per year since the early 1990s; the corresponding estimate for the euro area is in the order of $4 billion per year since 2002. In 2010, the United States is estimated to have benefited from a discount in its borrowing costs of $80 billion as a result of the dollar's international status.

- *Two opposing forces are affecting international monetary cooperation: on one hand, the contemporary international political system has broadened the scope for monetary cooperation across borders; on the other hand, the increasingly diffuse global distribution of economic power associated with multipolarity will render monetary cooperation more difficult.* In contemporary international politics—in which numerous national concentrations of power exist but no single center dominates—the deep connection between politics and currency arrangements that existed during the Cold War era has been replaced by an international monetary system ruled by economic interests. The prospect of successful international policy coordination in a multipolar world economic order, then, rests on the argument that economic interdependence has deepened with globalization, requiring strengthening of policy linkages. The feasibility of policy coordination depends on governments' ability to overcome the collective action problems of burden sharing and system maintenance.

In the years leading up to the 2008–09 financial crisis, the role of international economic policy making was confined to managing the symptoms of incompatible macroeconomic policies, such as exchange rate misalignments and payments imbalances. As capital markets have been liberalized and exchange rates made more flexible, balance of payments constraints on national economies have been considerably eased, thus shifting policy coordination toward the more politically sensitive sphere of domestic monetary and fiscal policies. Moving forward, countries with globally influential economies must be willing to accept the fact that their policy actions have important spillover effects on other countries. Thus, monetary policy initiatives that emphasize increased collaboration among central banks to achieve financial stability and sustainable growth in global liquidity would be particularly welcome. Agreeing on goals in such areas and communicating those goals to market participants would help anchor market expectations, reduce speculative capital movements, and bring about greater stability of exchange rates—the latter as the natural outcome, rather than the intermediate target, of enhanced international coordination.

- *The majority of developing countries, particularly the poorest countries, will continue to use foreign currencies to carry out transactions with the rest of the world, and thus will remain exposed to exchange rate fluctuations in a multicurrency international monetary system.* A multipolar global economy will not eliminate currency fluctuations, which disproportionately affect low-income countries with limited hedging possibilities. In fact, in the absence of coordinated efforts on behalf of the leading-currency economies, exchange rate movements may intensify, potentially leaving developing countries no better off than they are at present and continuing the great disparity between developing countries' growing strength in international trade and finance and their lack of influence in international monetary affairs. Alliance with one of the leading-currency countries, via a currency

peg or a monetary union, may reduce the risk for developing countries, however. In a best-case scenario, the evolving multicurrency regime would put into place mechanisms for limiting currency volatility through increased central bank coordination and the creation of instruments that facilitate hedging—for instance, through enhanced central bank swaps and the development of private markets for special drawing rights (SDRs). It is also important that the gains from international currency use be shared across countries of all income levels and that the adjustment of payments imbalances be made more evenhanded—that is, that such adjustments not fall mainly on the poorest countries, which are forced to conduct international transactions in currencies other than their own.

International Currency Use

For a national currency to serve an international role, the currency must garner demand beyond its own borders. The demand for an international currency, in turn, is related to its ability to satisfy the role of an international money with low transaction costs, while maintaining the confidence of private and official users in its value. A key property of financial markets is that the more the currency is used, the lower the transaction costs and the greater the liquidity associated with that currency become. Thus, there is a positive externality that tends to produce equilibria with only one or a few currencies in widespread international use (Hartmann 1998). Moreover, this externality can produce multiple equilibria, in which the circumstances of history lead to one currency being dominant for a number of years or decades (as the pound sterling was from 1860 to 1914), after which a triggering event may lead to a shift to another currency playing a dominant role (as the dollar has done from 1920 to the present). The property that currency use is reinforcing is more generally the property of networks in which there are economies of scale, and this property has been termed "network externalities" (Kiyotaki and Wright 1989). This property also helps to explain the continuing international use of the British pound even after the relative decline of the United Kingdom in the world economy: once a currency is widely used, it retains incumbency advantages that make it hard to displace.

International currency use parallels the domestic functions of money as the numéraire for establishing prices, serving as a means of payment, and providing a store of value (Cohen 1970; Kenen 1983). An international currency serves to invoice imports and exports, to anchor the exchange rate of currencies pegged to it, to effectuate cross-border payments, and to denominate international assets and liabilities (official foreign exchange reserves, private claims, and sovereign debt). In addition, just as domestic money serves as an alternative to bartering, an international currency can serve as a "vehicle currency" for trading between pairs of currencies for which the liquidity of the bilateral market is limited. Such uses are reinforcing, because currencies used for pricing are also likely to serve as means of payment.

The supply of international currencies is influenced by the actions of governments to allow international use and to provide the institutional and policy underpinnings that encourage the development of financial markets and produce macroeconomic stability (Tavlas 1991). Without the existence of markets in various financial instruments and a reasonable amount of investor confidence in accessing them, the currency's usefulness in the international realm is limited. But if those underpinnings exist, the supply of international currencies can be considered to be close to perfectly elastic: demand can be satisfied through facilities offered by banks and by issuance of domestic and foreign securities denominated in the currency. Conversely, attempts to stimulate international use of a particular currency will be unsuccessful in the absence of demand.

Several factors are correlated with the likelihood that a currency will become an international currency. In general, international currencies are issued by countries that have (1) low and stable inflation; (2) open, deep, and broad financial markets; and (3) a large share of world trade (and by implication, of world output).[1] The first and third factors are easy to measure, but the second factor is not, although market status is potentially no less important in determining whether a currency becomes an international currency.[2] Furthermore, the fact that inflation and trade tend to influence international currency use is by no means a new phenomenon; box 3.1 tracks those connections over more than 2,000 years.

From the perspective of an individual or entity holding an international asset, the attractiveness of a currency depends on both its ability to retain its value in terms of other currencies and its purchasing power. In addition, an international currency must be usable in the sense that official or privately held balances are easily convertible into other currencies through a variety of financial instruments with low transaction costs. Economic size is also linked to the development of international currencies, for at least two reasons. First, having a large economy gives a country market power and allows that country to denominate its trade in its own currency, forcing foreigners to absorb the impact of currency fluctuations; second, a large economy typically enhances the breadth and depth of domestic financial markets. Thus, the various economic factors are interdependent and reinforcing. By some accounts, wider political considerations (including military alliances and security) also play a role in determining international demand for a currency.

Measuring the importance of international currencies

At the present, the U.S. dollar remains the world's dominant currency. But since 2000, the euro has taken on a growing role in various international finance settings, most prominently as an issuing currency in global credit and debt markets (figure 3.1). The euro also represents an increasing proportion of the world's foreign exchange reserves (table 3.1) and more frequently serves as a vehicle currency for foreign exchange transactions than in the past (figure 3.2). *Global Development Finance 2006* (World

BOX 3.1 **Historically, one national currency has played a global role—or at most, a few national currencies**

Historical records indicate that the silver drachma, issued by ancient Athens in the fifth century B.C.E. was likely the first currency that circulated widely outside its issuing state's borders, followed by the gold aureus and silver denarius coins issued by Rome, even though the Athenian and Roman currencies circulated simultaneously for some time (see figure B3.1.1). The dominance of the Roman-issued coins was brought to an end as the long cycle of inflation that characterized the economy of the Roman Empire from the first century C.E. through the early fourth century led to a continuous devaluation of the Roman-issued currency, causing it to become increasingly less accepted outside the Roman Empire. Ultimately, the aureus became valued according to its weight rather than its imputed "face value," trading more as a commodity than a currency outside the Roman Empire and making way for the Byzantine Empire's heavy gold solidus coin to become the dominant currency in international trade in the sixth century. By the seventh century, the Arabian dinar had partially replaced the solidus in this role, although the solidus continued to circulate internationally at a debased value (reflecting the high financing needs of the Byzantine Empire) into the 11th century. Large fiscal costs also led to a gradual devaluation of the Arabian dinar starting at the end of the 10th century.

By the 13th century, the fiorino, issued by Florence, was widely used in the Mediterranean region for commercial transactions, only to be supplanted by the ducato of Venice in the 15th century. In the 17th and 18th centuries, the dominant international currency was issued by the Netherlands, reflecting that country's role as a leading financial and commercial power at the time. At that point, paper bills began replacing coins as the international currency of circulation, even though they were not backed by the Dutch government or any other entity under sole sovereign control.

It was only when national central banks and treasuries began holding gold as reserves, beginning in the 19th century, that bills and interest-bearing deposit claims that could be substituted for gold also began to be held as reserves. This development coincided with the rise of Great Britain as the leading exporter of manufactured goods and services and the largest importer of food and industrial raw materials. Between the early 1860s and the outbreak of World War I in 1914, some 60 percent of the world's trade was invoiced in British pounds sterling.

As U.K. banks expanded their overseas business, propelled by innovations in communications technology such as the telegraph, the British pound was increasingly used as a currency of denomination for commercial transactions between non-U.K. residents—that is, the pound sterling became a more international currency. This role for the pound was further enhanced

FIGURE B3.1.1   Historical Timeline of Dominant International Currencies

Source: Classical Numismatic Group, Inc., http://www.engcoms.com.

(continued)

BOX 3.1   (continued)

by London's emergence as the world's leading shipper and insurer of traded goods and as a center for organized commodities markets, as well as by the growing amount of British foreign investment, of which a large share was in the form of long-term securities denominated in pounds sterling.

At the beginning of the 20th century, however, the composition of foreign exchange holdings by the world's monetary authorities began to shift, as sterling's share declined and the shares of the French franc and the German mark increased. The beginning of World War I in 1914 is widely viewed as signaling the end of Great Britain's leading role in the international economy and the breakdown of economic interdependence. Despite attempts to revive the gold exchange standard after World War I and to restore an international monetary order based on fixed exchange rates, the restored system lasted only a few years.

The U.S. dollar's use internationally as a unit of account and means of payment increased during the interwar period, particularly during the 1920s, reflecting the growing role of the U.S. economy in international trade and finance. Although gold was officially the reserve asset (and the anchor) of the international monetary system following World War II, under the Bretton Woods system of fixed exchange rates, the dollar took on the mantle of dominant international reserve currency. By the early 1970s, however, following the breakdown of the system because of its inherent Triffin dilemma, the major economies moved to implement floating exchange rates.

During the 1980s, the global economy showed indications that it was moving to a multicurrency system in which the Deutsche mark was taking on an expanded role as a key currency, both in Europe and globally. This was due to a combination of factors—low and stable German inflation; credible government policies; deep, broad, and open financial markets; and a relatively high share of differentiated manufactured exports in Germany's trade. The introduction of the euro in 1999 and its adoption by a growing number of EU countries in the intervening years has only revived the debate about the dollar's future role as the dominant international currency.

FIGURE 3.1   Currency denominations of banks' international assets and international bonds outstanding, by percentage, 1999–2010

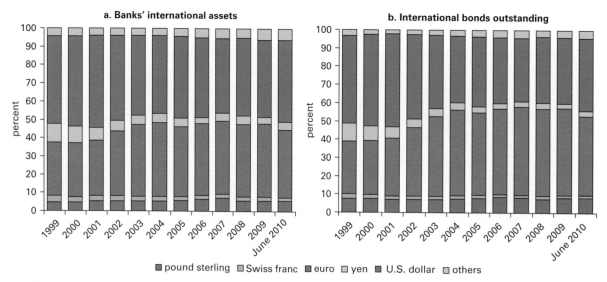

Source: World Bank staff calculations, based on Bank for International Settlements (BIS) Banking Statistics and BIS Securities Statistics.

Bank 2006) offers a detailed discussion of this issue.

Despite the increasing importance of the euro as a currency in which foreign exchange reserves are held, the share of reserves held in dollars remains well more than double the share held in euros.[3] But it is also clear that the proportion of reserves held in dollars has declined over the past decade, from 71 percent of reserves in 2000 to 67 percent in 2005 and to 62 percent in 2009 (table 3.1). Tellingly, the majority of the decline between 2005 and 2009 is reflected in the rise in share of reserves held in euros, which increased from 24 percent of reserves in 2005 to more than 27 percent in 2009. Although many countries now maintain floating exchange rate regimes, there is still strong global demand for reserve currencies for intervention and precautionary purposes. Since the breakdown of the Bretton Woods' fixed exchange rate regime in the early 1970s, global international reserve holdings as a share of global gross domestic product (GDP) have grown fourfold, from 3.5 percent of global GDP in 1974–78 to 14.5 percent in 2010.

Data on foreign exchange trading show a similar dominance, and a recent small decline, of the U.S. dollar. The amount of foreign exchange market turnover in dollars, at approximately $3.5 trillion per day, is still more than double the amount of turnover in euros in absolute terms. But the share of the market in dollars has declined, from 45 percent of the market in 2001 to 42 percent in 2010.

Other than the U.S. dollar and the euro, only three currencies have a truly international role at the present: the yen, the pound sterling, and the Swiss franc. In all three cases, their shares of international currency use are small. Moreover, usage of the yen as an international currency has undergone a steady decline in recent years—reflecting, in part, the slow growth of the Japanese economy.

Figure 3.3 offers a broad overview of the relative importance of international currencies: a composite indicator calculated according to shares of official foreign exchange reserves, turnover in foreign exchange markets, international bank credit, and outstanding international bonds[4] (annex 3.2 provides details related to the calculation, which is based on principal

FIGURE 3.2   Global foreign exchange market turnover, by currency (net of local, cross-border, and double counting), 1998–2007

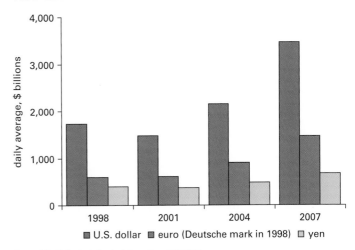

■ U.S. dollar ■ euro (Deutsche mark in 1998) □ yen

Source: World Bank staff calculations, from BIS 2010.
Note: Turnover includes spot, forward, and swaps transactions.

TABLE 3.1   Currency shares of foreign exchange reserve holdings, by percentage, 1995–2009

	1995	2000	2005	2009
All countries				
U.S dollar	59.0	71.1	66.9	62.1
Euro[a]	18.5	18.3	24.1	27.5
U.K. pound	2.1	2.8	3.6	4.3
Japanese yen	6.8	6.1	3.6	3.0
Other	13.7	1.8	1.9	3.1
Advanced countries				
U.S. dollar	53.9	69.8	69.3	65.2
Euro[a]	19.5	18.4	21.2	25.2
U.K. pound	2.1	2.8	2.7	2.8
Japanese yen	7.1	7.3	4.7	4.0
Other	17.5	1.8	2.1	2.8
Emerging and developing countries[b]				
U.S. dollar	73.7	74.8	62.7	58.5
Euro[a]	17.4	18.1	29.2	30.2
U.K. pound	2.2	2.6	5.1	5.9
Japanese yen	6.0	2.8	1.5	1.8
Other	2.8	1.7	1.5	3.6

Source: International Monetary Fund (IMF) COFER database, June 2010.
Note: Figures represent only the shares of reserves that have been allocated to individual currencies.
a. For 1995, the sum of shares of the Deutsche mark, French franc, and Dutch guilder.
b. IMF definition of emerging and developing countries.

FIGURE 3.3   Composite indicator of international currency shares, 1999–2009

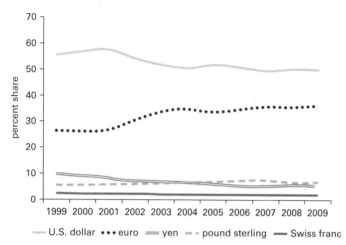

Source: World Bank staff calculations, based on BIS security statistics and IMF International Financial Statistics (IFS) database.

analysis confirm that trend growth of global trade and capital flows in excess of global GDP growth has a different effect on the four major international currencies (the same currencies included in the SDR basket). In particular, demand for M2 in the euro area appears to be positively affected by trade and capital flows, whereas demand for M2 in Japan appears to be negatively affected by trade.

The global currency role of emerging-market economies lags their shares of trade and economic activity

Considerable inertia exists in international currency use. It is thus not surprising that changes in the shares of reserve currencies lag behind changes in countries' shares of international trade and world output. Nevertheless, the disparity between currency use and countries' importance in trade and output is substantial. Figure 3.4, which shows the percentages of global foreign exchange reserves and turnover accounted for by the currencies of eight major industrial and developing countries, demonstrates this proposition powerfully. Despite the fact that the global share of U.S. exports is currently less than the global share of exports from China, whose currency essentially has no international role, the U.S. dollar scores much higher in measures of both reserves and turnover.

Even though the shares of turnover accounted for by several emerging-market currencies—the Brazilian real, the Indian rupee, the Korean won, and the Russian ruble—have grown in recent years, their roles in global currency markets remain extremely limited. In assessing the prospects for internationalization of leading emerging-market currencies, in addition to the general factors explaining international currency use discussed above, one also needs to consider each government's own policy stance and strategy in promoting the international use of its currency.

With a few exceptions, such as Japan in 1999 under its "Internationalization of the Yen for the 21st Century" plan, governments have not traditionally pursued deliberate policies to foster

components analysis).[5] The composite indicator shows an increase in the euro's importance by about 10 percent since its creation, the counterpart to a 6 percent decline for the dollar and a 5 percent decline for the yen. The pound sterling rose slightly over the same time period. The composite indicator also confirms the minor roles of the pound sterling, yen, and Swiss franc.

Another approach to gauging trends in global currency use is based on the idea that the various international uses of individual currencies contribute to global currency demand, where currency demand includes both domestic and international use.[6] Conventional money demand equations (for real money balances) capture domestic money demand by including explanatory variables such as domestic real GDP and interest rates. International transactions taking the form of exports and capital flows, however, may add to that demand for money. By including measures that drive global international transactions, one should be able to gauge demand for international currency use, regardless of whether the increased money balances are held by domestic or foreign residents. This is further discussed in annex 3.1, which applies such an approach to demand for M2 in G-20 countries. Results of the

FIGURE 3.4   Global currency shares relative to trade share and economic size

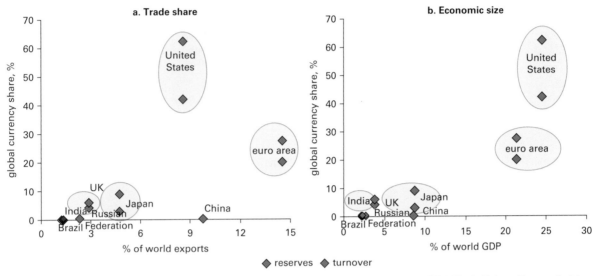

Sources: World Bank staff calculations, using data from IMF Direction of Trade Statistics, IMF Currency Composition of Official Foreign Exchange Reserves, Bank for International Settlements, and World Bank World Development Indicators.

a global role for their currencies.[7] The Japanese experience is illuminating. Despite growing capital transactions between Japan and other East Asian countries and the yen's influence on the exchange rate policies in the region, the yen has become less internationalized over the past decade. In fact, the dollar remains the most used currency in East Asia. Part of the explanation for why the international use of the yen remains muted in relation to Japan's economic size resides with the behavior of Japanese manufacturing firms, which have been reluctant to make full use of the yen so that they can avoid currency risks, preferring in many cases to use the same currency as their competitors for transactions—the U.S. dollar. Ito et al. (2010) find that Japan's production networks in East Asia have reinforced U.S. dollar invoicing of Japanese exports to other East Asian countries in large part because of country-specific foreign exchange regulations in those countries. The experience of Japan suggests that governments acting alone face great obstacles in promoting international use of their currencies, and that expanding the international role of a currency is likely to require enhanced regional cooperation, such as agreements concerning invoicing and settlement.

Moving to a Multicurrency International Monetary System

The U.S. dollar remains the preeminent international currency, as the British pound was before the U.S. dollar, for several main reasons: the size of the U.S. economy, the global influence of U.S. monetary policy, the breadth and depth of U.S. financial markets (table 3.2), and the fact that oil and other major commodities are priced in dollars on international markets. U.S. monetary policy has set the tone for global monetary conditions for most of the postwar era—at times, driving large, rapid flows of capital into or out of the United States. U.S. markets are also extremely liquid, meaning that assets can be sold with low transaction costs and liquidated in emergencies with little penalty. For such reasons, assets denominated in dollars, particularly U.S. Treasury securities, have for decades been viewed as safe by international investors.

The ability to issue a currency that is used internationally confers obvious benefits to the issuing country. In particular, since the dollar is a pure fiat currency—that is, its nominal value results from the fiat of the government rather than from being backed by a particular amount

TABLE 3.2   Importance of selected national financial markets

	Stock markets							Capital markets	
	Market capitalization (2009)			Capital market turnover[a]		Value traded (12-month cumulative)		Domestic debt securities, amount outstanding[b]	International bonds, amounts outstanding[c]
Growth pole country/region	$ billions	Rank	Capitalization as % of GDP	%	Rank	$ billions	Rank	$ billions	$ billions
Euro area	—	—	—	—	—	—	—	—	—
United States	15,077	1	106.8	348.6	1	46,736	1	24,978	6,675
China	5,008	2	107.9	229.6	3	8,956	2	1,478	52
Russian Federation	861	14	69.8	108.5	18	683	15	51	136
United Kingdom	2,796	4	128.4	146.4	6	3,403	4	1,194	2,853
Japan	3,378	3	66.6	128.8	11	4,193	3	9,764	364
Brazil	1,167	12	73.0	73.9	32	649	16	787	151
Canada	1,681	7	125.1	92.4	22	1,240	10	952	590
Australia	1,258	10	126.5	78.8	30	762	14	901	523
India	1,179	11	91.4	119.3	12	1,089	11	652	44
Korea, Rep.	836	15	99.5	237.6	2	1,582	6	1,141	125
Turkey	226	27	36.6	141.7	8	244	24	225	52
Mexico	341	20	38.8	26.9	53	77	31	394	103
Poland	135	33	31.1	49.5	41	56	35	190	55
Saudi Arabia	319	21	81.3	119.3	13	337	21	—	13
Argentina	49	—[d]	16.0	5.4	72	3	—[d]	57	50
Indonesia	178	31	32.7	83.3	23	115	28	105	35
Norway	227	26	59.2	140.3	9	248	23	—	180
Switzerland	1,071	13	216.8	82.3	25	796	13	255	428
Malaysia	256	25	132.4	32.9	49	73	32	203	37

Sources: World Bank staff calculations, Bank for International Settlements, and Global Stock Markets Fact book, Standard & Poor's.
Note: — = not available.
a. Ratios for each market are calculated by dividing total 2009 US$ value traded by average US$ market capitalization for 2008 and 2009.
b. Bonds, medium-term notes, commercial paper, treasury bills, and other short-term notes issued by residents in local currency on local market as of March 2010.
c. Issues of international bonds and notes in foreign markets and foreign currency based on nationality of issuer as of June 2010.
d. Detailed ranking data were available for only the top 40 countries.

of gold or other assets—the acquisition of dollar currency is, in effect, an interest-free loan to the U.S. government. In addition, because foreign governments acquire interest-earning U.S. dollar assets in the form of reserves, they lower the interest rate faced by U.S. borrowers. A careful analysis of these two advantages to the issuers of an international currency (the U.S. dollar and the euro) suggests that the advantages are non-negligible, but not enormous. In recent years, the seigniorage revenue of the United States from having an international currency has totaled roughly $90 billion per year (since 2007), and approximately $20 billion for the euro area (box 3.2). An additional potential advantage, though much more difficult to quantify, is the

ability of issuers of international currencies to avoid the painful adjustment of macroeconomic policies in response to balance of payments deficits. But this advantage also carries costs, since allowing financial imbalances to build up may also sow the seeds of a more serious crisis down the road.

Over time, the ease and security involved with investing in U.S. markets has led the rest of the world to take on massive levels of financial exposure to the United States: the value of foreign residents' investments in U.S. companies, real estate, capital markets, and government debt was nearly half of non–U.S. global GDP as of end-2008 (figure 3.5). Changes in U.S. monetary policy thus have a direct wealth impact on foreign residents,

BOX 3.2   Benefits from currency internationalization

Economies that have currencies with international status—at present, mainly the United States and the euro area—have the benefit of deriving income from that status. In particular, the circulation of an issuer's currency abroad provides seigniorage to the issuer, while at the same time demand for reserve assets by foreigners lowers the interest costs for the country's borrowers. Estimates of the value of these benefits are shown in figure B3.2.1. Other benefits that are not quantified here include the lower uncertainty resulting from being able to price exports and imports, and to hold assets and liabilities, in the domestic currency.

The value of seigniorage to the United States can be calculated as the savings from the Federal Reserve holding non-interest-bearing currency (instead of interest-bearing securities) on the liability side of its balance sheet, less the cost of maintaining the currency in circulation (Goldberg 2010). Detailed data on the composition of the debt securities portfolio held by the Federal Reserve show that the average maturity of debt securities was about three years in the period preceding the crisis, rising to about five years since 2009. Applying the corresponding U.S. Treasury yields to the stock of U.S. currency held abroad (64 percent of the total), one can conclude that since 1990, U.S. seigniorage income derived from the dollar's international

currency status has averaged $15 billion per year ($12 billion for 2010).

Another benefit derived from the international status of the dollar is the lower cost of capital enjoyed by borrowers in the United States as a consequence of foreign demand for dollar assets. A recent study by McKinsey & Company estimates the advantage that results from foreign official purchases of U.S. Treasury securities at 50 to 60 basis points (Dobbs et al. 2009). Applying the lower end of this range to the stock of U.S. interest-bearing liabilities with the rest of the world, the annual cost of capital advantage accrued to U.S. borrowers between 1990 and 2010 is estimated to be $33 billion ($81 billion for 2010).

Similarly calculated, the seigniorage gains from the international status of the euro averaged $4 billion per year for the euro area from 2000 to 2009. Just as in the U.S. case, seigniorage income for the euro area was lower in 2010 due to the fall in interest rates, amounting to $2.3 billion in 2010. For these calculations, central banks in the euro area are assumed to hold bonds with an average maturity of three years, and 20 percent of the stock of euro currency is estimated to circulate outside the euro area (ECB 2010). The annual cost of capital advantage for the euro area averaged $9 billion from 2000 to 2009.

FIGURE B3.2.1   Gains from the international status of currency

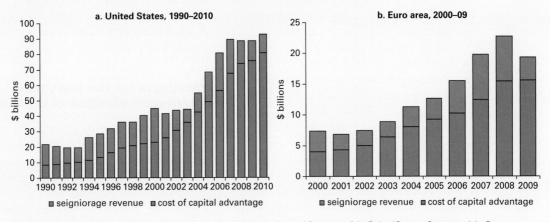

Sources: World Bank staff calculations, based on data from Bloomberg, the Board of Governors of the Federal Reserve System, and the European Central Bank.

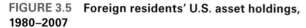

FIGURE 3.5   **Foreign residents' U.S. asset holdings, 1980–2007**

☐ foreign residents' asset holdings
■ foreign official assets in the United States
— U.S. liabilities as % of world GDP (excl. U.S.)

Sources: World Bank staff calculation based on IMF IFS, GEP 2011, and the U.S. Bureau of Economic Analysis.

influencing their expenditures. In addition, the vast majority—95 percent—of foreign holdings of U.S. assets are denominated in dollars, posing a difficult dilemma for foreign investors. Individually, foreign investors have an incentive to diversify their portfolios as a matter of prudent risk management; collectively, however, foreign investors have a strong incentive to maintain their holdings of dollar assets to avoid the risk of dollar depreciation that could undermine their investments.

Net U.S. liabilities to the rest of the world are the counterpart to past U.S. current account deficits, plus any valuation changes. Despite keeping its current account broadly in balance from 1944, the year the Bretton Woods system was established, to the mid-1960s, the United States has run a current account deficit for more than half of the years between 1944 and 2010, and for every year since 1992. The balance between resource availability and commitments to foreign economies in the United States began to unravel in the mid-1970s, when the U.S. trade account turned negative and the deficit began to expand rapidly, reaching $840 billion in 2006 (figure 3.6). The financial crisis of 2008–09 and the

deep economic recession that followed it narrowed the U.S. trade deficit to a still-substantial estimated $480 billion in 2010. But even the crisis, which originated in the United States, did not set off a flight from the dollar; to the contrary, the crisis resulted in extreme demand for dollar-denominated assets.

Demand for dollar-denominated assets notwithstanding, it is important to recognize that there are two potential challengers to the U.S. dollar as principal reserve currency, the euro and China's renminbi.[8] Both the euro area and China rival the United States in terms of output and trade flows. Figure 3.7 shows the concentration of trade of other countries with each of the three.

Trade concentration with the United States and European Union (EU) especially, but also with China, tends to be highest for neighboring countries. However, the United States, the EU, and China each has global reach, and each is an important trading partner with countries in other regions as well—a number of countries in Africa trade a great deal with China, for instance. In the years ahead, rapid economic expansion in China, where the pace of growth has exceeded that of the United States and the euro area by an average of at least 5 percent annually since the early 1980s, increases the likelihood that the renminbi will compete with the U.S. dollar as a reserve currency. It is predominantly in the remaining factor influencing international currency use—the stage of economic and financial development and depth of financial markets—that the U.S. dollar outshines its potential competitors.

Prospects for the increased internationalization of the euro

In the 11 years since its creation, the euro has become a legitimate rival to the dollar, gaining market acceptance as an important issuing currency in global debt markets. The elimination of intra-euro-area exchange rate risk has created a large single market for euro-denominated debt securities, attracting both sovereign and private borrowers not only from euro area entities and neighboring countries but also from major emerging-market economies such as Brazil,

FIGURE 3.6   **U.S. balance of payments, 1946–2008**

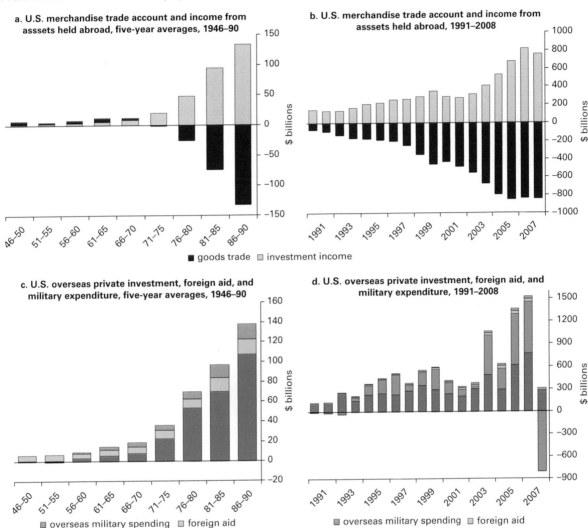

Sources: World Bank staff calculations, from U.S. Department of Commerce (Bureau of Economic Analysis), USAID *Greenbook*, and Cambridge University (*Historical Statistics of the United States*).

Note: Overseas military spending data before 1960 represent net military transactions. Foreign aid data represent the years 1991–2007.

China, Colombia, Mexico, and Turkey. Such has been the growth of the euro-denominated bond market that it now rivals dollar-denominated fixed income markets in size, depth, and product range. And the euro's investor base is still expanding. As of end-June 2010, outstanding international bonds and notes issued in euros amounted to $11.1 trillion, or 45 percent of the global total (table 3.3), compared to $10.2 trillion for the U.S.

dollar market. Although the governments of individual countries within the euro area collectively issue a large volume of debt, no single issuer is nearly as large as the U.S. Treasury—an obstacle to the increased internationalization of the euro that has been exacerbated by the global financial crisis of 2008–09.

One of the most serious follow-on effects of the financial crisis has been rising sovereign debt

FIGURE 3.7 The geographic distribution of trade concentration relative to China, the European Union, and the United States, 2005–09 period average

China

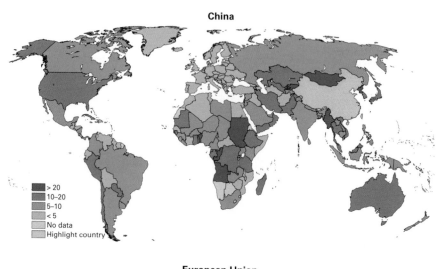

European Union

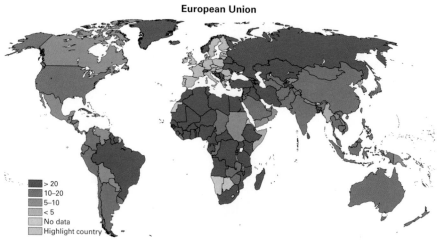

United States

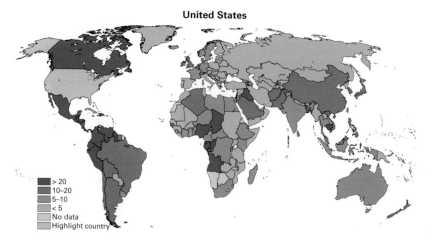

Sources: World Bank staff calculation based on IMF Direction of Trade and the World Bank WDI database.

Note: The trade concentration of country *i* relative to country or area *j* is calculated as

$$TC_{ij} = \frac{(export\ of\ i\ to\ j + imports\ of\ i\ from\ j)}{Total\ trade_i} \times 100,$$

where *j* = {China, European Union, U.S.}, and *i* = all other trade partner countries.

TABLE 3.3 International debt securities outstanding, by currency, 1999–2010

$ trillions

	1999	2000	2001	2002	2003	2004	2005	2006	2007	2008	2009	2010 (June)
U.S. dollar	2.6	3.3	3.9	4.3	4.7	5.1	5.6	6.7	7.9	8.6	9.8	10.2
Euro	1.6	1.9	2.4	3.5	5.1	6.5	6.6	8.7	11.0	11.4	12.8	11.1
Yen	0.5	0.5	0.5	0.5	0.5	0.5	0.5	0.5	0.6	0.8	0.7	0.7
Pound sterling	0.4	0.5	0.6	0.7	0.9	1.1	1.2	1.6	1.9	1.9	2.2	2.1
Swiss franc	0.1	0.1	0.1	0.2	0.2	0.2	0.2	0.3	0.3	0.4	0.4	0.4
Others	0.2	0.2	0.2	0.2	0.3	0.5	0.6	0.7	1.0	0.9	1.1	1.1
Total	5.3	6.3	7.4	9.0	11.4	13.5	14.1	17.7	21.7	23.0	25.9	24.5
US$ as % of total	49.6	51.4	52.1	47.2	41.3	37.8	39.7	37.7	36.4	37.4	37.6	41.6
Euro as % of total	29.8	30.6	32.6	38.3	44.8	48.4	46.9	48.9	50.7	49.6	49.5	45.4

Source: Bank for International Settlements.

concerns in several European countries, which have called into question the architecture supporting the single currency and have highlighted the need for greater coordination of fiscal policy (Bénassy-Quéré and Boone 2010). The crisis has led the EU to take steps considered extraordinary, such as intervening in secondary markets through the European Central Bank's (ECB's) Securities Market Program to purchase the government debt of the troubled countries and establishing the European Financial Stability Facility (EFSF), which provides country-level guarantee commitments intended to temporarily assist countries with budgetary needs and support the financial stability of the euro area as a whole. Such efforts are contrary to the spirit, if not the letter, of ECB statutes, which prohibit bailouts of governments. Subject to conditions to be negotiated with the European Commission, the EFSF was crafted with the capacity to issue bonds guaranteed by euro area members for up to €440 billion for on-lending to euro area member states in difficulty. The available amounts under the EFSF were intended to be complemented by those of the European Financial Stability Mechanism (EFSM) and of the International Monetary Fund (IMF).

Together, the EFSF (which is to be wound down in 2013) and the EFSM could create a more liquid market for euro-denominated public debt across a range of maturities, which in turn may increase the attractiveness of the euro as an international currency. But the size of the EFSF is much smaller than the outstanding amount of euro area government debt (about €5.4 trillion as of mid-2010). As of early 2011, it seemed likely that European governments would be reluctant to draw on the bailout fund at all (Reuters 2010),[9] instead treating the fund as a last resort, as Ireland did in November 2010. While a European summit in March 2011 boosted the effective lending capacity of the EFSF, the summit did not allow for the facility's purchase of government debt on secondary markets, as some had called for, leaving the ECB to continue in that role. In addition, the moral hazard created by bailouts of heavily indebted governments may well offset or reverse any favorable effect on the euro's international use. The ongoing process of overall European integration, however, eventually may lead to reforms that reduce moral hazard and enhance the attractiveness of the euro with respect to the dollar.

Prospects for the internationalization of the renminbi

Starting from a modest base, the renminbi's international role is poised to grow in the future, with prospects for internationalization dependent on how aggressively Chinese authorities pursue policy shifts promoting development of local capital markets and how quickly currency convertibility on the capital account is implemented. In some respects, China already satisfies

FIGURE 3.8   **Share of global manufacturing exports**

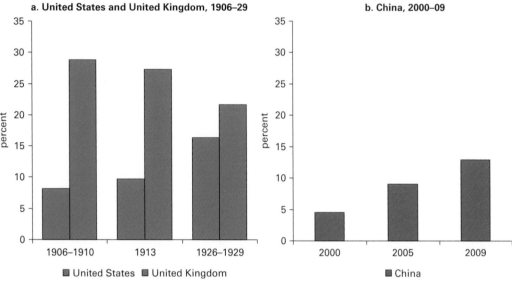

Sources: Hilgerdt 1945; World Bank WDI database.

the underlying trade and macroeconomic criteria required for its currency take on an international role: a dominant role in world trade, a diversified merchandise trade pattern, and a macroeconomic framework geared to low and stable inflation. From a historical perspective, China's current position in global manufacturing exports is similar to that of the United States in the interwar period[10], when the U.K. lead in manufacturing exports was steadily eroding (figure 3.8). On the remaining criterion—open, deep, and broad financial markets—the renminbi falls far short, however.

Restrictions on currency convertibility in China are one avenue by which the attractiveness of the renminbi as an international currency is constrained. Although the renminbi is convertible for current account transactions (that is, for payments for goods and services), capital inflows and outflows are subject to a wide range of restrictions. Renminbi balances acquired by foreigners (for instance, through the operation of subsidiaries located in China) or held by Chinese residents may be freely changed into foreign currencies and moved out of the country. But non-Chinese entities are restricted from freely acquiring Chinese assets in exchange for their foreign currencies.

Limitations in financial markets also curb use of the renminbi as an international currency. Domestic bond markets, except those for bonds issued by governments and state-owned enterprises are still underdeveloped. China's banking system remains under the control of the state, with deposit rates regulated administratively and banks required to set their lending rates within certain margins.

Although the capital market constraints to the renminbi's internationalization are undeniable, recent initiatives by Chinese authorities to actively promote the international use of the renminbi are beginning to have an effect. The envisaged strategy of "managed internationalization" (McCauley 2011) involves actions on two fronts: (1) development of an offshore renminbi market and (2) encouraging the use of renminbi in trade invoicing and settlement. Actions taken thus far seem to suggest that the authorities' initial focus is at the regional level, starting with promoting the renminbi's role in cross-border trade between China and its neighbors. To that end, China began a pilot arrangement of cross-border settlement of current account transactions in renminbi in July 2009, focusing on the Association of Southeast Asian Nations countries plus Hong

Kong SAR, China, and Macao SAR, China. This arrangement was extended in 2010 to include all countries and 20 provinces inside China (People's Bank of China 2010b). Still, cross-border trade settlements in renminbi amounted to Y 509.9 billion (about $75 billion) in 2010 (People's Bank of China 2010a), less than 3 percent of China's total annual trade in goods and services.

In simultaneously developing an offshore renminbi market and maintaining capital controls, Chinese authorities are using a novel approach, distinguished by China's pragmatism and gradual pace. The approach is intended to meet the growing demand by nonresidents for renminbi-denominated financial assets in both the banking and securities sectors. As such, authorities are now allowing the issuance of offshore renminbi bonds (so-called panda bonds) in Hong Kong SAR, China. Several multinational companies with operations in China, as well as international financial institutions (Asian Development Bank, International Finance Corporation, International Bank for Reconstruction and Development) have decided over the past year to issue renminbi-denominated bonds. As of January 2011, the Chinese government had issued Y 14 billion (about $2 billion), and Chinese corporations issued Y 46 billion (about $6.74 billion), in renminbi-denominated bonds (Dealogic DCM analysis).

With restrictions on bank deposits and currency exchange denominated in renminbi in Hong Kong SAR, China, being gradually lifted, the renminbi banking business has grown since 2008. In addition, the People's Bank of China has opened up swap arrangements with a number of other central banks (table 3.4). Several of those arrangements were made in the context of the Chiang Mai Initiative[11], which seeks to further East Asian monetary integration and eventually may lead to a common Asian currency.

From a policy perspective, the foreign currency exposure evident in China's external balance sheet provides a powerful incentive to the Chinese authorities to promote renminbi internationalization. In short, the strongest motivation for internationalization of the renminbi is not just related to the impact it would make in developing local capital markets in China, but also to

mitigation of the tremendous currency mismatch in its asset/liability positions vis-à-vis the rest of the world, as evident in the currency denomination of China's external balance sheet (table 3.5). As of end-2009, China had borrowed less than one-quarter of its $391 billion of outstanding foreign debt in renminbi, while the renminbi's share of China's international lending was negligible, at only 0.3 percent of the total. Part of the reason for the very low proportion of international lending that is denominated in renminbi is that foreign bonds could only be issued in foreign currency until mid-2007, at which point official and commercial borrowers were allowed to issue renminbi-denominated bonds in Hong Kong SAR, China.

In contrast to the situation in China, the United States borrows from and lends to the rest of the world predominantly in its own currency: 95 percent of total U.S. liabilities to foreigners (excluding derivatives) were denominated in dollars as of end-2009. While the U.S. Treasury issues debt solely in dollars, U.S. firms actively borrow abroad in foreign currency. Approximately $850 billion (30 percent) of the $2.8 trillion in U.S. corporate debt outstanding at the end of 2009 was denominated in foreign currency, mainly euros. On the asset side, 43 percent of the $14.9 trillion in U.S. claims on foreigners (excluding derivatives) was denominated in dollars at the end of 2009.

Thus, although the international use of the renminbi may undergo rapid growth, the task ahead remains challenging. Expansion of domestic debt markets, more complete convertibility of

TABLE 3.4   Renminbi local currency swap arrangements, July 2010

Date of agreement	Counterparty	Size (RMB billions)
December 12, 2008	Republic of Korea	180
January 20, 2009	Hong Kong SAR, China	200
February 8, 2009	Malaysia	80
March 11, 2009	Belarus	20
March 23, 2009	Indonesia	100
April 2, 2009	Argentina	70
June 9, 2010	Iceland	3.5
July 23, 2010	Singapore	150

Source: People's Bank of China.

TABLE 3.5   Currency denominations of the external balance sheets of the United States and China, end-2009

$ trillions

	United States			China		
	Liabilities	**Assets**			**Liabilities**	**Assets**
Debt & deposits	12.61	6.43	Debt & deposits		0.391	0.59
of which: in USD	11.75	5.54	of which: in CNY		0.09[b]	0.01[c]
FDI and portfolio equity	5.12	8.03	FDI and portfolio equity		1.17	0.28[d]
of which: in USD	5.12	0.86	of which: in CNY		1.17	—
International reserves		0.4	International reserves			2.45
of which: in USD		—	of which: in CNY			—
Derivatives	3.38	3.51	Other		0.07	0.14
Total	21.12	18.38	Total		1.64	3.46
of which: in USD[a]	16.87	6.39	of which: in CNY		1.26	0.01
Share in USD[a]	95.1%	43.0%	Share in CNY		76.9%	0.3%

Sources: World Bank staff calculations based on data from the Board of Governors of the Federal Reserve System, U.S. Bureau of Economic Analysis, U.S. Department of the Treasury, and IMF IFS. China State Administration of Foreign Exchange; government of Hong Kong SAR, China; BIS banking statistics; Dealogic DCM analysis.

a. Excluding derivatives.

b. An estimated $90 billion of China's foreign debt was denominated in renminbi at end-2009 (about 5 percent of total foreign liabilities).

c. Renminbi bank deposits outstanding in Hong Kong SAR, China, end-2009, which increased to about $42 billion at end-2010.

d. Assuming that all of China's foreign direct investment and portfolio equity outflows are in foreign currencies.

the renminbi, reinforced financial sector supervision, a more transparent framework for monetary policy, and increased flexibility of the renminbi are needed to make the renminbi an attractive international (not just regional) currency. But such reforms are far reaching and are likely to take considerable time to complete. Furthermore, even if such conditions were satisfied, network externalities suggest that the renminbi would not assume the role of international currency quickly. Prospects for the renminbi also depend on the direction of East Asian monetary integration—namely, whether it leads to a regional currency that will begin to replace national currencies, including the renminbi.

The Shape of Things to Come: Some Scenarios for a Future International Monetary System

Of the various aspects of contemporary international economic relations, it is in the monetary arena that the shift toward multipolarity is likely to have the strongest impact. In the unfolding multipolar order, in which several developing countries will attain global growth pole status

in the decades ahead and in which there will be an important shift in the distribution of global wealth, international monetary relations will need to accommodate an expanding role for major currencies other than the U.S. dollar (Dailami and Masson 2010).

The decade leading up to the global financial crisis of 2008–09 was associated with a major expansion in financial holdings and wealth in emerging markets. Following a downturn during the crisis, the upward trend is expected to continue through the forecast horizon of this book (box 3.3), bringing about changes in relative financial power. The expansion of financial holdings and wealth in emerging markets is most prominently reflected on the official side, in the accumulation of foreign exchange reserves by monetary authorities.[12] High levels of reserve holdings have, in turn, induced a buildup of assets held in sovereign wealth funds (SWFs)[13] and other state-controlled portfolios such as pension funds and financial holdings of state-owned enterprises.

Informed by the analytical work on changing growth poles and growth dynamics in chapter 1 and the previous discussion on international currency use and international policy coordination, this book envisions three possible international

BOX 3.3   The changing external financial position of developing countries

Years of structural reforms and improved macroeconomic performance combined with capital market liberalization have resulted in a significant improvement in the external financial position of developing countries, with both the private and official sectors now holding large amounts of overseas assets and investments. In 1999, developed countries' foreign exchange reserves represented approximately $1.1 trillion (62 percent) of the $1.8 trillion of global foreign exchange reserves and developing countries' reserves the remaining 38 percent. One decade later, these proportions had reversed: developing and emerging economies held approximately $5.4 trillion (66 percent) of the total global reserve stock of $8.1 trillion as of end-2010. At the same time, overseas asset accumulation by private firms in emerging markets expanded dramatically, as evidenced by large increases in cross-border mergers and acquisitions and greenfield investments (see chapter 2).

This trend of rising wealth in the emerging markets is expected to continue through to the end of the 2025 forecast horizon of this book. The baseline scenario presented in chapter 1 suggests that emerging economies are expected to accumulate substantial international investment positions (see figure B3.3.1), led by China (increasing from about 35 percent to 61 percent of GDP from 2009 to 2025), as well as Middle Eastern and East Asian economies. Malaysia and Singapore, for example, are expected to hold net foreign assets in excess of 100 percent of their GDP (with the United States, as the primary debtor, expected to hold a net international investment position of −69 percent of GDP in 2025). Even if policy rebalancing limits the widening of international investment positions, the same qualitative conclusion will remain: The difference in emerging-market net international investment positions between the baseline and rebalancing scenarios is only about $1.6 trillion in 2009 dollars (4.8 percent of emerging-market GDP), or a modest slowdown in their pace of asset accumulation.

FIGURE B3.3.1   Evolution of net international investment positions, advanced and emerging economies, 2004–25

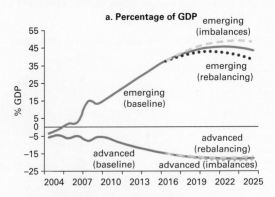
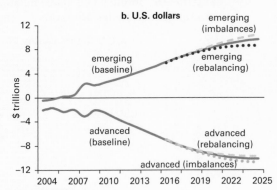

Sources: IMF IFS database and World Bank staff calculations.

Note: Developed countries included in the scenarios illustrated above are Australia, Canada, the euro area, Japan, Norway, Sweden, Switzerland, the United Kingdom, and the United States. Emerging countries and regions included in the scenarios are Argentina, Brazil, China, the Czech Republic, India, Indonesia, the Republic of Korea, Malaysia, the Mashreq economies, Mexico, Poland, the Russian Federation, Singapore, South Africa, Thailand, Turkey, Ukraine, and the República Bolivariana de Venezuela. Net international investment positions calculations assume constant asset prices in U.S. dollars, and a constant capital account/GDP ratio, and are depicted in constant 2004 prices relative to the basket of OECD exports.

currency scenarios. In each of the three scenarios, it is assumed that the major currencies will continue to float against each other (while allowing for some degree of intervention) and that capital accounts will continue to gradually liberalize. The three scenarios are as follows:

- *Dollar standard status quo.* The U.S. dollar retains its position as the dominant international currency, at least until the end of the forecast horizon of 2025. This scenario is the result of a combination of factors, including success by the United States in curbing unsustainable fiscal deficits and a delay by China and the euro area in making the reforms necessary to expand the international use of their currencies.[14] This scenario is reinforced by the presence of considerable inertia with regard to reserve currency switching and continued broad political economy factors supportive of the use of the currency of the predominant geopolitical and military power—that is, the United States (Drezner 2010; Eichengreen 2011; Posen 2008).

Under this scenario, the evolution of the U.S. economy is assumed to follow that outlined in the baseline scenario of chapter 1, where the United States is successful in gradually improving its fiscal position in the medium and long run (current projections by the U.S. Congressional Budget Office [CBO] place fiscal deficits at –9.8 percent in 2011, compared to the –8.2 percent in the baseline scenario considered here)[15] and achieving a sustainable current account balance (figure 3.9, panel a). In this case, even with the multipolar world of 2025, the output forecasts in chapter 1 point to the world's largest economy remaining that of the United States (in real terms); this trend, along with inertia in currency use, would be major justifications behind the persistence of the dollar standard status quo.

- *Multipolar international currencies.* The dollar loses its position as the dominant international currency at some point between 2011 and 2025, to be replaced by a global system with three roughly equally important currencies: the dollar, the euro, and an

FIGURE 3.9   **Implied U.S. fiscal balances and global economic sizes, dollar standard and multipolar currencies scenarios**

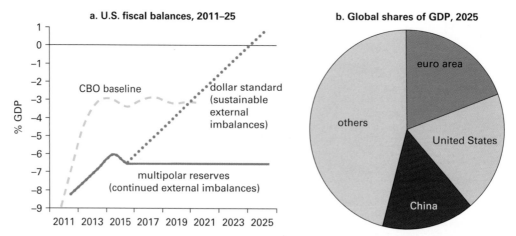

Sources: World Bank staff calculations; CBO 2011.
Note: U.S. fiscal balance paths assume that only fiscal balances adjust to bring about current account changes, so that other elements that affect the current account (official flows, net foreign assets, and net oil exports) do not deviate from their 2015 levels from 2016 onward. The chart for economic sizes in the dollar standard scenario is very similar to the multipolar currency scenario and, hence, omitted.

Asian currency. If current efforts to internationalize the renminbi continue apace, it will become the dominant Asian currency. Financial markets in China would need to expand in a manner supportive of an international currency, and successful efforts would need to be made to broaden the convertibility of the renminbi and access to renminbi-denominated assets. Together, these efforts would allow China to elevate its international monetary status to be on a par with the country's weight in global trade and economic output. The multipolar international currency scenario assumes that the euro area successfully puts the sovereign debt crisis to rest by instituting meaningful reforms that strengthen economic governance.

The likelihood of this second scenario playing out is buttressed by the probability, as outlined in chapter 1, that the United States, the euro area, and China remain the major three growth poles in 2025—thus diminishing the possibility that the Swiss franc and pound sterling expand beyond their currently small roles in the international currency environment. The expected GDP shares of the largest three economies over 2011–25 lend additional credence to this tripolar reserve scenario (figure 3.9, panel b). Slow progress in fiscal adjustment in the United States, which is consistent with the continued imbalances scenario outlined in chapter 1, also contributes to the likelihood of this scenario.

- *A single multilateral reserve currency.* Here, a single multilateral reserve currency, managed jointly rather than by a single national central bank, is at the center of the international currency system. Such an outcome would result from the recognition that the lower volatility afforded by a multilateral currency outweighs the potential costs of policy coordination necessary to manage the reserve currency, or the difficulty of achieving that coordination. While the current SDR would be the most likely

candidate to fill the role of such a reserve currency (Stiglitz and Greenwald 2010), a new monetary unit comprising a smaller set of constituent currencies (or a redefinition of the SDR) is another possibility, as is a currency whose value is not defined in terms of a basket of national currencies but, rather, is issued by the equivalent of a global central bank.

This scenario is consistent with the analysis of increased policy coordination discussed below, where it is argued that a marked strengthening of multilateralism is the necessary counterpart to increased economic globalization. The international monetary system thus would move away from the "nonsystem" that has characterized the global economy since 1973 and toward a new system involving the management of a multilateral, world currency.

Each of the three potential currency scenarios presents policy challenges, and the three are not equally likely. Under the *dollar standard status quo* scenario, the world would continue to exhibit some of the features that contributed to the nonsystem of the postwar era: inadequate incentives for the reserve currency country to adjust, leading to a skewed pattern of global demand, and incidence of acute dollar shortage, as was experienced during the recent crisis. The likelihood of this scenario would derive as much from the drawbacks of other currencies as from success by the United States in addressing its policy challenges. But the fundamental causes of global imbalances would remain, meaning that the risks of financial crisis would persist.

Given current trends, the *multipolar international currencies* scenario is the most likely to play out, and could constitute a more stable and symmetric global economic environment than the first scenario. However, this scenario, too, would embody risks. The danger exists that the existence of currency blocs might boost regional integration at the expense of multilateral liberalization.[16] In fact, during the postwar period, trade within major regional groupings has grown considerably faster than trade between blocs. This feature may undercut multilateralism by making cooperation to maintain a system of global free trade seem less essential for economic prosperity. Furthermore, in the second scenario, the vast majority of developing countries, including those with the lowest incomes, would continue to transact internationally in currencies other than their own, and thus would be exposed to the exchange rate risk. Only the largest emerging-market countries/regions would achieve the status of issuers of international currencies because of the liquidity advantages of size. The third, or *single multilateral reserve currency* scenario, is envisioned as a possible reaction to the perceived deficiencies of the other two scenarios, which provide few checks on national policies and may be associated with exchange rate instability.

The *single multilateral reserve currency* scenario is far less likely than the other two scenarios to materialize over the next 15 years, as the *multilateral reserve* scenario would necessitate developing a set of rules for managing international liquidity and moderating exchange rate movements and would require countries highly protective of their national monetary policy to relinquish full control.[17]

The need for enhanced policy coordination in an increasingly multipolar world

The three scenarios for the future of the international monetary system presented in this chapter can help focus the attention of policy makers on potential long-run outcomes and the type of international policy coordination responses that are desirable in order to prevent negative spillovers between countries that may result from major shocks to the global economy. At the current juncture of high uncertainty about medium-term global growth prospects and the emergence of competing power centers, coordination is essential. That coordination could take several forms, with varying degrees of difficulty and effectiveness.

Coordination may involve ad hoc meetings and occasional agreements to alter policy in the global interest (what has been called "episodic coordination"). On the other hand, coordination may lead to a formal revision of the workings of the international financial system to prevent destabilizing competitive behavior—what Artis and Ostry (1986) call "institutionalized coordination." Since the 1940s, there has been a steady rise in efforts at institutionalized coordination, as evidenced by a rise in the number of countries that participate in international organizations (figure 3.10). However, current disparities among countries in terms of economic conditions and policy objectives are likely to make reaching agreement difficult, and the emergence of a multipolar world with new power centers may even amplify impediments for achieving cooperation at the very time it is most necessary.

Disparities among countries' economic conditions and policy objectives that are likely to make reaching agreement difficult

In the absence of incentives for collective action,[18] countries may choose to make decisions unilaterally, but the final outcome easily could be one in which all countries are worse off. Under the present circumstances, it would be desirable to strengthen the institutional basis for cooperation—for instance, by expanding the

FIGURE 3.10   Membership in major international organizations, 1945–2010

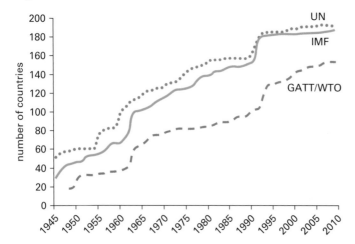

Sources: Membership rolls of General Agreement on Tariffs and Trade/World Trade Organization, the United Nations, and IMF, from their respective websites.

analytical component of G-20 discussions and monitoring and following up on policy agreements. International institutions, with their nearly universal membership, could help provide legitimacy and continuity to discussions in forums, such as the G-20.

Figure 3.11 illustrates the current large disparities in macroeconomic policy stance between advanced and emerging economies. Two key messages can be drawn from the figure. First, potential emerging-economy poles, except India, generally have lower fiscal deficits (with respect to their GDP) than do advanced-economy growth poles. Second, interest rates in emerging-market growth poles, including China, are much higher than interest rates in the advanced-economy growth poles. The two patterns reflect current global imbalances—namely, that deficits in developed countries, especially the United States, have been financed by developing countries in recent years. But the risk premium that developing countries pay for their own financing—the result of credit market constraints and immature financial markets—keeps their interest rates high. Developed countries, meanwhile, have enjoyed low levels of inflation, thanks in large part to low prices of imported goods from the developing world. In turn, those low-priced imports have helped developed

countries keep their nominal interest rates low despite their high levels of consumption.

Even if countries are willing to discuss such disparities, their sheer magnitude has the potential to make economic policy negotiations quite difficult. Nonetheless, countries should recognize that the persistence of disparities can have negative consequences on the global economy, and the major economies need to recognize the urgency of trading off some elements of national interest for the common good.

A Path toward Improved Institutional Management of a Multipolar World

In light of expanding multipolarity in the world economy, economic policy coordination can be strengthened and national policies improved along a number of avenues. For one, policy must be crafted with a mind toward potential spillover effects among countries. The G-20 is actively pursuing a framework of indicative guidelines for identifying imbalances that need to be addressed by policy measures, while at the same time recognizing that these guidelines are not themselves targets.[19] More generally, the G-20 is committed to the objective of achieving strong,

FIGURE 3.11   **Macroeconomic policy disparities, selected actual and potential growth poles among advanced and emerging economies**

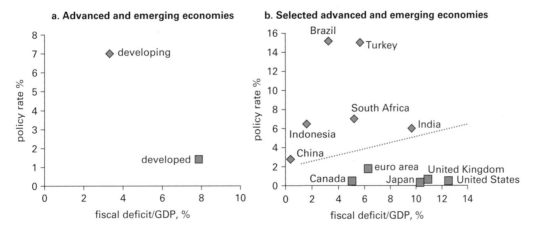

Sources: World Bank staff calculations, using IMF World Economic Outlook, OECD, and Datastream.
Note: Fiscal and monetary policy for all countries included is for the latest available year. The dotted line on the right panel is merely indicative, intended mainly to highlight the disparities between developed and developing countries.

sustainable, and balanced growth. In doing so, the G-20 needs to continue its focus on shared objectives rather than on instruments that lead to a zero-sum game. The G-20 also needs to institutionalize coordination, drawing on the in-house expertise and the institutional memory of official international economic institutions.

The form of policy coordination can be an important influence on its success in reaching and sustaining agreement. It seems clear that ad hoc coordination of policies, whether to inter-vene in exchange markets (such as those embod-ied in the 1985 Plaza Agreement) or occasional bargains to modify macroeconomic or structural policies (such as the 1978 Bonn Summit), have not been sufficient in preventing excesses such as uncontrolled global expansion of liquidity and global imbalances. Designing transparent, widely accepted triggers for economic policy coordina-tion thus would be desirable. Establishing such triggers also would represent an important step toward a more rules-based international mone-tary system, but designing appropriate rules pres-ents challenges.

At least three types of policy rules with auto-matic triggers have been proposed or used in the past to lessen negative spillovers on other coun-tries: rules on allowable exchange rate behavior; limits on balance of payments positions; and crite-ria for proscribing beggar-thy-neighbor macroeco-nomic policies (Masson forthcoming). Each rule type has limitations, however, due to the need to overcome conflict among countries in their efforts to cooperate. If countries are concerned with safeguarding their competitiveness, for instance, each country will make efforts to resist exchange rate appreciation, but the results are zero sum: depreciation for one country is appreciation for another. The challenge for policy coordination is therefore to find evenhanded criteria for choosing the appropriate values for the three variables listed above. A complementary approach is for policy coordination to emphasize targeting international public goods—that is, focusing on variables that reflect shared objectives. Low global inflation, sus-tained economic growth, exchange rate stability, and adequate global liquidity may draw the most support, as all four reflect objectives from which

many countries can benefit. The initial successes of the G-20 emphasized such common objectives and resulted from the recognition by all coun-tries that urgent action was needed—in the com-mon interest—to avoid a global recession and to address structural problems in the financial sector.

Linkages between countries occur in the first instance through changes in countries' external payments positions. Hence, there is consider-able interest at present in using some measure of external payments disequilibrium as a trigger for policy action by the country concerned (see, for instance, the proposal to the G-20 by U.S. Treasury Secretary Timothy Geithner[20]). Under such an arrangement, a country's current account surplus or deficit would be limited to some pro-portion of its GDP, say, to 4 percent. If a coun-try exceeded that threshold, that country would be required to take policy measures to bring its current account surplus or deficit back within the allowable range.

Earlier consideration of such rules, inspired in part by U.S. current account deficits and Japanese surpluses in the early 1980s, highlighted the importance of understanding the source of the current account deficits and surpluses. In gen-eral, imbalances are the outcome of the complex interaction of government policies and private sector behavior, and hence more robust analysis is needed to make a judgment concerning the causes and whether there is reason for concern. The G-20's current work program includes the objective of establishing indicative guidelines—not targets—for identifying unsustainable imbalances.

The G-20's attempt to exert peer pressure on its members' policies (the mutual assessment process) defines the contemporary approach to international policy coordination. But the cur-rent dispute over exchange rate levels and current account imbalances illustrates the problems of reaching agreement on targets for variables that are inherently zero-sum or the result of beggar-thy-neighbor policies (Masson 2011). The Bretton Woods regime ruled out such behavior, but no similar mechanism exists in the 21st century. Surveillance and ad hoc policy coordination are thus only a partial substitute for a rules-based international monetary system. Policy coordination would be facilitated if the focus is on goals that have the potential to benefit many countries in the same way: sustainable growth, financial stability, low inflation, and exchange rate stability. The initial successes of the G-20 have resulted from widespread concerns about the first two of those goals, along with a shared recognition that only a coordinated response could prevent a global economic meltdown during the financial crisis. Sustaining the momentum of cooperation will require a long-term commitment to these goals.

Implications for developing countries

Historically, country choices over the exchange rate regime revolved more around issues of whether they would choose to fix or float, with most pegs made vis-à-vis the U.S. dollar. With a multicurrency international regime, the choice of the reference currency—or currencies in the case of a basket—becomes more pertinent. The vast majority of developing countries, including those with the lowest incomes, would continue to transact internationally in currencies other than their own, and thus would be exposed to the exchange rate risk. Countries would therefore need to weigh standard considerations over the choice of a regime—such as the structural characteristics of the economy, the insulation properties of the regime, and the policy discipline conferred by a given choice (Frankel 1999)—along with whether pegging to a given international currency may be more optimal from the point of view of reducing volatility.

Leaving the confines of a relatively fixed-rate system would likely lead countries to experience significant increases in the volatility of both their nominal and real exchange rates. Developing countries with floating exchange rate regimes may experience heightened foreign exchange volatility, especially if exchange rate movements among the leading-currency economies are uncoordinated and if they possess limited hedging capabilities.[21] If the international currencies in a multipolar regime are indeed more volatile, then the volatility considerations that have

already induced a "fear of floating" (Calvo and Reinhart 2002) in emerging economies may be compounded. Successfully managing a flexible regime also calls for proper policy frameworks, market microstructure, and financial institutions that can ensure the smooth functioning of foreign exchange markets (World Bank 2006). The fact that many developing countries, especially least developed countries, lack these necessary elements is probably why many have continued to choose some form of pegged regime (figure 3.12), and are likely to continue to do so even in a multicurrency system.

However, whether the diversification benefits of pegging to a basket of the three main international currencies outweighs the costs of managing such a basket—as well as the optimal choice of weights within a basket—remains an open question. Furthermore, a move by a significant number of developing countries toward a non-dollar-pegging regime—either via a peg to one of the other international currencies or to a basket—could also have implications for the system as a

FIGURE 3.12   Exchange rate arrangements of developing countries, 2000 and 2010

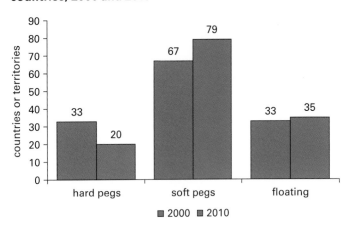

Source: IMF 2000, 2010.

Note: Classifications are based on the exchange rate arrangement classifications defined by the IMF (2010). Hard pegs include exchange rate arrangements of no separate legal tender and currency board; soft pegs for 2000 include other conventional fixed peg arrangement, pegged exchange rate within horizontal bands, crawling peg, crawling band, and managed floating with no preannounced path for the exchange rate; soft pegs for 2010 include exchange rate arrangements of conventional peg, stabilized arrangement, crawling peg, crawl-like arrangement, pegged exchange rate within horizontal bands, and other managed arrangement; floating arrangements include floating and free floating.

whole, especially with regard to global current account imbalances. Such issues will require further research and consideration.

Enhancing the role of the SDR

Over the years, numerous proposals to stimulate the attractiveness of the SDR (see Mussa, Boughton, and Isard 1996; von Furstenberg 1983) have been made by academics and officials, some of whom have argued for changes in the basket definition and the calculation of interest rates paid to holders of SDRs and charged to borrowers of SDRs. The proposal made by the BRICs (Brazil, the Russian Federation, India, and China) in 2008, for example, revived the idea of making the SDR an important reserve currency by encouraging its use by the private sector. This process could involve linking private and official SDRs and allowing central banks to transact in SDRs with private holders—for instance, when performing currency intervention. Another option would be for governments to issue marketable debt in SDRs, which would enhance market liquidity for the SDRs in the process. So far, however, no concrete actions have increased the private use of the SDR, and the current (2010) stock of official SDRs is

only about 4 percent of global foreign exchange reserves (figure 3.13).

The International Monetary Fund (IMF) periodically reviews the composition of the SDR and the rules governing its use. The IMF staff recently concluded that the SDR could play an enhanced role in addressing some of the challenges facing the international monetary system (IMF 2011).

The expansion of global liquidity in recent years has been accompanied by dramatic changes in the distribution of reserves, further undercutting the case for SDR allocations. Comparing the distribution of all countries' reserves-to-imports ratios at the end of 1999 (the year of the introduction of the euro) with comparable figures for 2008 (the last year for which relevant data are available for an adequate number of countries), it is clear that the number of countries with reserves of less than three months' worth of import cover has declined substantially, while the number of countries with a more comfortable cushion of three to six months of import cover has increased (figure 3.14).[22] Moreover, many of the countries with the lowest reserve ratios are advanced countries, as these countries intervene little in foreign exchange markets and are able to borrow reserves when needed. The proportion of advanced countries with low reserve levels (less than three months of import cover) actually increased over the decade from 1999 to 2008, to 63 percent of the total. The countries with the highest reserve ratios are the emerging-market countries and Japan, where flexibility of exchange rates is limited to a greater or lesser extent.

Although the objective of making the SDR the primary reserve asset of the international monetary system does not seem to be within sight in the foreseeable future, greater focus on alternatives to national currencies gradually may create the preconditions for greater management of the monetary system, with advantages for systemic stability along the way. A liquid international asset could also supplement dollar liquidity, minimizing the problem of dollar liquidity shortage that occurred during the recent crisis. Even in the absence of major reforms, countries have the potential to col-

FIGURE 3.13   SDRs as a percentage of the world's foreign exchange reserves, 1970–2010

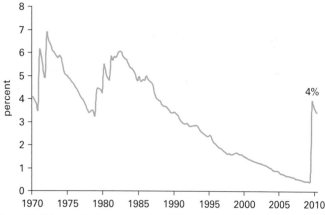

Source: World Bank staff calculations, from IMF IFS database.

laborate to encourage use of the SDR in a number of ways:

- By issuing public debt linked to the value of the SDR
- By encouraging the creation of clearing mechanisms for private SDRs
- By changing the SDR basket, for instance, to include the renminbi or other major emerging-market currencies
- By expanding the set of prescribed holders of official SDRs
- By intervening directly in SDR-linked instruments to develop the liquidity of the private SDR market

In addition, the provisions for approving SDR allocations could be modified to make them more flexible and subject to less stringent conditions,

also conceivably allowing the IMF to hold SDRs in escrow and issuing or withdrawing them when needed (IMF 2010c). Such reforms, however, would require an amendment to the IMF's Articles of Agreement.

Conclusion

The world economy is going through a transformative change in its growth dynamics, industrial landscape, and management of international monetary and financial affairs. How the international monetary system evolves in the future matters crucially for development policy, agenda, and practice. In setting the context for global growth and financial stability, the international monetary system conditions not only developing countries' access to international sources of capital, but also the stability

FIGURE 3.14   Distribution of foreign exchange reserves, 1999 and 2008

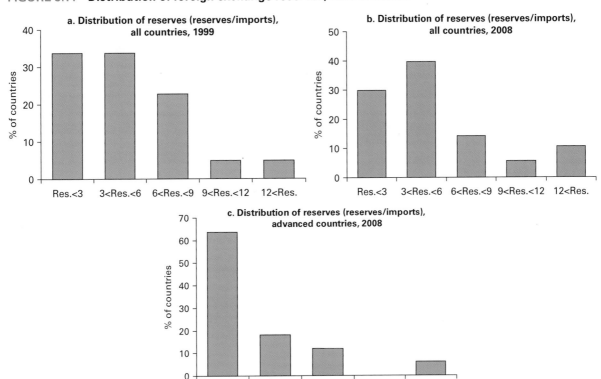

Source: World Bank staff calculations, from IMF IFS database.

of their currencies. The 2008–09 financial crisis exposed some of the structural weaknesses of the previous international monetary system, and underscored the need for reform in line with the growing roles of developing countries on the global stage.

There remains a wide disparity, however, between developing countries' roles in international trade and finance and their importance in the international monetary system. Addressing these disparities in the international monetary system is an area in need of urgent attention, both in terms of the management of the system—in which the IMF continues to play a leading role—as well as in the understanding of long-term forces shaping the future working of the system.

International currency use has lagged the increasing importance of emerging-market economies. None of their currencies is used internationally to any great extent. That situation may change in the coming decades, but the shift will be limited by the inertia in currency use explained by network externalities, which dictate that a currency is most attractive if it is already in widespread international use. Recent moves by the Chinese authorities, for example, to encourage international use of the renminbi can be expected to gradually increase use of that currency in East Asia. But to become a true international currency, the renminbi would have to be supported by capital account liberalization, exchange rate flexibility, and domestic reforms that would encourage liquid and deep financial markets and transparent and effective financial regulation and supervision. The future international role of the renminbi will depend importantly on whether the Chiang Mai Initiative multilateralization leads to the development of a regional currency, and whether such a regional currency is a new one issued by a regional central bank or one of the existing currencies.

Emerging-market economies other than China will need to evaluate whether internationalization of their currencies is in their best interest. Internationalization of currencies would impose constraints on monetary policies, open up new sources of financing, and reduce exchange rate risk. The very different situations of the potential emerging-market growth pole countries—in terms of institutions, regional linkages, and macroeconomic conditions—suggest that answers to this question vary substantially according to the country and region being considered.

In the meantime, it is the euro, rather than any emerging-market currency, that has the potential to rival the U.S. dollar as a true international currency—provided the euro area can strengthen its institutions and overcome the severe fiscal crisis afflicting several EU countries that is weakening the credibility of the euro system as a whole. It is also the case that large U.S. fiscal and current account deficits, and concerns about further dollar depreciation, have dented the dominance of the dollar as the main international currency. Views are sharply contrasting, however, as to the seriousness of the challenge posed by other currencies. Some believe that the euro will overtake the dollar in importance quite soon and that the renminbi will do the same at a more distant horizon. But others believe that the dynamism of the U.S. economy, the depth of U.S. financial markets, and the position of the United States as the world's only superpower—as well as inertia in currency use—make the dollar's position at the top of the currency pyramid unshakable in the foreseeable future.

With such factors in mind, three possible international currency scenarios for the period 2011–25 emerge. In the first of those scenarios, the U.S. dollar's dominance remains without a serious challenger. In the second, a more multipolar international monetary system emerges, most likely with the dollar, euro, and renminbi at the center of the system. In the third, dissatisfaction with an international currency system based on national currencies leads to reforms that make supply of the world's currency the result of multilateral decisions—a role intended for the SDR when it was created. These three scenarios have different costs and benefits and are not equally likely to occur.

The creation of the G-20, and its development into the primary forum for economic cooperation among the world's major economies, recognizes the importance of the challenges facing the global economy, and the G-20 successes have been the result of the shared objectives of limiting the scope of the financial crisis, reviving global growth, and improving financial regulation. The G-20 needs not only to replace the G-8, but also to improve on the G-8 when it comes to effective policy coordination, and the G-20 should consider over the long term whether to move to a more rules-based system in anticipation of trends toward multipolarity.

More specifically, in the international monetary arena, gains in central bank cooperation—which have improved as a result of the financial crisis—need to be consolidated. Financial stability, it is now widely recognized, is a primary responsibility of central banks. Because of a high degree of financial interdependence, central bank cooperation must be addressed through enhanced exchange of information and coordination. Several decades of experience, however, have shown the limitations of attempting to coordinate policies around zero-sum variables, such as exchange rates and balance of payments, because of disagreements over appropriate levels: one country's depreciation corresponds to other countries' appreciation, and balance of payments deficits need to be matched by surpluses. It would be more promising to emphasize coordination around global public goods, such as sustained growth, financial stability, low inflation, and exchange rate stability.

Annexes

Annex 3.1: Using global money demand to determine the extent of international currency use

A simple model framework. The international roles of a currency ultimately should lead to an increase in the global demand for money of the currency in question, where global demand is defined as encompassing both international and domestic demand. A conventional error-correction specification for money demand for transaction purposes would postulate that nominal money balances m (in logs) should depend positively on the price level p and real GDP y (both in logs) and negatively on the short-term interest

rate i. Money holdings would adjust gradually to their long run level:

$$\Delta m = \alpha + \beta \Delta p + \sigma \Delta y \\ + \varphi(a_1 i_{-1} + a_2 y_{-1} + a_3 p_{-1} - m_{-1}) + u$$

If some transactions are international, however, then one should include variables that capture the demand for money balances to carry out those transactions, if that currency is in international use. Globalization increases the volume of international transactions relative to GDP, and hence the amount of money needed to carry them out, holding the transactions technology constant. Let xs be the share of global exports in global GDP, and ks be the corresponding share of (gross) capital flows in global GDP. Additionally, let country subscript j be used to distinguish countries. Consistent with the pooled mean group (PMG) estimator (Pesaran, Shin, and Smith 1999), the long-run money demand coefficients (a_1, a_2, a_3) are constrained to be the same across countries, while allowing the short-run adjustment and the degree of internationalization (as well as the constant term) to vary. The above equation then can be augmented as follows:

$$\Delta m_j = \alpha_j + \beta_j \Delta p_j + \sigma_j \Delta y_j + \gamma_j xs + \delta_j ks \\ + \varphi(a_1 i_{j,-1} + a_2 y_{j,-1} + a_3 p_{j,-1} - m_{j,-1}) + u_j$$

where the coefficients α_j, β_j, σ_j, γ_j, δ_j, ϕ_j include a country subscript to indicate that they vary across countries. The variables xs and ks do not have country subscripts, as they are measures of global transactions. But their coefficients vary depending on the extent to which demand for the country's currency reflects global transactions.

Data issues. Annual data for G-20 countries from 1990–2009 are used in the analysis, with two major qualifications. First, the data begin in 1996 for Russia, 1992 for Argentina, and 1994 for Brazil in order to remove the effects of massive structural changes and hyperinflation. Second, the M2 of G-20 euro area countries (France, Germany, and Italy) are included in the M2 of the euro area rather than analyzed individually (for years before 1999, the series is a composite

M2 for the countries that joined the euro area in 1999). Money holdings are measured as M2, which includes notes and coins in circulation (M1) plus, typically, checking accounts, savings deposits, and time deposits. The interest rate is that of three-month Treasury bills or similar instruments.

The internationalization variables xs and ks are calculated as ratios of global exports to global GDP, and the first difference of Bank for International Settlements international claims, divided by global GDP, respectively.

Estimation results. Table 3A.1 summarizes the results of preliminary estimation using PMG, focusing on the long-run demand relationship, which is constrained to be the same for all countries, and the effects of the globalization variables, which are allowed to differ. Results are reported only for the U.S. dollar, euro, pound sterling, and Japanese yen.

Assuming that both international trade and asset flows continue to grow more strongly than GDP, the results are suggestive of future trends in currency use. International trade and capital flows would seem to favor the use of the euro strongly, and trade growth to discourage use of the yen and encourage that of the dollar.[23] These trends are consistent with the reported decline in use of the yen for foreign exchange reserves and in currency turnover data (as discussed in the text).

Indeed, research has found that Japanese exporters have a strong tendency to choose the importer's currency when exporting to other industrial countries and to use the dollar for invoicing when exporting to Asia (Ito et al. 2010).

Annex 3.2: A composite indicator of shares of international currency use

To aggregate the four indicators reported in the text—reserves, turnover, international bank credit, and international securities issues—principal factor analysis was used to generate the weights on each to create a single series that maximizes the common variance in the series. The first factor calculated in such a manner explains 93 percent of the variance (table 3A.2, top panel). The remaining factors (which were not retained) are orthogonal both to the first factor and among themselves. They explain little of the variance, and one of the criteria for retention of factors (only those with eigenvalue greater than unity) strongly suggests that only the first factor is needed. The resulting weights (or factor loadings) for the first factor are almost equal for the four series—slightly higher for reserves and credit, with international bonds having the lowest weight (table 3A.2, bottom panel). Using these weights, the principal factor was calculated and then renormalized to give proportions that sum to unity for each of the years in the sample. The series for the composite indicator based on the principal factor are plotted in figure 3.3.

Annex 3.3: A short history of the SDR

The SDR is an international reserve asset that was created by the IMF in the 1960s to palliate a perceived shortage of reserves and to address the so-called Triffin dilemma, a potential confidence problem associated with the use of the U.S. dollar as the predominant reserve currency. The dilemma resulted from the fact that the United States needed to run a balance of payments deficit to provide adequate global liquidity, but the deficit, in turn, undermined the attractiveness of the dollar and the credibility of the U.S. commitment

TABLE 3A.1 Estimates of long-run global money demand for the U.S. dollar, euro, pound sterling, and yen

Coefficient	United States	Euro area	Japan	United Kingdom
a_1	1.761*	1.761*	1.761*	1.761*
	(0.0668)	(0.0668)	(0.0668)	(0.0668)
a_2	−0.0003	−0.0003	−0.0003	−0.0003
	(0.0022)	(0.0022)	(0.0022)	(0.0022)
a_3	0.7179*	0.7179*	0.7179*	0.7179*
	(0.0663)	(0.0663)	(0.0663)	(0.0663)
γ_j	0.0034*	0.0043*	−0.0084*	0.0021
	(0.0013)	(0.0010)	(0.0046)	(0.0011)
δ_j	0.0012	0.0012*	0.0016	−0.0000
	(0.0007)	(0.0005)	(0.0021)	(0.0007)

Source: World Bank staff estimates.
Note: Standard errors are shown in parentheses below the estimated coefficients.
*Indicates significance at the 10 percent level or better.

to maintain dollar convertibility into gold. By the time of approval of the first allocation of SDRs in 1969 (which occurred in three installments over 1970–72), the United States had in fact restricted convertibility to foreign central banks; rather than the perceived shortage of reserves, there was now a glut of foreign dollar holdings. President Nixon suspended gold convertibility completely on August 15, 1971, to bring about a readjustment of exchange rates. However, the new set of parities that resulted from the December 1971 Smithsonian Agreement lasted less than two years, and by March 1973 there was generalized floating of exchange rates.

The First Amendment to the IMF's Articles of Agreement creating the SDR envisioned that it would become "the principal reserve asset in the international monetary system" (Art. XXII). This has not occurred. Although the first allocation of SDRs was followed by a second general allocation over 1979–81, no further allocations were made until August/September 2009, when approval of the Fourth Amendment authorized a special allocation for countries that had joined the IMF after 1981 (as they had not benefited from previous allocations); a general allocation also was made to all members of SDR 161.2 billion. Between 1981 and 2009, however, SDRs fell from 7.3 percent of nongold foreign exchange reserves to 0.4 percent. The new allocations raised the proportion to 3.9 percent.

As the name implies, the SDR is not really an asset, but rather the unconditional right to obtain usable currencies through the IMF.[24] The SDR's attractiveness is greatest for countries that have limited ability to borrow reserve currencies (or only at a high interest rate). For countries that have market access, the SDR has limited appeal either as an asset or as a source of credit. The interest rate charged on the use of SDRs and its valuation are related to those of the component currencies of the basket that define it—currently, the dollar, the euro, the pound sterling, and the yen.[25] Until 2009, agreement on new SDR allocations has foundered on the need to prove "a long-term global need [for reserves]" (Article XVIII), which has been difficult to provide given the tremendous expansion in holdings in reserve currencies, especially U.S. dollars.

TABLE 3A.2 **Principle factor analysis of international currency use**

Factor	Eigenvalue	Difference	Proportion	Cumulative
1	3.69331	3.42583	0.9349	0.9349
2	0.26748	0.27014	0.0677	1.0026
3	−0.00267	0.00508	−0.0007	1.002
4	−0.0077	−0.0020		1
		Observations		55

Factor loadings (first factor)

Variable	Factor 1	Uniqueness
Reserves	0.96285	0.07291
Turnover	0.95806	0.08212
Credit	0.98433	0.0311
Bonds	0.93778	0.12056

Source: World Bank staff estimates.

According to the IMF's articles, the SDR is limited to official users, namely, governments and central banks, although for a time around 1980 there was considerable issuance of private SDR deposits and bonds (these use the same basket definition as the official SDR, but interest rates can differ from the interest rates of official SDR). This private market was virtually nonexistent as of 2010. The SDR also has been used as an exchange rate peg, allowing countries to avoid some of the volatility associated with single currency pegs. By 2007, the use of basket pegs (including the SDR) virtually had disappeared. The SDR's current role is mainly to serve as a unit of account for international institutions.

Notes

1. This issue has been much researched (see Cohen 2000; Tavlas 1991; and references therein to earlier literature).
2. Empirical work by Chinn and Frankel (2005) shows that a currency's share in world foreign exchange reserves is linked to two main explanatory variables: the GDP share of the economy (positive correlation) and the economy's inflation rate relative to the world average (negative correlation). Chinn and Frankel (2005) also find a high degree of inertia in currency use, reflected in the

slow effect of changes in the explanatory variables on currency use.

3. The proportions relate to allocated reserves only and exclude those countries (China, in particular) that do not report the currency composition of their reserves.

4. The components were first converted to shares of the total for the five currencies, and the first principal component was normalized so that shares summed to unity across the five.

5. A similar approach is reported in ECB (2010, 55–58).

6. An alternative methodology suggested by Thimann (2008) is to broaden the definition of international use beyond bonds issued to international investors to include foreigners' purchases of domestic instruments, as well as measures of the size and stage of development of financial markets. The latter elements, however, raise measurement problems and require one to weight together very different qualitative variables.

7. In some periods, however, the status of an international currency has been maintained by negotiation, in particular within the sterling zone following World War II and during the 1960s, when the United States introduced various controls to discourage exchanging dollars for gold (see Helleiner 2009).

8. To quote a recent paper discussed at the IMF's Executive Board (IMF 2010b, 18), "As the world becomes more multipolar in terms of GDP, the drive for a multicurrency system that mimics global economic weights is likely to increase—e.g., a dominant dollar zone, euro zone, and a formal or informal Asian currency zone."

9. The euro area and IMF rescue package for Greece, agreed on in April 2010, is covered by a separate facility.

10. In terms of total exports, China's share of world trade, despite its rapid growth, has not yet reached the corresponding figure for the United States a century ago. The United States already accounted for 12.2 percent of global merchandise exports in 1906–10, and 12.5 percent in 1913–20. During the second part of the 1920s, this U.S. share was already 15.5 percent (surpassing the United Kingdom's) and by 1950, the U.S. share was at an all-time high, at 20.6 percent.

11. See   http://www.mof.go.jp/english/if/regional_ financial_cooperation.htm#CMI for more information.

12. The extent of reserve accumulation has attracted much attention in recent years. Developing countries as a group (especially those that are commodity exporters) are now stockpiling reserves at a far greater rate and on a much larger scale than advanced economies. Some of this reflects the self-insurance motives of emerging countries in the aftermath of the East Asian financial crisis in the late 1990s, and some reflects their desire to limit the flexibility of their exchange rates. For further discussion of the demand for reserves, see Lin and Dailami (2010) and Obstfeld, Shambaugh, and Taylor (2010).

13. Despite the substantial debate that has raged over the motivations and investment behavior of SWFs, their mere existence does not, in itself, pose a threat to the international financial system. For example, SWFs likely played a valuable stabilizing role during the financial crisis, as SWFs acquired stakes in U.S. financial institutions that provided capital injections at a time of scarce global liquidity and may have contributed to U.S. institutions' continued viability. Nevertheless, if emerging-market governments attempt to take large positions in sectors viewed as sensitive, these concerns may come to the fore once again; thus, agreement on a multilateral framework governing cross-border investment flows, as elaborated in chapter 2, becomes all the more important.

14. Chinn and Frankel (2005) maintain that this scenario is consistent with the likely case where no exits from the European Monetary Union occur, while smaller Eastern European economies meet the Maastricht criteria and choose to join the European Monetary Union. However, they assume that the United Kingdom retains its currency independence and dismiss the possibility of the renminbi becoming an international currency. In a later paper, Chinn and Frankel (2008) argue that since much of London's business is done in euros, the importance of that financial center would provide a further boost to the euro.

15. It should also be noted that the scenarios here anticipate somewhat slower short and medium-term adjustment in U.S. fiscal balances, compared to projections in 2011 by the CBO. However, it is clear that the CBO baseline for fiscal adjustment falls neatly between the two international currency scenarios considered.

16. The danger of greater currency instability is based on both historical experience and analytical models. Giavazzi and Giovannini (1989), for example, suggest that greater symmetry in the size of countries or economic blocs will produce greater global instability. This is consistent with political

economy models of hegemonic stability, in which a single dominant country has the incentive and means to make the system work smoothly (Cohen 1998; Kindleberger 1973). Assuming, as does the second scenario, that the ability of the United States to guide the evolution of the international monetary system continues to decline, the resulting lack of a hegemon likely will lead to attempts by other major powers to assert their influence. From a historical perspective, the experience between the two world wars suggests that rivalry between financial centers can exacerbate exchange rate instability (Eichengreen 1987).

17. Some of the same concerns facing the economic policy-making community today—namely, the potential instability of a multiple currency system, the unchecked expansion of global liquidity, the trade-offs between financing and adjustment, and the asymmetric position of reserve currency countries—also motivated extensive discussions of reform of the international monetary system in the late 1960s (see, among many proposals for reform, Cohen 1970; Hawkins 1965; Machlup 1968; Triffin 1964) and led to the creation of the SDR. At the time of its creation, the SDR was intended to become the main reserve currency of the international monetary system—a role it never assumed (annex 3.3).

18. There is considerable scholarship on cooperation theory in international relations. The main insights emphasize the role of three factors affecting the willingness of governments to cooperate: mutuality of interest, the shadow of the future, and the number of actors involved in the cooperation (see Axelrod and Keohane 1985; Fearon 1998). The G-20, for example, as a vehicle of international coordination, needs to reconcile the tension between efficiency in its decision-making processes, which argues for a small number of members, and the legitimacy imparted by wider participation. Although the G-20 does not satisfy the universality principle of multilateralism entrenched in the postwar economic order, the G-20 comes much closer to meeting the universality principle than did its predecessor, the G-7, as the G-20 also includes emerging countries in Africa, Asia, Latin America, and the Middle East.

19. Communiqué, Meeting of Finance Ministers and Central Bank Governors, Paris, February 18–19, 2011, G-20 website.

20. See http://graphics8.nytimes.com/packages/pdf/10222010geithnerletter.pdf.

21. High level of exchange rate volatility can deter exports (see Mundaca 2011).

22. A traditional rule of thumb was that holding reserves equal to six months' imports gave an adequate cushion for trade-related shocks, but a more complete analysis of reserve adequacy needs to account for exposure to short-term debt (Jeanne and Rancière 2006). The Greenspan-Guidotti rule suggests that reserves should be at least equal to debt maturing within the coming year; see Greenspan (1999) and Guidotti (1999).

23. While international payments should only increase, not decrease, total currency use, the negative coefficient should be interpreted as being relative to the average behavior displayed by all international currencies and embodied in the common coefficients.

24. Thus differing from the conditional credit extended by the IMF through its various lending facilities.

25. The composition of the SDR has evolved over time. Originally it was valued in terms of gold, and then it was defined as a basket of 16 currencies, which was reduced to five currencies in 1980 and to four in 1999, with the creation of the euro.

References

Artis, Michael J., and Sylvia Ostry. 1986. *International Economic Policy Co-ordination*. London: Routledge.

Axelrod, Robert, and Robert Keohane. 1985. "Achieving Cooperation under Anarchy: Strategies and Institutions." *World Politics* 38 (1): 226–54.

Bénassy-Quéré, Agnès, and Laurence Boone. 2010. "Eurozone Crisis: Debts, Institutions, and Growth." La Lettre du CEPII 300 (June).

BIS (Bank of International Settlements). 2010. "Triennial Central Bank Survey: Foreign Exchange and Derivatives Market Activity in April 2010: Preliminary Results." Basel, Switzerland: BIS.

Calvo, Guillermo A., and Carmen M. Reinhart. 2002. "Fear of Floating." *Quarterly Journal of Economics* 107 (2): 379–408.

Cambridge University Press, 2006. "Historical Statistics of the United States." Millennial edition online. Ed. Susan B. Carter, Scott Sigmund Gartnerm, Michael R. Haines, Alan L. Olmstead, Richard Stuch, and Gavin Wright.

CBO (Congressional Budget Office). 2010. "The Long-Term Budget Outlok." Washington, DC: CBO.

Chinn, Menzie, and Jeffrey Frankel. 2005. "Will the Euro Eventually Surpass the Dollar as Leading

International Reserve Currency?" NBER Working Paper 11510, National Bureau of Economic Research, Cambridge, MA.

———. 2008. "Why the Euro Will Rival the Dollar." *International Finance* 11 (1): 49–73.

Cohen, Benjamin J. 1998. *The Geography of Money.* Ithaca, NY: Cornell University Press.

———. 2000. "Life at the Top: International Currencies in the Twenty-First Century." Princeton Essay in International Finance 221, International Economics Section, Department of Economics, Princeton University, Princeton, NJ.

Cohen, Stephen D. 1970. *International Monetary Reform: The Political Dimension, 1964–69.* New York: Praeger.

Cooper, Richard N. 1976. "International Monetary Reform after Three Years." *Trialogue* 10: 2–3.

Dailami, Mansoor, and Paul Masson. 2010. "Toward a More Managed International Monetary System?" *International Journal* 65 (2): 393–409.

Dobbs, Richard, Susan Lund, James Manyika, and Charles Roxburgh. 2009. "An Exorbitant Privilege? Implications of Reserve Currencies for Competitiveness." Discussion Paper, McKinsey Global Institute. http://whatmatters. mckinseydigital.com/file_download/11/ McKinsey_MGIReserve_Currency.pdf.

Drezner, Daniel W. 2010. "Will Currency Follow the Flag?" *International Relations of the Asia-Pacific* 10 (3): 389–414.

ECB (European Central Bank). 2010. *The International Role of the Euro, July 2010.* Frankfurt: ECB.

Eichengreen, Barry. 1987. "Conducting the International Orchestra: Bank of England Leadership under the Classical Gold Standard." *Journal of International Money and Finance* 6 (1): 5–20.

———. 2011. *Exorbitant Privilege: The Rise and Fall of the Dollar and the Future of the International Monetary System.* New York: Oxford University Press.

Fearon, James D. 1998. "Bargaining, Enforcement, and International Cooperation." *International Organization* 52 (2): 269–305.

Frankel, Jeffrey A. 1999. "No Single Currency Regime is Right for All Countries or at All Times." Essays in International Finance 215 (December 1998).

Giavazzi, Francesco, and Alberto Giovannini. 1989. "Can the EMS Be Exported? Lessons from Ten Years of Monetary Policy Coordination in Europe." CEPR Discussion Papers 285, Centre for Economic Policy Research, London.

Goldberg, Linda S. 2010. "Is the International Role of the Dollar Changing?" *Current Issues in Economics and Finance* 16 (1): 1–7.

Goldstein, Morris. 2002. "Managed Floating Plus." Policy Analysis in International Economics 66, Institute for International Economics, Washington, DC.

Greenspan, Alan. 1999. "Currency Reserves and Debt." Remarks before the World Bank Conference Recent Trends in Reserve Management, Washington DC, April 29. http://www.federalreserve.gov/ BoardDocs/Speeches/1999/19990429.htm.

Guidotti, Pablo. 1999. Remarks to the G-33 Seminar, Bonn, Germany, March 11.

Hartmann, Philipp. 1998. *Currency Competition and Foreign Exchange Markets: The Dollar, the Yen, and the Euro.* Cambridge, U.K.: Cambridge University Press.

Hawkins, Robert G., ed. 1965. *A Compendium of Plans for International Monetary Reform.* New York: C. J. Devine Institute of Finance, New York University.

Helleiner, Eric. 2009. "Enduring Top Currency, Fragile Negotiated Currency: Politics and the Dollar's International Role." In *The Future of the Dollar,* ed. Eric Helleiner and Jonathan Kirshner, 69–87. Ithaca, NY: Cornell University Press.

Hilgerdt, Folke. 1945. *Industrialization and Foreign Trade.* Geneva: League of Nations.

IMF (International Monetary Fund). 2000. *Annual Report on Exchange Rate Arrangements and Exchange Restrictions.* Washington, DC: IMF.

———. 2010a. *Annual Report on Exchange Rate Arrangements and Exchange Restrictions.* Washington, DC: IMF.

———. 2010b. "Reserve Accumulation and International Monetary Stability." Strategy, Policy and Review Department, IMF, Washington, DC.

———. 2010c. "Reserve Accumulation and International Monetary Stability: Supplementary Information." Strategy, Policy and Review Department, IMF, Washington, DC.

———. 2011. "Enhancing International Monetary Stability—A Role for the SDR?" Strategy, Policy, and Review Department, IMF, Washington, DC.

Ito, Takatoshi, Satoshi Koibuchi, Kiyotaka Sato, and Junko Shimizu. 2010. "Why Has the Yen Failed to Become a Dominant Invoicing Currency in Asia? A Firm-Level Analysis of Japanese Exporters' Invoicing Behavior." NBER Working Paper 16231, National Bureau of Economic Research, Cambridge, MA.

Jeanne, Olivier, and Romain Rancière. 2006. "The Optimal Level of International Reserves for Emerging Market Countries: Formulas and Applications." IMF Working Paper WP/06/229, International Monetary Fund, Washington, DC.

Kenen, Peter. 1983. *The Role of the Dollar as an International Currency*. Washington, DC: Group of Thirty.

Kindleberger, Charles P. 1973. *The World in Depression, 1929–39*. Berkeley, CA: University of California Press.

Kiyotaki, Nobuhiro, and Randall Wright. 1989. "On Money as a Medium of Exchange." *Journal of Political Economy* 97 (4): 927–54.

Lin, Justin Yifu, and Mansoor Dailami. 2010. "Comments on Dealing with Global Imbalances." In *Reconstructing the World Economy*, ed. Olivier Blanchard and Il SaKong, 111–20. Washington, DC: International Monetary Fund and Korea Development Institute.

Machlup, Fritz. 1968. *Remaking the International Monetary System: The Rio Agreement and Beyond*. Baltimore, MD: Johns Hopkins Press.

Masson, Paul. Forthcoming. "The Evolution of Exchange Rate Regimes and Some Future Perspectives." In *The Handbook of Exchange Rates*, ed. Jessica James, Ian W. Marsh, and Lucio Sarno. New York: Wiley.

McCauley, Robert N. 2011. *The Internationalisation of the Renminbi*. Basel, Switzerland: Bank for International Settlements.

Mundaca, Gabriela. 2011. "Exchange Rate Uncertainty and Optimal Participation in International Trade," Policy Research Working Paper Series 5593, World Bank, Washington, DC.

Mussa, Michael, James Boughton, and Peter Isard, eds. 1996. *The Future of the SDR in the Light of Changes in the International Financial System*. Washington, DC: International Monetary Fund.

Obstfeld, Maurice, Jay C. Shambaugh, and Alan M. Taylor. 2010. "Financial Stability, the Trilemma, and International Reserves." *American Economic Journal: Macroeconomics* 2 (2): 57–94.

People's Bank of China. 2010a. *China Monetary Policy Report, Quarter Four*. Beijing: People's Bank of China http://www.pbc.gov.cn/publish/english/3511/index.html.

———. 2010b. "Supporting Pilot Program for RMB Settlement of Cross-Border Trade Transactions to Facilitate Trade and Investment." People's Bank of China, Beijing. http://www.pbc.gov.cn/publish/english/955/2010 /20101216101630952838958/20 101216101630952838958_.html.

Pesaran, M. Hashem, Yongcheol Shin, and Ronald P. Smith. 1999. "Pooled Mean Group Estimation of Dynamic Heterogeneous Panels." *Journal of the American Statistical Association* 94 (446): 621–34.

Posen, Adam S. 2008. "Why the Euro Will Not Rival the Dollar." International Finance 11 (1): 75–100.

Stiglitz, Joseph E., and Bruce Greenwald. 2010. "Towards a New Global Reserve System." *Journal of Globalization and Development* 1 (2). http://www.bepress.com/jgd/vol1/iss2/art10.

Tavlas, George S. 1991. "On the International Use of Currencies: The Case of the Deutsche Mark." Princeton Essays in International Finance 181, International Economics Section, Department of Economics, Princeton University, Princeton, NJ.

Thimann, Christian. 2008. "Global Roles of Currencies." *International Finance* 11 (3): 211–45.

Triffin, Robert. 1964. *The Evolution of the International Monetary System: Historical Reappraisal and Future Perspectives*. Princeton Studies in International Finance 12, International Economics Section, Department of Economics, Princeton University, Princeton, NJ.

USAID (U.S. Agency for International Development). "U.S. Overseas Loans and Grants, Obligations and Loan Authorizations (Greenbook)." July 1, 1995– September 30, 2009.

von Furstenberg, George, ed. 1983. *International Money and Credit: The Policy Roles*. Washington, DC: International Monetary Fund.

Williamson, John. 1993. "Exchange Rate Management." *Economic Journal* 103 (416): 188–97.

World Bank. 2006. *Global Development Finance 2006: The Development Potential of Surging Capital Flows*. Washington, DC: World Bank.

ECO-AUDIT
Environmental Benefits Statement

The World Bank is committed to preserving endangered forests and natural resources. The Office of the Publisher has chosen to print *Global Development Horizons* on recycled paper with 50 percent post-consumer waste, in accordance with the recommended standards for paper usage set by the Green Press Initiative, a nonprofit program supporting publishers in using fiber that is not sourced from endangered forests. For more information, visit www.greenpressinitiative.org.

Saved:
- 14 trees
- 6 million Btu of total energy
- 1,379 lb. of net greenhouse gases
- 6,220 gal. of water
- 394 lb. of solid waste